A HAND BOOK OF ISLAMIC ARCHITECTURE

A HAND BOOK OF ISLAMIC ARCHITECTURE

Amir Ansari

CYBER TECH PUBLICATIONS
4264/3, Ansari Road, Daryaganj, New Delhi-110002 (India)
Ph.: 011-23244078, 011-43559448 Fax: 011-23280028
E-Mail: cyberpublicationsdelhi@yahoo.com
Website: www.cybertechpublications.com

A HAND BOOK OF ISLAMIC ARCHITECTURE

Amir Ansari

First Edition 2011

Published by :

G.S. Rawat for **Cyber Tech Publications**
4264/3, Ansari Road, Daryaganj, New Delhi-110002 (India)
Ph.: 011-23244078, 011-43559448 Fax: 011-23280028
E-Mail: cyberpublicationsdelhi@yahoo.com
Website: www.cybertechpublications.com

CONTENTS

CONTENTS

Preface

Babur, the first mughal emperor, was a descendant of the Turkish conqueror Timur on his father's side and of the Mongol (in Persian, mughal) conqueror Genghis Khan on his mother's side. The Islamic Dynasty is a line of Muslim emperors who reigned in India from 1526 to 1858. From 1526, when Babur defeated Sultan Ibrahim Lodi, the ruler of Delhi, and established himself in neighbouring Agra, until 1638, when his great-great-grandson Shah Jahan built a new capital city in Delhi again, Agra was a repository for all the wealth and talent of one of the most extensive empires in the medieval world.

The many elements that led to the creation of the Taj Mahal had their roots in the reigns of the earlier monarchs: 1) Humayun, Akbar, Jehangir, Shah Jehan, Aurangzeb, each of whom contributed his particular aesthetic interests and endeavours to the establishment of what we have subsequently called the Mughal Style, a style which blended the Persian patterns brought by the Mughals with the indigenous genius for fine craftsmanship. The amazing achievements in the Mughal architectural tradition owe much to the great talent of Indian artisans and the wealth of material found in India, including the abundance of stone. Each emperor used local materials and indigenous forms and craftsmanship to nurture and bring to fruition an unique enduring beautiful architectural tradition.

The Mughal style found triumphant fulfilment in the building of the Taj Mahal, the most splendid expression of the centuries of Mughal rule in India. The Taj Mahal was the last and greatest architectural flowering of the Mughal period in Agra, before its builder, Shah Jahan (1592-1658) shifted the imperial centre of power and administration to what is now called Delhi.

— *Author*

1

Precedents for Mughal Architecture

Mughal architecture, an amalgam of Islamic, Persian and Indian architecture, is the distinctive style developed by the Mughal Empire in India & Pakistan in the 16th and 17th centuries.

The Uzbek dynasty began with the emperor Babur in 1526. Babur erected a mosque at Panipat to celebrate his victory over Ibrahim Lodi. A second mosque, known as the Babri masjid, was built in Ayodhya and was demolished in 1992 by Hindu extremists. A third mosque also built by Babur during the same period was constructed in Sambhal in Distt Moradabad

Some of the first and most characteristic examples that remain of early Mughal architecture were built in the short reign (1540-1545) of emperor Sher Shah Suri, who was not a Mughal; they include a mosque known as the Qila i Kuhna (1541) near Delhi, and the military architecture of the Old Fort in Delhi, Lal Bagh (Dhaka) in Bangladesh , and Rohtas Fort, near Jhelum in present-day Pakistan. His mausoleum, octagonal in plan and set upon a plinth in the middle of an artificial lake, is in Sasaram, and was completed by his son and successor Islam Shah Suri (1545AD-1553AD).

In 1526 a descendant of the Iranian house of Timur, Zahir al-Din Muhammad Babur, better known today simply as Babur, defeated the last ruler of the Lodi dynasty in a battle at Panipat, about 90 km north of Delhi. The Lodis were one of many short-lived Islamic houses that had ruled over much of the Indian subcontinent since the Islamic conquest of this area in 1192. Babur and his successors, who continued to rule north India until 1858, were known as the Mughals, a term Babur would not have liked, for originally it had a pejorative connotation.

In contemporary eyes Babur's victory over Ibrahim Lodi was no more consequential than the frequent campaigns that brought changes in ruling power. However, well before the year 1600, during the reign of Babur's grandson, Akbar, it was clear that Mughal rule made a substantial impact on the cultural, economic, and political development of the lands it controlled - an area then called Hindustan. In the realm of architecture, the Mughals achieved master-builder status, producing monuments such as the Taj Mahal, which even today is considered one of the world's most magnificent buildings. Unlike the contemporary and powerful Islamic rulers of Iran and Turkey, the Safavids and Ottomans, the Mughals ruled a land dominated by non-Muslims, largely Hindus. Just as indigenous religions and traditions were tolerated and in many cases even respected by the Mughal rulers, so, too, they incorporated in their patronage of the arts, literature and music many indigenous elements.

Over their 300-year rule, Mughal attitudes toward the indigenous Indian population - Hindu and Muslim - varied; so did Mughal adaptation of earlier Indian art forms. During the earliest days of Mughal patronage, little attention was paid to India's non-Islamic architectural traditions; however, during the reign of the third Mughal ruler, Akbar (15 56-1605), indigenous Indian elements, both Hindu and Muslim, were incorporated consciously into Mughal structures. In subsequent Mughal architecture, patrons often abandoned the use of indigenous elements, seeking instead forms and symbols that might affirm the Islamic character of the Mughal house.

Mughal architecture is the product of innovative genius that borrowed from Indian, Timurid and even European sources. The Mughal artists interpreted these borrowed forms, both in terms of symbolism and style, to their own purposes. However, to imagine, as many do, that Mughal architecture was the first to make extensive use of indigenous motifs along with standard Islamic forms - for example, domes and arches - is to overlook the heritage bequeathed to them by earlier Indo-Islamic dynasties.

SOURCES OF MUGHAL INSPIRATION

Indian Muslim Aources

The Delhi Sultanate, 1192-1451

Among the earliest remaining Islamic monuments in India are the foundations of walled city and mosque at Banbhore near Thatta in Sind, Pakistan. The site was commenced shortly after the birth of Islam, and is probably the earliest Arab settlement in the South Asian continent. Other remains indicating an early Islamic presence include a tomb dated to the mid-twelfth century found at Bhadreshvar in the coastal regions of Gujarat in western India. Another aspect of Islamic presence was the periodic incursions, more destructive than constructive, intended to take booty, not to build any record of a permanent presence. The incursions into India made by Mahmud of Ghazni in the eleventh century were of this sort. However, in 1192, Qutb al-Din Aibek, a military commander of the Afghan Ghorid dynasty, defeated the last Hindu ruler of Delhi. Within a few years, a great deal of north India was under Ghorid control, and in 1206 Aibek asserted his independence from the Ghorids, declaring himself sultan of India. He and his successors built architecture that served as one foundation of Mughal art.

Among the first concerns of the conqueror was the construction of a congregational (Tamic) mosque, necessary for the legitimization of the sultan in this newly acquired territory as well as for the establishment and spread of Islam. Aibek's first mosque, significantly now called the Quwwat al-Islam or Might of Islam, was erected in Delhi, the capital of the new Muslim rulers (Plate 1). Constructed from the architectural members of temples, the mosque in its first phases appears to be modeled loosely on a common form of Ghorid-period mosques. Such mosques, following a general Iranian fashion, had a central open courtyard surrounded by cloistered halls on three sides; the prayer chamber was on the fourth side. Each side had a central vaulted entrance or aiwan. Hence, such mosques are known as iom-aiwan types. In India their appearance is somewhat modified, and by the Mughal period the term aiwan assumes a different meaning. During this early period entrances are not vaulted. The prayer chamber is situated on the west, the side that in India faces Mecca, thus the direction toward which all Indian mosques are oriented. Variations of this Iranian iour-aiwan plan continue to be constructed even through the Mughal period. In elevation, however, the Quwwat al-Islam mosque initially followed traditional Indian building techniques. That is, the building in its initial phase was strictly trabeated, built in the post-and-lintel system. This contrasts to the more common arcuated or vaulted building types found throughout most Muslim-dominated lands. In Indo-Islamic architecture, however, trabeated buildings continued even through the Mughal period as one major mode of construction. As we shall see, to assume as most writers have done that all trabeated structures, especially in the case of Akbar's Fatehpur Sikri, are a revival or even conscious adaptation of Hindu forms is erroneous.

Aibek was evidently aware that his mosque, constructed entirely of elements pillaged from Hindu and Jain monuments, resembled more a rearranged temple than a traditional mosque. In 1198 he thus constructed an arched screen (Plate 2) across the front of the prayer chamber so his mosque might more closely mirror those in his homeland. This screen is richly adorned with vertical bands of carved calligraphy and naturalistically growing vines. While Arabic lettering, in this case verses from the Quran, typically embellishes the facade of prayer chambers throughout the Islamic world, the appearance of naturalistic, organic forms is a good deal more unusual. These naturalistic forms, in lieu of the more flattened, abstracted patterns generally found in the Ghorids' Iranian homelands, doubtless can be traced to Indian masons continuing to work in indigenous modes.

A rapidly growing Muslim population necessitated a larger mosque. Thus Aibek's structure was doubled in size by his son-in-law and successor, Iltutmish. Before the prayer chamber he also constructed an arched screen whose ornamentation differed from that of Aibek's. The motifs on Iltutmish's screen relate closely to those seen on Ghorid structures, for example the Shah-i Mashhad Madrasa in Ghargistan, north Afghanistan. They are more abstract than those on Aibek's screen and carved in a deep flat relief. The overall appearance is that of a rich tapestry, almost a horror vacui design. This tendency toward intense patterning over an entire stone-carved surface reappears in the early phases of Mughal architecture. Profuse surface decoration is characteristic of much Islamic ornamentation, not just that of India. Under Iltutmish, the subcontinent's first monumental tombs were built.

One, known today as the Sultan Ghari tomb, was constructed for his son, and a second was built for himself, both in Delhi. The interior of Iltutmish's own square-plan tomb was embellished in a fashion similar to his screen at the Quwwat al-Islam mosque. Some thirty chapters of the Quran are engraved on the tomb's interior walls. The themes of the chapters selected from these inscriptions include the oneness of God, the obligations of the devout, and the power of God - all themes of inscriptions on the Quwwat al-Islam mosque and its minaret, the Qutb Minar, both constructed under Aibek and Iltutmish. A new theme was introduced in the inscriptions of Iltutmish's tomb, one that became especially important for the Mughals, that is, eternal paradise as a reward for the true believer on the Day of Judgment. Thus commences in India the tradition of paradisical imagery for tomb construction. Under the Mughals and culminating with the Taj Mahal, this theme came to be used with extraordinary effect, not only in inscriptions but in the entire conception of the monument. No major Islamic structures remain in India that date between the death of Iltutmish in 1235 and the beginning of the fourteenth century. However, under the Khalji Sultan Ala al-Din (ruled 1296-1316), architecture assumed renewed importance. Focusing on the monument that remained symbolically paramount, Ala al-Din expanded the Quwwat al-Islam mosque to triple its original size. Although the project was never completed, its vast scale mirrors the ambitions of a prince who wished to become a second Alexander the Great.

He sought to incorporate not only south India into his domain, but China as well. In fact, the only remaining parts of the Khalji addition to the Quwwat al- Islam mosque complex are an enormous unfinished minaret, pillared galleries and an entrance portal on the south, known commonly as the Alai Darwaza (Plate 3). Dated 13 n , many epigraphs on this gate are not Quranic, but hyperbole praising its patron, Sultan Ala al-Din Khalji. Although it is not a monumental structure, it is one that later builders, among them the early Mughals looked upon as a source of inspiration. A square-plan gate, its layout adheres closely to that of Iltutmish's tomb. In ornamentation, however, major differences exist. The exterior of Iltutmish's tomb is austere, composed largely of plain dressed stones. In contrast, the Alai Darwaza's facade as well as interior is entirely faced with carved stones. This ornamentation appears to be based on both indigenous Indian traditions as well as non-Indian Islamic patterns. For example, the Arabic lettering, flat-cut stencil-like arabesques, battlement motifs {kungura) and geometric patterns derive from earlier Iranian traditions, while the carved lotus medallions and budded creepers are adaptations of earlier Indian motifs.

By the Khalji period, Indo-Islamic culture had come into its own. Underscoring this is the contemporary work of Amir Khusrau, still considered one of the greatest Indian poets. Writing in Persian, the official language of most Muslim courts and kings in India, Khusrau used motifs such as the parrot, mangoes and flowers only found in India to supplement Persianate imagery, such as cedars and tulips, alien to the subcontinent. By this time, many motifs - architectural and literary - had no strictly sectarian connotation. To call a motif Hindu or Muslim has little meaning, for elements such as the lotus or even trabeated architecture, still found in parts of Ala al-Din's extension to the Quwwat al-Islam mosque, are now part of a well-established architectural tradition developed under the Indian sultans.

The Alai Darwaza is covered with carved stones and calligraphy that give the appearance of a richly textured surface. Long strips of white marble, used frequently for calligraphic bands, effectively stand out against the red sandstone ground of the facade. This concern for contrasting colors on a facade, also seen for example on the Khalji-period Ukha mosque in Bayana, probably ultimately is derived from the architectural traditions of the Turkish Seljuks. A memory of Seljuk design was brought to India by nobles, intellectuals and artisans fleeing the invading Mongols. Multi-colored facades of inlaid stone are seen rarely over the next 200 years; however, beginning in the early sixteenth century, facades inlaid with multi-colored stone are seen with greater frequency. There is reason to believe that the Alai Darwaza served as a direct source of inspiration for these structures, which in turn were the inspiration for the ornamentation on buildings such as the tomb of Ataga Khan (Plate 16), constructed early in Akbar's reign, or the Fatehpur Sikri Jamic mosque. Following the Khaljis, the Tughluqs emerged as the ruling power. Assuming control in 1320 over an area that included much of the Indian subcontinent, their territory quickly diminished as provincial governors declared independence from central authority, leaving them little more than Delhi and its suburbs. While the dynasty nominally survived until 1412, Delhi was sacked in 1399 by the invasion of Timur, the ancestor of the Mughals.

The Tughluqs were prolific providers of architecture, especially under the third ruler, Firuz Shah (r. 1351-88), whose extensive building campaigns were in a sense a cover for his politically weak regime. In general, architecture under the Tughluqs became increasingly austere into the fourteenth century. For example, richly carved stone facades and interiors were replaced with plain stucco veneers, and Quranic inscriptions rarely embellished any structure. While Tughluq buildings may have been painted, multi-colored stones on their surface were rare. With the exception of the iour-aiwan mosque type, few of the architectural forms and little of the ornamentation developed in their reign appear to have had any direct bearing on Mughal buildings.

Nevertheless, the work of the Tughluqs foreshadows aspects of Mughal architecture. Firuz Shah Tughluq constructed extensive earthworks, mosques, schools for religious instruction (madrasa), as well as other edifices that were aimed at enhancing the religious and economic well-being of his subjects. While such projects fit well with the theoretical duty of a good Islamic ruler, in India no sultan hitherto had built public works so extensively. The Mughals subsequently did so, and like their Tughluq predecessors, they also provided support for the benefit of all subjects. For example, the Tughluq sultans and nobles endowed Hindu temples;3 so, too, under the Mughal dynasty, was patronage provided for Hindu monuments. Even the Mughal Aurangzeb, traditionally considered an iconoclast and temple destroyer, gave orders for the protection of Hindus and their temples. And some Hindu nobles under the Mughals provided funds for Islamic buildings. The tomb of the first Tughluq ruler, Ghiyas al-Din, reflects a further development in paradisical imagery. While not unique to India, this imagery is developed most fully in funereal architecture during the Mughal period. Ghiyas al-Din's tomb is located slightly to the west of this sultan's massive Delhi fortress, Tughluqabad. Originally connected to it by a long arched bridge, the tomb is situated within pentagonal walls that mirror the nearby larger fort. Today the square-plan tomb sits in the midst of grain fields, but originally it was surrounded by a vast body of water, making the tomb, already protected by sloping enclosure walls, even more inaccessible.

It has been suggested that the tomb's fortress-like design reflects the political instability of the time and that it was constructed during Ghiyas al-Din's own life so that he could use it to protect himself against foes. However, such a structure could not provide long-term protection; rather, its setting in a pool of water evokes numerous references in the Quran to the abundant waters of paradise, an image so precious to the desert dwellers of Arabia, Islam's birthplace. This pool refers to the tank at which believers quench their thirst when entering paradise. The association of water with funereal structures to denote paradise will continue as a major motif in Mughal architecture.

While Iltutmish's tomb is a virtual storehouse of Quranic verse and Ghiyas al-Din Tughluq's tomb is a private vision of paradise, Firuz Shah Tughluq's tomb is austere, appropriate for its location in the midst of an Islamic theological college. Also in the grounds of this madrasa, in close proximity to Firuz Shah's tomb, are small kiosk-like structures known as chattris. They have domed superstructures supported by six or eight pillars. These chattris mark the graves of deceased saints or men of sufficient piety to be buried in the school's grounds. The nearby tomb of Firuz Shah overlooks a large tank, an appropriate location for a tomb. The tomb, characteristic of its period, is square in plan. The exterior walls have a thick unembellished stucco veneer. The interior is also stucco faced, generally plain, although the interior of the dome is incised and polychromed to evoke an image of the heavens. In addition to medallions and floral designs, the dome is inscribed with verses from the Quran and sayings attributed to the Prophet Muhammad (hadis). The hope of paradise is a principal theme of these verses, a theme that will dominate the iconography of Mughal tombs.

THE SUCCESSOR STATES OF THE TUGHLUQS

As central Tughluq authority over regional territories weakened, Tughluq governors asserted their independence, creating a series of successor states. In the case of Deccani and Bengali governors, ties were severed with the Tughluq masters as early as the mid-fourteenth century. Gradually through the early fifteenth century other governors declared independence. Most of these regions remained autonomous until the very beginning of the Mughal period. Artistic trends to a large extent reflect political ones.

That is, structures constructed in these areas during Tughluq domination or shortly thereafter are modeled closely on the Tughluq architecture of Delhi. For example, the first congregational mosque of the Ilyas Shahi dynasty (1352-1415; 1433-86) in Bengal, the Adina mosque of Pandua built in 1374, is inspired in both plan and overall appearance by Muhammad Shah Tughluq's congregational mosque in Delhi, commonly known as the Begumpuri mosque (c. 1343). So is the earlyfourteenth century Atala mosque in Jaunpur, the first congregational mosque of the Sharqi dynasty. However, buildings constructed after the initial phase of independence generally use plans and motifs indigenous to their area. This, as we shall see, is a pattern also reflected in some of the late Mughal architecture of the provinces.

The most dramatic examples of distinctly regional style are found in the architectural traditions of Bengal and Gujarat. In Bengal, the form of the village hut with its sloping roof, well suited for heavy rains, was adapted for tombs and mosques, for example the mosque of Baba

Adam (1483) in Rampal, today located in Dhaka District, Bangladesh, and the Eklakhi tomb in Pandua, West Bengal, datable to the fifteenth century. Probably the curved roof was used in palace architecture as well, but we have no surviving examples. Similar roofs are common in Mughal architecture commencing around the mid-seventeenth century. Such roofs were called bangala in Mughal documents and were often used by the end of the seventeenth century far from Bengal in Mughal architecture.

Few other connections link architecture produced under the independent sultans of Bengal with monuments subsequently erected under the Mughals. For example, the delicate brick work seen in the Tantipora mosque in Gaur or the exquisite stone carving on the Adina mosque in Pandua had little influence on subsequent Mughal monuments. While a few motifs - among them the bell and chain - are common to the architecture of both Sultanate Bengal and the Mughals, these motifs are seen also in the Sultanate architecture of other realms, notably Gujarat. Thus the claim of Akbar's chronicler, Abu al-Fazl, that the "fine styles of Bengal" were crucial in the development of Akbari architecture is little substantiated by the remains themselves.

In Gujarat, as in Bengal, architecture under the newly established Ahmad Shahi dynasty (1408-1578) assumed a distinctly regional character. Features found commonly on tombs, mosques and saints' shrines (dargahs) include ones such as serpentine-like gateways (toranas) or lintels above prayer niches (mihrabs), bell-and-chain motifs carved on pillars and walls, pillars supporting corbelled domes and ceiling insets, and carved panels often depicting trees, all ultimately derived from Gujarati temple traditions. Because of these borrowings, some scholars have assumed a conscious and continued Hindu influence. More likely, however, these features were first used by local Hindu artisans contracted to work on the Islamic architecture of the area, and their form, but not their original meaning, became assimilated into the standard architectural repertoire. Thus when many of these same ideas appear in the architecture of Akbar, there is no reason to associate them with any particular sectarian tradition.

Such features are not limited to Gujarat. They are also features of architecture in Mandu, related politically and geographically to Gujarat, and in Chanderi. For example, serpentine brackets, seen on the mid-fifteenth-century mosque at Sarkhej, Gujarat, also appear on the Jamic mosque in Chanderi and on the tomb of Hoshang Shah in Mandu. Similarly, inlaid white marble was a dominant building material in both Gujarat and Mandu. The concurrent use of such features throughout western and part of north-central India has significance for Mughal architecture, where these features are common. It is generally assumed that artisans for Akbar's palaces came from Gujarat, but the widespread use of such motifs opens the possibility that they came from a greater area.

More important than the borrowing of individual motifs from Gujarat is the overall influence of the fifteenth-century dargab of Shaikh Ahmad Khattu of Sarkhej on the design of Mughal tombs. This tomb, situated outside of Ahmadabad, is a white marble shrine whose facade is embellished with pierced carved screens (jalis). Both the material and screens became major features of Mughal architecture. In addition, the tomb's plan as well as the juxtaposed colored stones used on the flooring had a major impact on Mughal mausolea.

The early structures erected by the independent rulers in the Deccan, as in the north, adhered closely to Tughluq models. However, unlike the monuments of Gujarat and Bengal, Deccani architecture was subject to the influence of Iranian Seljuk and Timurid forms in the course of developing its own regional styles. Although this Seljuk influence has no bearing on Mughal art, the Timurid influence is of concern here, for the Deccan felt the impact of Iranian Timurid tradition before north India.

For example, intersecting pendentives, a Timurid device, appear in Bidar on the tomb of Sultan Kalim Allah (d. 1527), shortly before they are used in north India. It is thus possible that the Mughals, descended from Timurid ancestors, did not directly import the tradition of their heritage when they came to India but adopted Timurid forms from the Deccan. There is, however, no real evidence for the movement of artistic styles from south to north.

IMMEDIATE MUGHAL PRECEDENTS: THE LODI AND SUR TRADITIONS

After some hundred years, during which Delhi enjoyed little prestige, the Afghan-descended Lodi dynasty (1451-1526) made vigorous efforts to revive the city's status. They vanquished their enemies, the Sharqis of Jaunpur, and soon afterward commenced extensive building in Delhi itself. Certain motifs on Lodi buildings are identical to those seen earlier only at Jaunpur. This is the case, for example, with engaged colonettes embellished with an interwoven pattern on the Bara Gumbad, almost certainly built as a ceremonial entrance to the Bagh-i Jud, known today as Lodi Gardens, the burial grounds for the Lodi rulers.

This suggests that artists were taken to Delhi from Jaunpur, until then considered the cultural center of Islamic India, in an attempt to revive the prestige of the traditional capital. The revival of Delhi was accelerated under the reigns of the first two Mughals, Babur and Humayun, who succeeded the Lodis. Their architecture is the subject of the next chapter. Following their reign, however, Mughal authority in India was briefly interrupted when the Delhi throne was assumed in 1540 by the Afghan ruler, Sher Shah Sur and his successors (1538-55). Although fifteen years of Mughal rule separated the periods of Lodi and Sur authority, the architecture produced under these two Afghan dynasties can be discussed simultaneously since it is close in form and spirit.

Under the Lodis a new type of mosque developed, one that ultimately became a major type in Mughal India. In lieu of the large congregational mosque favored under earlier Sultanate dynasties, small single-aisled mosques composed usually of three or five bays were constructed. Although it is not fully understood how or why this type was developed, a Jamic mosque constructed by Sultan Sikandar Lodi and dated 1494, commonly known as the Bara Gumbad mosque in Delhi's Lodi Gardens (Plate 4), appears to be the first example. Subsequent examples include the Moth-ki Masjid, built in Delhi about 1510 by Sikandar Lodi's prime minister, and the Jamali mosque, probably built shortly after the Mughal conquest of India but in this Lodi style. The Jamali mosque was built adjacent to the house of Jamali (d. 1536), a poet and saint favored by the Lodis as well as by the first Mughals, Humayun and Babur. It represents a mature example of the small single-aisled type. The facades of these mosques show one or more of the following features not seen on mosques in Delhi since the Khalji era, yet important for the subsequent development of much Mughal mosque architecture: inlaid colored stones Qamali mosque), calligraphy (Sikandar Lodi's Jamic mosque), and a high central portal (pishtaq) on all these mosques, suggesting a renewed interest in the monumental appearance of the facade.

Within the walls of Sher Shah Sur's citadel, known today as the Purana Qalca in Delhi, is a magnificent single-aisled mosque that was probably the Jamic mosque of this Sur sultan (Plate 5). The citadel was commenced by the second Mughal, Humayun, but was probably finished by Sher Shah (r. 1538-45), an Afghan usurper, after he expelled the Mughals from Hindustan in 1540. Although this mosque, today known as the Qalca-i Kuhna mosque, is attributed by some to Humayun, it follows forms and utilizes motifs seen on at least one other building of Sher Shah, the tomb he erected for his grandfather at Narnaul.

Moreover, it shares little in common with any extant building of Humayun. Its use of calligraphy and contrasting colored stones on the richly textured exterior evokes the appearance of Ala al-Din Khalji's Alai Darwaza. Significantly, Sher Shah's government revived many of the administrative features of Ala al-Din's own government. Sher Shah associated these features with the revival of the Delhi Sultanate's prestige. Abu al-Fazl, Akbar's official chronicler, guardedly applauded these revived administrative features in spite of Mughal contempt for this Afghan upstart. Not only is the overall appearance of this mosque's facade important for the future development of Mughal architecture, but also many details found there influence subsequent building. On the mosque, many features are presented in an only slightly less sophisticated manner than in Akbar's own architecture. They are here more developed than on any prototype, thus in a sense serving as a bridge to subsequent Mughal ornamentation.

The single-aisled plan is used exclusively for Lodi- and Sur-period Jamic mosques and for many lesser mosques in those periods as well. Still, simple multi-aisled multi-bayed mosques, often trabeated and flat-roofed, continued to be constructed across India. Examples include the Sangi mosque in Phulwari Sharif, Bihar, dated 1549-50, and the Chowk-ki Masjid, dated 1553, in Nagaur, Rajasthan.

Trabeated, flat-roofed structures continue a long-standing Indian tradition. They in no way represent a style that can be classified as non-Islamic. Before the Lodis, elaborate tombs were built only for kings, members of the royal family and highly venerated saints.

Although there were only three Lodi kings, more than a hundred large tombs constructed under Lodi auspices remain in Delhi alone, many times the number of tombs built under earlier regimes. Since surely there were not a hundred saints worthy of elaborate tombs during this brief period, the explanation appears to lie in the attitude toward kingship under the Lodis. The sultan under earlier Indo-Islamic dynasties had been regarded as autocratic, a ruler whose power was absolute. The Lodis, however, were a tribe from Afghanistan.

Although they were long settled in India, members of other Afghan tribes formed their support. These tribal chiefs viewed a king not as an absolute but rather as a comrade who was first among equals. In this same manner, these nobles felt that they, too, should merit tombs, formerly a royal perquisite. Often the tombs of these nobles are even larger than royal ones. Generally the royal tombs were octagonal, while those of the nobles were square in plan.

A typical square-plan tomb is that of Mubarak Khan in Delhi's South Extension, dated to 1481-82. Its facade is marked with multiple tiers of arched niches and windows divided by rows of string coursing, giving this single-storied structure the appearance of several stories. Mubarak Khan's tomb is surmounted by a single dome, and chattris mark each corner of the roof. Square-plan tombs adhering to this general plan were constructed by the Mughals as well, even into the eighteenth century. For Sher Shah Sur the association of tomb construction with status assumed even greater importance. The only

Indian sultan descending from a lowranking heritage, Sher Shah wished to fabricate an elevated genealogy to indicate that he had the requisite piety and high birth demanded of Islamic sovereigns.

Shortly after he assumed the Delhi throne in 1540, this sultan constructed for his grandfather and father, each long-deceased and lowranking, enormous magnificent tombs that posthumously implied elevated status. His grandfather's tomb in Narnaul is of special interest, for not only is it a square-plan tomb of the type that had been reserved for high-ranking Lodi nobles, but also it is larger and more carefully crafted than Lodi prototypes.

This enormous tomb is exquisitely rendered with contrasting grey and red stones on the facade. It serves as an immediate model for the finest Mughalperiod square-plan tombs. In Sasaram Sher Shah built for his father a huge three-tiered octagonal mausoleum, a type generally reserved for royalty, yet much larger than any Lodi prototype. Situated in the middle of a walled compound with structures usually found in a saint's shrine - a mosque, a madrasa, a serai, a hall for religious meditation and step-well - this tomb bestowed upon Sher Shah's low-ranking father the trappings of both a saint and a king.

The monumental octagonal mausoleum, completed in 1545, that Sher Shah constructed for himself, also in Sasaram, was at that time the largest tomb ever built in all India. Its setting, in the middle of an artificial lake, is a visual allusion to the abundant waters of paradise described in the Quran. Specifically this tank refers to the pool at which believers quench their thirst when entering paradise, a reference made lucid by the presence of these particular Quranic verses (108: 1-3) carved on the tomb's interior.

The tomb's octagonal shape is again an allusion to the eight levels that comprise the Islamic notion of paradise. The eight-sided ambulatory around the tomb permits circumambulating the deceased, an act of veneration in itself. The symbolism apparent in this tomb anticipates that of Mughal tombs. Thus the roots of Mughal mausolea do not lie exclusively outside of India.

SOURCES OF MUGHAL INSPIRATION

Non-Islamic Sources

Although the Sultanate period is generally believed to be one of little tolerance for non-Muslims, Hindu and Jain architecture continued to be built in north India during this time. For example, at least three temples in Bihar are either dated or datable to the Sultanate period. One of them, in the Hindu pilgrimage city of Gaya, even bears an inscription praising the Muslim overlord, Firuz Shah Tughluq, a ruler traditionally considered belligerently anti-Hindu. Some temples of this period are domed, as indicated by paintings illustrating a 1516 Aryanyakaparvan. Thus domed architecture cannot be considered exclusive to the Muslims.

Secular architecture erected at this time under Hindu patrons had a substantial impact on subsequent secular buildings, notably those of the Mughals. One example, a magnificent one, is the Man Mandir palace built in Gwalior about 1500 by Raja Man Singh Tomar. Among the few buildings admired by Babur in India, the palace is rightly regarded as having influenced Akbar in the design of his own palaces. Situated atop the high flat plateau of the ancient Gwalior fort, the palace's exterior is marked with a series of circular buttresses each surmounted by a high domed chattri, and the facade is embellished with tiles glazed predominantly blue or yellow.

While the Gwalior palace's exterior influenced the inlaid mosaic facade of the Delhi gate in Akbar's Agra fort, the interior of this palace had an even greater impact on Akbar's architecture. The main body of the palace consists of a series of small connecting courtyards around whose perimeter are galleries containing rooms. These rooms are never arcuated, but have essentially flat roofs, a type that reappears in Akbar's Agra and Fatehpur Sikri palaces. Like subsequent Mughal palaces, the Gwalior palace makes use of animal brackets supporting the gallery eaves (chajjas), probably ultimately modeled on torana motifs, that are used both as wall ornamentation as well as functional devices. While Man Singh's palace, not far from Agra and Fatehpur Sikri, had an apparent impact on Akbari architecture, it is wrong to consider the Gwalior palace uniquely Hindu in form. Rather, it belongs to a type of domestic architecture that late in the Sultanate period was utilized by both Hindus and non-Hindus.

THE IRANIAN TRADITION

In spite of a long-standing Islamic heritage in India, Mughal rulers considered themselves the rightful heirs of the Iranian Timurid tradition, which they felt was superior to Indo-Islamic culture. Important among Timurid artistic traditions adopted by the Mughals are those that had been maintained and further refined by a Timurid successor state, the Shaibanis of Bukhara. Their rule was contemporary with the beginnings of a Mughal domination of India. Thus, despite the fact that Safavid rule and artistic expression dominated most of the Iranian world, the Shaibanis provided a conduit for the transmission of Timurid architectural forms.

Mughal architecture adopted from Timurid antecedents possesses a sense of grandeur and an extremely sophisticated realization of geometrical proportion. Timurid architects had developed an understanding of how interconnecting and stacked transverse arches could be used in lieu of solid walls to create new spatial organizations. This resulted in structures with a large central room surrounded by smaller chambers and arched entranceways of various sizes. Such a plan is seen in the Timurid cIshrat Khana, a dynastic mausoleum in Samarqand; it was built for women of the Timurid house and finished around 1464. Frequently imperial Mughal tombs were designed on a similar plan, specifically one consisting of nine bays. That is, a central chamber is surrounded by eight smaller rooms whose placement, size and shape depended on a geometric division of the whole.

The Ak-serai tomb in Samarqand was of this type, as were some garden pavilions known from written descriptions. Other Timurid examples of this type include the khanqah of Qasim Shaikh in Kirman dated 15 58-59 and the tomb of Uleg Beg Miranshah in Ghazni (d. 1506). Since the architect of Humayun's tomb, the first Timurid-inspired tomb in Mughal India, came from Bukhara, where he had designed a variety of building types, the Timurid inspiration for this and later Mughal tombs is not surprising. In mature phases of Timurid architecture, the surrounding chambers became symbolic of the eight levels of paradise, a concept adopted for Mughal mausolea as well. The complex geometrical formulae used for Timurid building plans and the arcuated systems of the walls allowed a proportionately large floor space to be covered by a narrower superstructure. New vaulting systems consisting of arch-nets in the squinches were created to cover angles formed by intersecting arches. Stellate forms, frequently based on the structure's geometrical proportions, adorned interior domes and vaults. These are found first in Timurid and then in Mughal architectural vaulting.

Following a long-standing Iranian tradition, the garden, symbolic of paradise, was developed by the Timurids and subsequently by the Mughals. Informally planted walled gardens with running streams, pools and often pavilions were an inherent part of the large Timurid cities. Babur, the first Mughal emperor, lists in his memoirs numerous gardens that delighted him in Timurid Herat, a city whose splendid palaces and gardens went a long way in influencing Babur's own building schemes in India.

These gardens were called char bagh (literally: four gardens), although their actual layout is open to dispute since none remains today. While some believe that this type of garden was divided into four sections as at the Mughal tombs, others believe that the term derives from the practice of planting in sets of four beds and that quartering a garden by waterways was a Mughal innovation. The type of Jamic or large congregational mosque developed under the imperial Mughals derives from large Timurid mosques. These are iour-aiwan structures in whose center is an open courtyard. The prayer chamber of these mosques is entered through a large vaulted portal. The side wings are pillared corridors. This type of Timurid mosque, for example the Bibi Khanum in Samarqand (i398-1405), or the Kalan mosque (fifteenth-sixteenth century) in Bukhara, adheres closely to earlier Seljuk models that had been the prototype as well for the mosque (Plates 1 and 2) erected by the Ghorid rulers who had conquered Delhi in the late twelfth century. This would explain why early Mughal mosques ideally modeled on Timurid types often appear to resemble in plan many earlier Sultanate mosques of India.

MUGHAL TASTE ANTICIPATED

The heritage bequeathed to the new Mughal rulers and their subjects was a rich and varied one. It included Iranian, indigenous Indian and eventually even European forms and symbolism. Attitudes toward this heritage during the subsequent 300 years, on both an imperial and a sub-imperial level, will formulate a Mughal aesthetic and create a unique cultural expression. Mughal architectural taste and idiom evolves from the center outwards. It is triggered by imperial predilection, rarely arbitrary but embedded in political and cultural ideology. The ruler is not often solely responsible for construction outside central urban areas; rather, it is the nobility, usually high-ranking, wealthy and sophisticated, that are responsible for building there.

They built, often prolifically, on their landholdings that were granted in lieu of salary, even though these lands were shifted about every two years to prevent the establishment of threatening power bases. Such construction, almost always rooted in a current Mughal idiom but often reflecting local taste as well, was essentially a way to curry favor with the emperor and to buy power and success. In return, the mosques, temples, palaces, gardens and other works erected served as symbols of Mughal presence and authority. Even during the eighteenth and nineteenth centuries, when the capital, Delhi, increasingly became both the heart and perimeter of the Mughal empire, imperial Mughal architectural aesthetic and taste served as the model for construction in developing splinter states. Mughal style eventually came to represent not Mughal authority, but the cultural and social values established under the Mughals. These values were cherished by Muslim subjects living increasingly under western colonial rule. How, why and where this transpired is the story of the next five chapters.

2

The Beginning

BABUR

Born in what is today the southern Soviet province of Uzbekistan, the Timurid Babur inherited the throne of a small principality known as Ferghana in 1494. He was then eleven years old. By the time he was twenty-one, he twice had held neighboring Samarqand, albeit briefly. For two years after his second loss of Samarqand, Babur, homeless and supported only by a tiny band of loyal followers, sought a principality. In 1504 his luck improved, and he captured Kabul and surrounding territories. In 1511, Babur tried for a third time to extend his rule to Samarqand, this time with support from the Safavid king Shah Ismacil. The Safavid extended his support only because Babur, a Sunni, had agreed to adopt trappings of the Shia creed, a heretical notion to the orthodox Sunni Muslims of Samarqand. Babur was able to enter the city and establish himself as its ruler. But within less than a year, the Sunni subjects of Samarqand withdrew support from Babur. After unsuccessful attempts to gain Bukhara, Babur returned to Kabul in 1512, once again holding only this province, nothing more.

While Babur's tenure in Samarqand had been short, the city's impact upon him was profound, shaping his attitude toward architecture and, even more significantly, toward landscape. Samarqand, embellished by Timur and his immediate successors with splendid char bagh gardens, mosques, madrasas and tombs, was one of the wonders of the fifteenth century. Babur was also deeply impressed by Herat, the seat of most cultured Timurid princes, which he had visited in 1507. Its many gardens and magnificent buildings are recorded in tourist-like fashion in his memoirs. These memoirs are not only intimate observations of his own exploits and travels, but also carefully observed descriptions of nature, be it human or the flora and fauna which abounded in his native Central Asia as well as in India. It thus comes as no surprise that among Babur's first enterprises in the province of Kabul was the layout of terraced, planted gardens with running streams. These doubtless were inspired by the gardens of Samarqand and Herat and reflected Babur's deep love of nature.

A true Timurid in spirit, Babur preferred to camp in gardens than reside in any permanently constructed palace. Throughout his small principality, he either refurbished already existing gardens or created new ones. However, the creation of such gardens was not simply an indulgence in a personal pleasure or a whimsical pastime. They were used as camp sites, situated at a day's or halfday's horse ride from one another in the manner that other rulers built serais. The fruit of the gardens was consumed by Babur and his men, for frequently he refers to bananas, oranges or pomegranates eaten by his followers or given as special gifts. But such gardens probably had a greater significance. That is, the manipulation of natural untamed landscape into a rational, ordered creation was for Babur a metaphor for his ability to govern. Underscoring this is the allusion by Babur's faithful noble, Zain Khan, to "the garden of his [Babur's] powerful state," using other garden and floral imagery to proclaim Babur's regal character.

The locations of many of these gardens, such as the ones at Nimla or Istalif, are known from Babur's writings as well as those of Zain Khan. They indicate the types of trees, flowers and fruit that grew in these terraced settings. Natural springs were formalized with stone edgings, streams were diverted through man-made watercourses and pavilions were constructed for the joy of the beholder. Of all Babur's gardens in Kabul province, the Bagh-i Wafa, or Garden of Fidelity, must have been his favorite, for he writes about it most frequently. Located near Jalalabad in modern Afghanistan, this garden lay close to the Khyber Pass, the only break in the mountain barrier between Kabul and Hindustan.

Babur halted at the Bagh-i Wafa at various times over the next fifteen years. It was divided into four parts by running streams and planted with oranges, limes, pomegranates, bananas, sugar cane, jasmine, tulips and hyacinths, among other plants. Today none of these Afghan gardens exists in its original state, and even the location of many of them remains in doubt.

Babur's Conquest of India

Babur had long contemplated a conquest of India. As early as 1505 he made an initial foray as far as the Indus River, but until 1514 he largely aspired to retake his Central Asian territories. With this dream effectively quashed, Babur's thoughts turned again toward India. He then engaged a Turkish artillery-man and fortified his army with guns, weapons his Indian opponents lacked. He secured Qandahar, necessary in order to protect Kabul during long absences, and invaded India five times. Using innovative military tactics learned from Ustad Ali, his current head artillery-man, Babur's army defeated Sultan Ibrahim Lodi's more numerous foot and cavalry forces. Babur killed the Indian sultan himself at the battle of Panipat in April, 1526.

Declaring himself emperor of Hindustan, Babur established Agra as his capital. His first and most serious opponent was a Rajput Hindu, Rana Sangam of Mewar, leader of a largely Hindu-Rajput confederacy. A renowned warrior, Rana Sangam had also aspired to replace the Lodi sultans. His troops were defeated by Babur in March 1527 in close proximity to Fatehpur Sikri, a victory commemorated by the construction of large stepped wells. For the next several years until his premature death in 1530, Babur's career was devoted to conquering northern and eastern India. When he died, Babur bequeathed to his oldest son, Humayun, a shaky and as yet unconsolidated empire that extended from Afghanistan into Bihar.

Babur's Indian Gardens

Even before the battle of Panipat, Babur considered the Punjab, that is, the north-western territory between Delhi and Kabul, rightfully his since earlier it had been conquered by his ancestor, Timur. There, on a bitter cold, rainy day in February 1526, two months before his victory over the Lodis, Babur discovered a site near the Ghaggar river that he deemed ideal for a char bagh.

The garden, which he designed himself, was finished in 1528-29. Although it no longer survives, literary reports indicate that Babur's first Indian garden was built around a natural spring and that the garden itself was situated in a narrow mountain valley, a terrain close to that of Babur's own Kabul. However, after his victory at Panipat in the hot summer month of April 1526, the morale of Babur's troops declined markedly. While Babur himself detested the heat, dust, flies and violent winds of the Indian summers, he was determined to stay, rallying the support of his followers. He responded to the climate by building gardens and baths.

Gardens, ordered and regular, could shape the terrain to Babur's own liking and expectations. Running water required for all Mughal gardens was supplied by constructing Persian water wheels, in conjunction with deep stepped wells called baolis. Baths piped with hot and cold water were built in these gardens, for, as Babur states, inside such baths the heat and flying dust are shut out. In Agra no suitable land for a garden existed, but Babur nevertheless laid out a char bagh that he named Hasht Behisht, the four-quartered Garden of Eight Paradises. It was situated on the east bank of the Jumna river. Although not stated explicitly, Babur's memoirs suggest that it served as his main residence and court, for it included baths, a large tank, an audience hall and private dwellings.

A second garden was constructed just inside the city's old fort. By the end of 1526 this garden, its well, several stone structures and a mosque were completed. Babur disliked the mosque, for it was designed "in the Hindustani fashion," but the well pleased him, and he dedicated its completion to his victory over the Rana Sangam. Some have associated this well with an extant baoli in the Agra fort, but that is probably a later project.

A second baoli, an octagonal one, is located at the base of the Fatehpur Sikri rock scarp about a kilometer from the Hiran Minar

(Plate 27) constructed by Akbar later in the century. This was probably the original site of a well-known epigraph commemorating Babur's Fatehpur Sikri victory. A deep flight of stairs leads to the octagonal well; pillared and arched passageways mark each level of its shaft. These red sandstone corridors, which remain cool during the hot season, are embellished with rosettes, simply carved brackets and cbandrashalas (elaborate niche-like forms) on pillar bases typically found during this period. While some writers confuse this baoli with the one Babur's memoirs describe in the Agra fort garden,6 he probably constructed a baoli in each place, recording only one in his memoirs.

Agra, Babur's capital, figures large in his memoirs, but he much loved Fatehpur Sikri, which he named Shukri, or Thanks, for its large lake with water much needed by Mughal troops. Following his defeat of the rana on the outskirts of Fatehpur Sikri, Babur constructed a garden there called the Garden of Victory. In it he built an octagonal pavilion which he used for relaxation and writing. In the center of a nearby lake he built a large platform. Only two of Babur's Indian gardens can be identified with any certainty. One is in Agra, today called the Ram Bagh. Although its original name is open to some dispute, it was probably the Gul Afshan garden, which served as Babur's burial site until his body was transferred to a garden in Kabul in accordance with his final wishes.

A water-course with pools symmetrically dividing the terraced garden is still evident, although it belongs to Jahangir's reign (1605-27), when the garden underwent extensive renovations. The second of Babur's gardens that can be identified is at Dholpur, today in Bharatpur District, Rajasthan. It is his Bagh-i Nilufar, or Lotus garden, described in his memoirs. Located atop the red sandstone ridge that looms high above the Chambal river, the Lotus garden is situated some 50 km south of Agra. The site, like all the settings for his gardens, was chosen by Babur personally, spotted when the emperor was examining a Lodi-period reservoir.

Babur describes the process of building the garden in some detail and refers to a mosque, bath, well, twenty-six rock spouts, pillars, watercourses cut terracelike into the terrain, and stone platforms. The bath, well and water channels are still extant, although little remains of the garden's original character; however, a centrally situated large lotus-shaped pool (Plate 6) as well as smaller pools, some with edging resembling lotus petals, are still visible. Lotus-shaped pools and tanks had been used earlier in India, for example in the Sultanate of Mandu, but the notion of terraced symmetrical gardens divided into four quarters by courses of running water was introduced into India by Babur.

No traces of the original planting remain, but the placement and choice of plants at the Lotus garden, as at all Babur's gardens, were probably by the emperor.

For example, melons brought from Kabul were grown successfully in Agra, grapes were introduced into India, trees were grafted and flowers especially cultivated for their color. His memoirs reveal a deep personal involvement with the cultivation of plants and flowers for his own gardens, and one section is devoted solely to a discussion of the fruits and trees of Hindustan. In short, Babur knew all potential plantings for his garden, and he demonstrated himself ultimate master and creator of each garden. Recalling that Zain Khan uses the garden metaphor for Babur's state, Babur's portrayal of himself as its master assumes special significance. Babur issued orders that regular, symmetrical gardens and orchards were to be laid out in all large cities.

A garden constructed in conjunction with a mosque was completed in Panipat upon imperial order. In Gwalior, Rahim Dad, superintendent of Gwalior fort, constructed his own garden. It no longer remains, although a madrasa constructed in a local style adjacent to the garden does. Doubtless other gardens not mentioned in the memoirs were built as well. This introduction of a new aesthetic and ordering of the land, a land that Babur refers to as "disorderly Hind," should be construed as concrete evidence of the Mughals' Timurid heritage.

That these four-part, ordered gardens represented a. Timurid tradition, even in the eyes of Babur's Indian subjects, may be surmised from their names. The area in Agra developed under Babur's nobles, Zain Khan, Yunus Ali and Khalifa, was called Kabul by local inhabitants;

and today the area in Panipat where Babur's garden originally stood is still called Kabuli Bagh.

The Quest for a Mughal Style

Babur's memoirs indicate that the construction of permanent buildings assumed less importance for him than the construction of gardens. Just as he camped in gardens in Kabul when moving from site to site, so too in India the garden served as his camp. Moreover, his precarious financial situation - where the payment of troops had to be his first priority - left fewer resources for large stone monuments. Nevertheless, buildings were constructed, enough to employ almost 1,500 stone cutters at work on projects throughout his north Indian domain.

Babur's view of indigenous Indian architecture is only partially reflected in his comment about a mosque within his Agra fort garden. He considered the building unattractively constructed in the "Hindustani fashion." While his objections are vague, Zain Khan elaborates that the foundations as well as the walls of this Agra mosque were strong, constructed of brick and stone, but the "composition was not conformable,"16 that is, not harmonious, referring to the spatial organization, doubtless much less sophisticated than that of Timurid prototypes. But Babur did not dislike all Indian architecture, for he describes favorably at some length the palaces of the Gwalior fort, praising especially those of Man Singh Tomar discussed in the previous chapter. Its special appeal lay in the carved stone walls, tiled facades and exterior chattris.

Just as Timur had admired Indian stone masons and some 225 years earlier had carried some back to work on his own buildings in Samarqand, so Babur - who had noted this in his memoirs - also favored the work of these artisans and employed them freely. Still today the hand of Indian masons is evident on the tanks at the Dholpur Lotus garden. These masons had been rewarded with gifts by Babur, who admired their craft. He was astonished at the ability of Indian masons to inlay and bond pieces of colored stone without the use of mortar. In spite of his admiration for Indian craftsmen,

Babur was concerned that the overall design of his structures in India should be modeled on Khurasani, that is, Timurid examples. Such models, for example, were probably followed in the design of one structure in the Agra Hasht Behisht garden. Although it is only known from textual description, it appears to have had a large pishtaq on each of four sides, connecting galleries and four small interior chambers. Possibly to insure fidelity to Timurid models, two artisans from Central Asia came to work for Babur in India.

One was Mir Mirak Ghiyas, identified as a stone cutter in Babur's memoirs, possibly identical with Mirak Sayyid Ghiyas, the designer of Humayun's tomb, who came from Herat and owned much land in Khurasan. A second stone cutter, Ustad Shah Muhammad, first had served Babur in Qandahar before his incursions into India and continued in his employ until at least 1529, the year before Babur's death. These men doubtless enjoyed a status far higher than that of ordinary craftsmen, for routine workers would not have been identified by name. Among the buildings of Babur's time that survive are one imperially patronized mosque and two others constructed by nobles on Babur's orders. These were all built in the final years of his reign. This is notable, for until Babur's conquest of India there is no evidence for his patronage of religious structures.

The mosque that Babur himself provided is in Panipat, today in Karnal District of Haryana State (Plates 7-8). Inscriptions indicate that the mosque was well under way, if not finished, by the end of 1527, and its gate, well and garden were finished by 1528. The mosque is not mentioned in literary sources; Babur's memoirs contain lacunae for this period, and Zain Khan's work ends abruptly with the events of early 1527. Nevertheless, we can certainly assume that the complex commemorates Babur's decisive victory over Sultan Ibrahim Lodi at Panipat and thus the Mughal conquest of Hindustan. Since the garden has disappeared, the mosque's location within it is not known. However, the building's large size suggests that it, rather than the garden, dominated the complex.

The rectangular prayer chamber, measuring Plate 7. Babur's mosque, today known as Kabuli Bagh mosque, Panipat 53. by 16.

meters, is dominated by a large central domed bay flanked on either side by three-bayed triple-aisled side wings. Each bay of the side wings is entered by an arched opening supported on massive piers. Over the mosque's brick construction is a heavy stucco veneer, reminiscent of that covering much Sultanate architecture. The northwest and southwest corners of the mosque were marked by octagonal towers crowned by domed pavilions, although only one survives. Each of the mosque's bays is surmounted by a dome, those over the westernmost aisle being smaller than those on the east.

The large central bay's qibla wall, the one oriented toward Mecca, is stonefaced, but elsewhere the veneer on the mosque's interior is stucco over a brick core. This central bay is the mosque's focal point, visible even from the outside through the wide entrance. Attention is drawn to the mihrab by an epigraph - including the Throne Verse from the Quran, and an historical inscription dated 1527-28 - rendered dramatically in black stone against white marble. While the chamber itself is a simple domed structure, recalling the Lodi Bara Gumbad built in Delhi's Lodi Gardens in 1494, the appearance of net pendentives here used only decoratively, evokes a Timurid flavor. Each side wing is divided into two aisles by massive brick piers; the resulting bays are crowned by domes resting on brick pendentives that are covered by a thick stucco veneer modeled to resemble net squinches, introduced to north India by the Mughals. A stone gate stands in the courtyard's north wall. It is carved in the tradition of earlier Lodi gates, for example that at the Lodi-period tomb of Khwaja Khizr dated 1522-24 in nearby Sonepat. Most of the enclosure wall has disappeared, but remains suggest that the entire courtyard was walled and that each side had similar gates.

The Panipat mosque's prayer chamber appears to have been loosely modeled on the type of congregational mosque used by the Timurids. It also incorporates features of mosques built by the pre-Lodi sultans in this region. This mosque type, however, was favored by Babur not because of any earlier Indian associations, but for two rather different reasons. First, it is decidedly different from the single-aisled multi-bayed type used exclusively by Babur's immediate predecessors, the Afghan Lodis. Notably at Panipat, the site of this mosque, Babur had defeated the Lodis. Second, it is a type that, although somewhat transformed in the process of Indian translation, had been constructed by Timur, for example in his Bibi Khanum mosque in Samarqand. As the Mughal Babur was the only surviving Timurid ruler, it must have been especially important for him to preserve at least a vestige of Timurid architectural forms. A vestige it is, no more, surprising in light of Babur's admiration for the architecture of the great Central Asian Timurid cities Samarqand and Herat. Despite his regard for Timurid architecture, it could not be replicated on Indian soil. It appears that there were only a few artists trained in the Timurid homeland and probably no architect capable of introducing the complex Timurid engineering principles. Moreover, Babur lacked the wealth needed for such construction. Instead, local architects and artisans relied closely on older but familiar Indian techniques.

Two other mosques remain that were constructed by leading nobles following Babur's orders. Probably these orders were general ones, not commands to erect specific mosques. One of these mosques is at Sambhal (Plate 9), about 140 km east of Delhi. It was constructed in 15 26 by Mir Hindu Beg, an important noble in the court of both Babur and Humayun. Built a year before Babur's Kabuli Bagh mosque in Panipat, the Sambhal mosque is the first extant Mughal building in India. The complex is entered through a gate on the east that opens to a large walled courtyard. The prayer chamber, like the one of the Panipat mosque, is rectangular with a large square central bay. Its entrance is set into a high pishtaq, recalling those of Sharqi mosques at Jaunpur. The chamber is flanked on either side by three-bayed double-aisled side wings. A single dome surmounts the central bay, and a small flatish dome surmounts each bay of the side wings.

The mosque's pishtaq and other features resembling fifteenthcentury Sharqi structures in nearby Jaunpur suggest a reliance on local artisans and designers. Even though the Sambhal mosque was renovated at least twice in the seventeenth century, enough of its original state remains to show that the plan and general appearance anticipate Babur's Panipat mosque commenced the following year. The size (40. by 12. meters), too, anticipates the scale of Babur's imperial mosque, thus making this mosque at Sambhal the largest one constructed in the Delhi region since Timur's sack of that city in 1398. This mosque is situated high on a hill and dominates the city for a considerable distance. According to Hindu lore that was known to the Mughals, the tenth and last incarnation of Vishnu will appear in Sambhal at the end of this era.

A second mosque (Plate 10) probably built in response to Babur's general orders, not a specific command, stands at Ayodhya, today in Faizabad District, on the banks of the Ghaghara river. Three inscriptions indicate it was constructed by Mir Baqi, a noble, in 1528-29, that is, after the mosques at Sambhal and Panipat. Unlike the other mosques built under Babur's auspices, this one at Ayodhya is a single-aisled three-bayed type. It is also considerably smaller than the other two. The central bay's pishtaq is much higher than the flanking side bays, but all three bays contain arched entrances. Most of the mosque is stucco-covered, over a rubble or brick core, but carved black stone columns from a pre-twelfth-century temple are embedded into either side of the central entrance porch.

The mosque is surmounted by three prominent domes. The site today is highly charged. Many claim the mosque, situated on a hillock, replaces a temple which Babur had destroyed. Today this mound popularly is considered the birthplace of the Hindu deity Rama. An important Mughal chronicler, writing about seventy years after the mosque's construction, acknowledges Ayodhya's sanctity as Rama's dwelling, but says nothing about the exact site of Rama's birth. It is thus difficult to disentangle recent popular passion from historical accuracy.

All the same, Ayodhya was a site of great importance to Babur's Hindu subjects in the Mughal period. The incorporation of older Hindu architectural members prominently displayed on the mosque's facade, at a period when the reuse of Hindu material was highly unusual, suggests the patron, Mir Baqi, was attempting to make a general statement of Muslim superiority.

This mosque, then, like the others of Babur's time, appears to be located in an area that had a charged significance. Babur's own mosque in Panipat was built on the site of Lodi defeat and Mughal victory, while the other two sites were both associated, however loosely, with ancient Hindu tradition. Babur's choice of Panipat for a mosque is not difficult to understand. However, the construction of mosques on sites associated with non-Islamic tradition is less comprehensible for a ruler who claimed his right to sovereignty based on his Timurid heritage and Turkishness, not on religious grounds. While such rhetoric predominated in his pre-India conquest, once he established himself permanently in India, Babur added the establishment of Islam as a mission of his rule.

He referred to Hindus as kafirs, that is, pagans or infidels, and war against his greatest Indian threat, Rana Sangam, was termed jihad or holy war. Shortly after his victory over Rana Sangam, Babur assumed the title Ghazi, that is, a warrior dedicated to the cause of Islam, and wrote a verse stating his resolve to defeat Hindus and pagans. All this rhetoric followed the long-established practice of Islamic rulers conquering non-Islamic lands. The placement of the Ayodhya and Sambhal mosques by his nobles in generally charged locales was well in keeping with the spirit of Babur's new legitimizing rhetoric. Babur ruled Hindustan for less than five years before his death in December, 1530. Although he ruled for only a short time, he introduced Timurid architectural concepts and, most importantly, the rationally organized four-part paradise garden. This latter in particular was to become a Mughal trademark.

3

Architecture in Humayun's Reign

In 1530 Humayun, designated by Babur as his successor, acceded to the throne. Humayun was sensitive, kind and intelligent, but lacked long-term wisdom and a mature understanding of statecraft. He had proven himself capable in warfare; however, he was inclined to lose the fruits of his victory by abandoning himself to long periods of pleasure and celebration. For example, after victories in Gujarat, Mandu and Gaur, Humayun remained in the palaces of the defeated for extended periods. Meanwhile the Mughal opponents' strength increased, giving them time to plot Humayun's downfall. The most serious of these adversaries was the Afghan, Sher Shah Sur, based in eastern India.

Humayun underestimated Sher Shah's potential and occupied himself with lesser rivals in western India. In 1536, Humayun, alarmed by reports of Sher Shah's activities, headed toward Bihar and Bengal, where he captured Gaur, the Bengal capital. Apparently unaware that Sher Shah had proclaimed himself sultan, Humayun spent the next nine months in pursuit of pleasure in Gaur, even renaming the city Jannatabad, or Abode of Paradise.

This led to his defeat in 1538 in a decisive battle with Sher Shah at Chausa, in Bihar. The Mughal emperor managed to escape across the swollen Ganges river, although most of his retinue drowned in its waters. He was then forsaken by his brothers, each of whom sought the Mughal crown for himself. As a result of this division, Humayun was again defeated by Sher Shah, this time at Kanauj in 1540. Sher Shah then assumed the throne of Delhi and drove Humayun from

Hindustan. Homeless, Humayun and his wife, Hamida, were pursued through Rajasthan, where their first son, Akbar, was born in 1542. Reaching Kabul in 1543, they left the prince Akbar there in the charge of one of Humayun's brothers. Although Humayun himself was not safe from his brothers' treachery, Timurid custom protected the young child.

BEGINNINGS OF MUGHAL ARCHITECTURE

By 1544, Humayun reached Iran and found refuge in the Safavid court of Shah Tahmasp. The relationship between the deposed Mughal and this Safavid ruler was not a comfortable one, since Shah Tahmasp insisted that Humayun embrace Shiism just as Babur had been forced to do some years earlier. Nevertheless, Shah Tahmasp's support eventually enabled Humayun to regain the Mughal throne in 1555. These years in Iran introduced Humayun not only to Safavid painters and painting but also to the architecture of Herat and Samarqand and to the Timurid-Safavid Iranian traditions that Babur had so admired.

Humayun's Patronage

With the exception of a single inscribed mosque in Agra, no other surviving structure indisputably results from Humayun's patronage. Some hold that the Delhi Purana Qalca, its mosque and octagonal pavilion (Plate n) also are his. Despite the dearth of remaining buildings from Humayun's time, contemporary sources refer to his architectural output. They describe, for example, his unique conceptions, although they are based on Timurid design concepts. One of them was a floating palace formed from four barges each bearing an inward facing arch and attached in such a manner that an octagonal pool formed the central portion. In addition, he designed three-storied collapsible palaces, gilded and domed.

More traditional palaces were constructed at Gwalior, Agra and Delhi. Neither the Gwalior palace, constructed of chiselled stones, nor the multistoried Agra palace, with its octagonal tank, connected via subterranean passages to other parts of the palaces, survives. Much controversy centers around Humayun's role in erecting the fortified enclosure today known as Delhi's Purana Qalca. Humayun commenced a walled city and imperial palace on this site in 1533. The city, named Din-Panah or Refuge of Religion, was auspiciously situated upon the age-old site known as Indraprastha, long associated with the traditional Hindu epic Mahabharata. The city was also located in very close proximity to the shrine of Delhi's most revered saint, Nizam al-Din Auliya. The choice of the site must have been made with its history in mind, for Humayun, superstitious yet religious, sought advice from learned men as well as astrologers. Even after Humayun's victorious return to India in 1555, this site remained symbolic for the Mughals, for, as we shall see, Humayun's tomb was constructed in this same area.

Khwand Amir, a noble in Humayun's court, reports that by 1534 the "walls, bastions, ramparts and gates" of Humayun's Din-Panah were nearly completed, adding that it was hoped that the "great and lofty buildings" of the city soon would be finished. It is difficult to tell from Khwand Amir's bombastic prose exactly how much of the city in reality was ready by 1534; moreover, it is impossible to judge how much was completed before Sher Shah's accession to the Delhi throne in 1540, for Humayun was constantly engaged in defending the Mughal domain and struggling to maintain his crown.

Sher Shah probably completed the fort and constructed its interior Qalca-i Kuhna mosque discussed in the previous chapter. Humayun almost certainly built the fort's small octagonal pavilion, known as the Sher Mandal (Plate 11) and traditionally associated with the library upon whose steps Humayun fatally fell in 1556, less than a year after his successful return to India. Abu al-Fazl, the official chronicler of Humayun's son and successor, Akbar, writes that the building in which Humayun had his fatal accident had only recently been completed,35 presumably by Humayun. The pavilion's design, close to Timurid garden pavilions and unlike Sultanate architectural types, suggests Mughal patronage. So does the appearance of the net pendentives in the structure's vaulting.

The sole inscribed monument belonging to Humayun's patronage is a mosque in Agra known after the name of its locality, Kachpura

(Plate 12). Two inscriptions indicate that the mosque was completed in 1530, the year of Humayun's accession to the throne. Its location, across the Jumna from the land on which the Taj Mahal was later built, may have been the site of the Hasht Behisht garden, or Garden of Eight Paradises, used for Babur's court.

This garden also most likely continued to serve as Humayun's court until he constructed his Delhi citadel. Like Babur's mosques, this one in Kachpura is mentioned in no text. It resembles Babur's Panipat mosque (Plates 7 and 8) in general plan and appearance, although the central pishtaq is much higher and the central vaulted chamber achieves a greater sense of open space than did the only slightly earlier Mughal mosques. The open character of the central bay with low flanking bays recalls earlier Timurid mosques, for example the Jamic mosque at Nishapur. As at Babur's Panipat mosque, stucco covers a brick core. On Humayun's mosque, eight-pointed stars and lozenge patterns are imprinted into the rectangular facade; possibly these were once painted to emphasize the design, evoking the brightly colored glazed tile ornamentation of Herat and Samarqand.

The mosque today is ruined, so it is unclear how many bays originally composed the double-aisled side wings. The interior central bay is surmounted by a dome supported on kite-shaped pedentives and net squinches. The smaller domes of the resulting side wings are similarly supported. While no traces of enclosure walls and entrance gates remain, they were almost certainly part of the original plan. The overall appearance and plan of this structure suggests that it, like Babur's Panipat mosque, was intended to emulate older Timurid types.

NON-IMPERIAL ARCHITECTURE UNDER BABUR AND HUMAYUN

Architecture erected in the Delhi region by those close to Babur and Humayun appears little influenced by Timurid concepts; rather, what remains reflects the older Lodi style. The most significant examples are at the shrine (dargah) around the tomb of Nizam al-Din Auliya. Belonging to the Chishti order, Nizam al-Din is Delhi's most esteemed Muslim saint. This shrine gained renewed significance in the Mughal period. In it is the tomb of Amir Khusrau (d. 1325), considered the greatest Persian poet of Hindustan.

This tomb was restored by Babur's brother-in-law, who provided an inscribed marble slab next to an open-air grave. In Humayun's reign, in 1531-32, a red sandstone screened enclosure (Plate 13) was built around the grave. This screen, carved with geometric and floral patterns, recalls Lodi-period tombs, for example that of Yusuf Qattal, also in Delhi. Other monuments of this time include the mosque of Ghazanfar, constructed in 1528-29 during Babur's reign near the Delhi airport in Palam. In another part of Delhi, Malvianagar, a residential center for spiritual study (khanqah) was built in 1534-35 to honor Shaikh Farid al-Din Ganj-i Shakar, a long deceased saint. That makes it contemporary with Humayun's Din-Panah, although it reveals no awareness of new imperial forms.

Both the mosque and khanqah are squat single-aisled three-bayed structures notable for neither their proportions nor ornamentation. Inscriptions indicate that mosques, tombs and other structures continued to be erected by men of all ranks and classes outside of Delhi during the early Mughal period. However, few of these remain in their original state. Like subimperial monuments in the Delhi area, they reveal little or no Timurid influence. For example, the tomb of Tardi Kochak in Hisar, dated 1537-38 by a stucco inscription incised on its facade,38 is a square-plan structure whose facade is articulated by a series of slightly recessed niches closely resembling the Lodi-period tombs of Delhi.

One more structure suggests the persistence of the older Lodi style. It is a small three-bayed single-aisled mosque in Fatehabad (Hisar District, Haryana), known as the Humayuni mosque (Plate 14). An inscription now detached from the structure bears the date 1539 and describes the construction of a mosque during Humayun's reign. This is probably the very mosque identified in the inscription. Although another inscription on the mosque indicates that it was renovated in the nineteenth century, features from the time of Humayun are quite apparent. Small glazed tiles on the east facade, for example, are reminiscent of those on two sixteenth-century buildings in Hansi, about 30 km away: the Barsi gate restored in 1522 and the tomb of Ali Mir Tijara.

Ibn Khaldun, the fourteenth-century Islamic political thinker and historian, observed that the founders of dynasties generally channel substantial effort into consolidating their political strength, leaving little time for extensive architectural construction. Nonetheless, the architecture of both Babur and Humayun sowed the seeds for future construction under the Mughals. This is especially true for the types of works built, although the purpose and meaning will change somewhat as the state matures and evolves its unique notions of legitimacy. Babur introduced the char bagh garden, which for him was a visual metaphor for his ability to control and order the arid Indian plains and ultimately its population. Subsequently such gardens gain even greater popularity, especially when used as a paradisical setting for funereal monuments. Before his conquest of India, Babur had built no mosques. In Hindustan, however, he built mosques, probably because of his newly assumed role as a warrior in the cause of Islam.

Humayun, too, built at least one mosque; however, his construction of palaces and pleasure pavilions reflected his apparent selfindulgence. The palace and its role as the center of regal ceremony, increasingly significant in each ruler's interpretation of the nature of Mughal kingship, continues as a major architectural form through the eighteenth century. Babur and Humayun, each keenly aware of their Timurid heritage, attempted to introduce Timurid-inspired architectural forms and spatial conceptions into India. Although the outcome was not necessarily successful, the ideology behind such forms is maintained by their Mughal successors.

4

Akbar Period Architecture

MUGHAL THEORIES OF KINGSHIP AND STATE POLITY

Akbar is generally recognized as the greatest and most capable of the Mughal rulers. Under him Mughal polity and statecraft reached maturity; and under his guidance the Mughals changed from a petty power to a major dynastic state. From his time to the end of the Mughal period, artistic production on both an imperial and sub-imperial level was closely linked to notions of state polity, religion and kingship.

Humayun died in 1556, only one year after his return to Hindustan. Upon hearing the call to prayers, he slipped on the steep stone steps of the library in his Din-Panah citadel in Delhi. Humayun's only surviving son and heirapparent, Akbar, then just fourteen years of age, ascended the throne and ruled until 1605 the expanding Mughal empire. Until about 1561, Akbar was under the control of powerful court factions, first his guardian, Bhairam Khan, and then the scheming Maham Anga, a former imperial wet-nurse. Between about 1560 and 1580, Akbar devoted his energies to the conquest and then the consolidation of territory in north India. This he achieved through battle, marriage, treaty and, most significantly, administrative reform. Concurrent with these activities, Akbar developed an interest in religion that, while initially a personal concern, ultimately transformed his concept of state.

Many of the policies he adopted, such as the renunciation of the poll-tax (jiziya) for non- Muslims, had a solid political basis as well as a personal one, for Akbar, much more than his Mughal predecessors, saw every advantage in maintaining good relations with the Hindu majority. Moreover, during this period, Akbar equally was interested in winning over the sympathy of orthodox Indian Muslims. In part, his goal was to reduce the power of the dominant Iranian nobles, that is, Persian and Central Asian nobles, by including Indians, both Hindu and Muslim, in his administration.

Always interested in religious affairs, Akbar showed a deep reverence for saints belonging to the Islamic Chishti order. His devotion to them peaked between 1568 and 1579. This coincides with the period that he commenced the khanqah and palace at Fatehpur Sikri, whose construction was stimulated by his spiritual guide (pir) who resided there. Commencing about 1575, Akbar's interest in religions and religious matters broadened. First, he invited learned men from diverse Islamic sects and later Christian priests, Hindus, Jains and Zoroastrians to join him in discussions, which more often than not turned into petty disputes, particularly among the leading Muslim thinkers. The result led Akbar increasingly away from formalized religion and into a deep personal spiritualism with strong mystical overtones, but one that was rooted within the font of Islam.

The events of the later part of his reign were marked by an attempt to control the Deccan plateau of central south India and territory in the northwest including Kashmir, Qandahar and Baluchistan. His final years were spent in conflict with his only surviving son, Salim, the future Jahangir, who rebelled against his father, establishing his own court in Allahabad. Eventually Salim and Akbar were reconciled, but it is believed by some that Akbar died poisoned by his son. Our knowledge of Akbar's thought and policy comes from the writings of Abu al-Fazl, Akbar's chronicler and close companion. The first part of his massive Persian text commenced about 1589 was the Akbar Nama, or the Book of Akbar; it is a eulogistic chronicle of the events of Akbar's reign.

The second part, known as the A 'in-i Akbari, or Regulations of Akbar, is a manual of statecraft. Together these present Akbar's mature concept of kingship and state. These, in large measure, continued to serve as the basis of the Mughal state. Abu al-Fazl presents Akbar as a divinely inspired ruler who traced his lineage not only to his esteemed ancestor, Timur, but back further to a Mughal princess whose offspring were the products of a miraculous impregnation by light. Describing Akbar as an emanation of God's light, Abu al-Fazl plays upon light imagery, presenting the emperor as a superior being who had a special relationship with God. By contrast, earlier Islamic kings were considered but shadows of God on earth.

Abu al-Fazl's writings indicate that Akbar, adhering to well-established Perso-Islamic concepts of sovereignty, believed that the ultimate justification for the Mughal empire was the propagation of justice. He presents Akbar not only as divinely inspired, but also as a paternal figure concerned for his subjects' welfare. As patriarch of the state, Akbar's mantle does not only extend to Muslims, traditionally the only valid subjects of an Islamic state, but to non-Muslims as well.

For example, in 1579, he issued a declaration (mahzar) allowing in some instances the emperor, rather than Islamic judges, to decide matters that affected the lives of all his subjects. Akbar further underscored toleration as a major concern of state by declaring his policy of sulh-i kul, universal toleration. That extended the canopy of justice to all, regardless of religious affiliation, thus establishing the groundwork for the successful and long-term domination of an Islamic state in the midst of a non-Muslim majority.

Under Akbar, Mughal administration was divided into three categories: the household, the army and the empire. Akbar was the head of each of these, and it was to him personally that all high-ranking nobles answered. To further perpetuate his role as the head of state and as father to his people, Akbar established the Din-i Ilahi, a disciple-like relationship between himself and his most trusted nobles. Many have interpreted the Din-i Ilahi as a new religion. This is a misunderstanding, resulting in part from the nature of Akbar's relationship with his highest-ranking nobles. This relationship can be likened to that between an Islamic spiritual guide (pir) and his devotees (murids), or a master and his slave. Understanding the nobles' commitment to Akbar helps explain the diffusion of a uniform aesthetic across Mughal territory.

Architecture in Delhi (1556-76)

Delhi, the traditional capital of north Indian Islamic rulers, served as Akbar's capital until 1565, when he commenced his massive Agra fort. This was followed by the construction of other forts in strategically important locations signaling the diminishing importance of Delhi, until its revival in the midseventeenth century.

While ruling from Delhi, Akbar continued to reside in Humayun's citadel, Din-Panah. There is no example of Akbar's architecture from these early years, but leading members of his court built mosques and tombs close to the Din-Panah. For example, the Khair al-Manazil mosque and madrasa were constructed in 1561 by Maham Anga. She had been one of Akbar's wet-nurses and had considerable influence over the young king during this early period.

Erected under the supervision of Shihab al-Din Ahmad Khan, her son-in-law, the mosque closely follows the plan and elevation of the nearby Qalca-i Kuhna mosque probably built by Sher Shah. Her mosque is embellished with incised stucco and paint in lieu of inlaid stone. Its courtyard is enclosed with high cloistered walls used as a madrasa. The dominant feature of the mosque, however, is not the prayer chamber, but its monumental east gate (Plate 15).

It is faced with red and white stones like those on the entrance gates into the Din-Panah. This gate, which lay on a main thoroughfare linking the fort with the city walls, commanded a dominant position in the city. Nearby is the shrine (dargah) of Nizam al-Din Auliya. Restorations had been made there in Babur's and Humayun's reigns, and further renovations were made in Akbar's time.

In 1562 a noble of Akbar's court, Farid al-Khan, rebuilt Nizam al-Din's tomb. The walls of this square-plan tomb consist of marble screens (jalis) supported by intricately carved pillars; the carved geometric patterns are more finely rendered than those on the nearby tomb of Khusrau (Plate 13) carved in Humayun's reign. It is with this tomb that marble, probably in emulation of the tomb of Mucin al-Din in Ajmer, becomes an emblem of sanctity in Mughal architecture.

In the dargah of Nizam al-Din is the tomb of Ataga Khan (Plate 16), built in 1566-67 by his son Mirza Aziz Koka. Ataga Khan, Akbar's prime minister and the husband of one of his wet-nurses, was murdered in 1562 by the jealous son of Maham Anga. The square plan of this tomb follows the older Indian tombtypes, while its red sandstone exterior inlaid with multi-colored stones and white marble slabs carved with Quranic verses reflects the influence of the exquisite Qalca-i Kuhna mosque (Plate 5). This is the first Akbar-period monument for which we know the names of both the architect, Ustad Khuda Quli, and the calligrapher, Baqi Muhammad of Bukhara. The verses on the tomb were chosen carefully, referring specifically to the nature of Ataga Khan's demise, which Akbar's court chronicler Abu al-Fazl likens to martyrdom.

Ataga Khan's murderer, Adham Khan, was immediately punished by death. Adham Khan's large octagonal tomb (Plate 17), containing his grave and that of his mother, who died a few months later, was erected by imperial order 15 km south of Akbar's Delhi. By contrast to Ataga Khan's tomb, reflecting the apex of Mughal technology and taste, his murderer's tomb, stucco covered and octagonal in format, represents the end of this older type. Octagonal tombs once had been associated with royalty, for example by the Surs, considered traitors by the Mughals. Thus a tomb-type associated with traitors was particularly suitable for the once-leading, now disgraced, noble, Adham Khan. Timurid features are often evident in some of the most important Akbari buildings in Delhi, including his finest work there, his father's tomb. Many of these features are, however, largely dropped in Akbar's buildings constructed after moving the capital to Agra.

Among the works that recall architecture in the Mughal homeland is the Sabz Burj, located south of the citadel. The tomb is probably a product of Akbar's reign, although it may date as early as Humayun's reign. It is designed as a Baghdadi octagon (see glossary) with a high dome resting on an elongated neck; originally green tiles covered its surface. At least as clearly based on Timurid prototypes is the largest structure erected in Delhi during the early years of Akbar's reign, the tomb of the deceased emperor Humayun (Plates 18-19). Situated just south of the Din- Panah citadel and in close proximity to the esteemed dargah of Nizam al-Din, the mausoleum even today dominates its surroundings. A contemporary Mughal source indicates that the tomb was finished in 1571 after eight or nine years of work.

Tradition states that a devoted wife, Hajji Begum, was responsible for its construction; recently, however, Akbar has been proposed as the patron,5 even though the tomb resembles none of Akbar's other architectural enterprises. Its Timurid appearance must be credited to its Iranian architect, trained in the Timurid tradition and known from contemporary texts as both Mirak Sayyid Ghiyas and Mirak Mirza Ghiyas. His masterpiece came to be influential in the design of Mughal mausolea through the eighteenth century. Mirak Mirza Ghiyas, originally from Herat, may have been a stone cutter who had worked for Babur. He worked extensively in Bukhara, where he excelled at buildings and landscape architecture. Around 1562, he returned to India to design Humayun's tomb. Before its completion, however, he died. His son completed the great project in 1571.

Today the tomb complex is entered by a large gate on the west, although in Mughal times the southern gate was widely used. Upon entering any gate, the centrally situated tomb and its char bagh setting are visible. Each of the four garden plots is further sub-divided by narrower waterways. Based on the char bagh types established in Iran and more fully developed in Babur's own concept of the ideal garden, such formalized and geometrically planned garden settings became standard for all the imperial Mughal mausolea and for those of many nobles as well. Char bagh gardens long had been associated with paradisical imagery. But at Humayun's tomb, the association is all the more explicit, for the water channels appear to vanish beneath the actual mausoleum yet reappear in their same straight course on the opposite side. This evokes a Quranic verse which describes rivers flowing beneath gardens of paradise.

The mausoleum is square in plan, 45 meters on a side. Crowned with a white marble bulbous dome and flanking chattris, the tomb sits on a high elevated plinth 99 meters per side. Each facade, faced with red sandstone and trimmed with white marble, is nearly identical and meets at chamferred corners. The west, north and east facades are marked by a high central portal flanked on either side by lower wings with deeply recessed niches. The south entrance, probably the main one, consists of lower wings on either side of a high central pishtaq, underneath which is a deeply recessed niche.

The seeming simplicity of this tomb's exterior is belied by the interior. There, on the ground floor, the mausoleum has a central octagonal chamber containing a cenotaph. This chamber is surrounded by eight ancillary rooms, a radical departure from the single chamber of earlier Indian tombs. Passages connect these smaller chambers with the main one and with the outside. The second story of the tomb is similar. Such a spatial arrangement is based on geometric principles first applied in Timurid architecture and seen in structures such as the cIshrat Khana built about 1464 and used as a dynastic mausoleum for women.

These eight ancillary chambers are intended to evoke the paradises of Islamic cosmology. The passages connecting them are probably intended to facilitate circumambulation of the cenotaph in the central chamber. This ritual, drawn from sufic rites, was a common practice at Mughal imperial tombs. The tomb's adherence to geometric principle and the complexity of its internal organization bear a clear imprint of Timurid tradition. This is not surprising since the architect himself had worked extensively in Bukhara, the last bastion of Timurid artistic traditions. Coupled with the fact that Humayun and his wife had long been exiled in Iran and developed a taste for an Iranian aesthetic, this easily explains the tomb's appearance.

Moreover, the Mughals were extremely proud of their Timurid ancestry, and it is not without significance that this Timurid-inspired tomb and setting continued for the most part to serve as an important model for imperial tombs. Some believe that Humayun's tomb was conceived as a Mughal dynastic mausoleum in the tradition of the great Timurid dynastic mausolea, for example, the Gur-i Amir in Samarqand.

It was, however, not used as the tomb for subsequent rulers, although some members of the royal house were buried there. In 1565, only three years after its commencement, Akbar began construction on his massive Agra fort and moved his administration there.

Moving the imperial headquarters from Delhi did not signal its abandonment by either the emperor or highly influential court members. For example, Akbar in 1571 visited his father's tomb upon its completion and in 1572-73 gave orders for the restoration of the Jamacat Khana mosque at the Nizam al-Din dargah. In 1575-76, Akbar's chief theologian (sadr), Shaikh Abd al-Nabi Khan, who wielded tremendous power until his fall from favor about 1580, constructed a mosque not in Agra or Fatehpur Sikri, then imperial residences, but in Delhi, suggesting that the city still was envisioned as a major urban center. This mosque, situated north of the Mughal Din-Panah, closely resembled Maham Anga's madrasa, although today few of its original features remain. The structure's epigraph, composed by Akbar's poet laureate, Faizi, the brother of Abu al-Fazl, does not specifically identify the structure's function, but its close adherence to the earlier madrasa suggests that it was intended as a theological school, indicating Delhi's continuing role as an intellectual center.

Imperial Forts and the Formulation of Akbar's Taste

While Humayun's Timurid-inspired tomb was still under construction, Akbar commenced a series of fort-palaces in a very different style at strategic locations across north India. The first of these was his great fort at Agra, which he commenced in 1565 and completed around 1571. Others that followed include Ajmer, the gate to Rajasthan, in 1570, and Lahore, traditionally guarding the northwestern portion of the subcontinent, in 1575. Later, in 1583, Akbar built a fort at Allahabad, situated east of Agra in the fertile Gangetic plain, a response to widespread uprisings throughout eastern India two years earlier. Beside these is his palace at Fatehpur Sikri, the most renowned of his capitals, although not a fortified one. Few Akbari structures remain within most of these forts. In Ajmer, two Akbar-period palaces remain, each stone constructed.

One is a trabeated structure today known as the Badshahi Mahal. Better known is a small palace, today used as a museum (Plate 20). There a nine-bayed pillared pavilion is enclosed within a fortified appearing quadrangle. In the Lahore fort Akbar's structures were replaced by subsequent rulers, and in the Allahabad fort, today still used as a major military headquarters, only one of the Akbari structures remains well-preserved. This is a baradari (pillared pavilion) situated in the center of a courtyard. The first floor of this three-stoned pillared structure bears a large central chamber surrounded by eight ancillary ones and an encompassing veranda. Buildings of such design had been used earlier at the Fatehpur Sikri palace, and appear to have been specifically intended for imperial use.

Abu al-Fazl states that more than 500 stone buildings were constructed in the Agra fort's interior. While that number may be exaggerated, all the same, very few buildings remain. The fort was commenced in 1565 and completed in eight years under the direction of Qasim Khan Mir Barr o Bahr. It was intended to replace an older brick fort, so Akbar directed Qasim Khan to construct a stone fortification that would have unprecedented strength. The plan of the buttressed and crenellated walls, 22 meters high, roughly resembles a semicircle about 2. km in circumference. According to contemporary sources, thousands of workers, many of them stone masons, were employed on the project. The red sandstone facing inlaid with white marble detail gives a sense of majesty to the massive Delhi gate, the fort's main entrance.

The fort's entire exterior, constructed with finer materials and crafted more meticulously than any other Indian fort, including Humayun's Din-Panah, imparts an awesome sense of the patron's power. It was the role of architecture to impress, according to traditional Islamic views of statecraft, and here Akbar succeeded immeasurably. That was his intention, as his biographer, Abu al-Fazl, makes clear. Within the fort the so-called Jahangiri Mahal (Plate 21) is the most notable remaining building of Akbar's time. Overlooking the river, this palace was probably one of a series that originally lined the waterfront. Palaces closest to the water in later periods are reserved for the king and his chief queens. This is probably the case here, too. However, the use of particular rooms and courtyards remains elusive, and indeed spaces that could serve multiple functions appear to have been typical in Akbar's palace architecture.

In plan and elevation the exterior of this Jahangiri Mahal closely resembles the so-called Jodh Bai's palace at Fatehpur Sikri or what remains of the small fortified appearing enclosure at Akbar's Ajmer palace. The main fabric of the exterior is intricately carved red sandstone trimmed with white marble. The heavily carved surfaces recall the Khalji-inspired Qalca-i Kuhna mosque or pre- Mughal monuments from Kanauj and Bari. The main entrance of the edifice opens onto a large central courtyard flanked on its north and south sides by pillared halls, whose red sandstone bracketed supports are even more intricate versions of the sort of brackets seen on the Qalca-i Kuhna mosque (Plate 5).

The interior walls, too, are ornately carved. Abu al-Fazl comments that the red sandstone, quarried in the ridge of Fatehpur Sikri, hence known as Sikri sandstone, can be chiseled so skillfully that it is superior to wood. Indeed, the brackets of the Jahangiri Mahal have wooden prototypes, but they appear earlier in stone on Man Singh Tomar's Gwalior palace, built at the turn of the sixteenth century. Both the layout and many of the motifs used on this earlier palace, much admired by the Mughals, appear instrumental in the design of this Agra palace and others built under Akbar's auspices. Typical of several Islamic palaces in Central Asia, the Jahangiri Mahal's interior is symmetrically arranged around a central courtyard; a second courtyard on the east overlooks the river. A number of ancillary chambers and passages lead off from the central courtyard. Among these on the north is a large chamber with a flat roof supported by serpentine brackets. The source for such brackets is usually cited as Gujarat, especially Hindu or Jain architecture there. But such brackets long had been used in the Sultanate architecture of Gujarat and Bengal as well as at the Gwalior palace.

On the roof of this multi-storied building is a small rectangular pavilion with a veranda on three of its sides, whose exquisitely carved brackets in the shape of peacocks earlier appeared on the Gwalior palace. The attention to all stories, not just the ground floor, underscores the extraordinary quality of this palace. It was one of the few Akbari buildings in this fort that Shah Jahan maintained. Aspects of this palace, especially the carved geometric patterns and even its trabeated form, may draw from the Timurid tradition.

But its overall appearance reflects the form of domestic architecture, both Hindu and Muslim, popular across north India prior to Akbar's time. For example, trabeated structures, the most common type in all Akbari palaces, were used for the palaces of the sultans of Chanderi. And residential structures in fifteenth- and early sixteenth-century paintings executed for both Hindu and Muslim patrons across north India were depicted as flat-roofed, not arcuated. While Akbar's trabeated palaces may have Timurid origins, contemporary writers recognized their form as Indian.

For example, Abu al-Fazl indicates a pan-Indian secular basis for Akbar's buildings in the Agra fort. He remarks that the Agra fort was built in the "fine styles of Bengal and Gujarat," commonly taken to indicate that Akbar based his palaces on Hindu buildings from Bengal and Gujarat. Akbar's architecture, however, was not based on any particular sectarian form. While some features of Akbar's buildings may be Bengali in origin or explicitly Gujarati, most of these motifs are found widely.

Therefore, Abu al-Fazl's statement may be taken more on a figurative level than a literal one. That is, the architecture of Bengal and Gujarat was considered the most exquisite of the age, as we can tell from Babur's enthusiasm for the edifices of Chanderi built in the Gujarati style and Humayun's love for the palaces of Gujarat and Bengal.

Thus "the fine styles of Bengal and Gujarat" is probably a metaphor for that which was deemed the ultimate in architectural perfection. Moreover, as Bengal and Gujarat at the time that Abu al-Fazl was writing essentially marked the eastern and western boundaries of the Indian subcontinent, he may have been alluding to styles that found favor throughout north India and symbolically were brought together with the construction of Akbar's palace-fort in Agra, which he terms "the center of Hindustan."

The New Capital at Fatehpur Sikri

Akbar remained heirless until 1569 when his son, the future Jahangir, was born in the village of Sikri, 38 km west of Agra. That year Akbar commenced construction there of the religious compound as a sign of his esteem for the Chishti saint, Shaikh Salim, his spiritual adviser who had predicted the birth of his son. After Jahangir's second birthday, probably considered an adequate period to test his stamina since all the emperor's other offspring had died in infancy, Akbar commenced construction at Sikri of a walled city and imperial palace. He shifted his capital from Agra to this city, which came to be called Fatehpur Sikri. Just as Humayun's tomb earlier had been placed close to the Chishti dargah, Nizam al-Din, so Akbar situated his palace at a Chishti site. By constructing his capital at the khanqah of his spiritual adviser, Akbar associated himself with this popular sufi order and so brought further legitimacy to his reign through affiliation with popular yet orthodox Islam.

The city is surrounded by about 11 km of walls except on the south, where there was a lake. Situated atop a rocky ridge (about 3 km in length and 1 km wide), the royal enclave, consisting of the Chishti khanqah and palace, form the focal point of the city and the best preserved area (Plate 22). The numerous structures comprising this area are made from locally quarried red sandstone, known as Sikri sandstone. Although the site has been carefully studied, the identification and original purpose of many buildings there remain in question. The names they bear today were invented, largely for the benefit of nineteenthcentury European visitors to the site. Probably, in fact, the buildings had no single purpose, in keeping with Islamic tradition, but were adaptable to serve many functions. This matches well with Akbar's fluid and spontaneous approach to court ceremony.

Akbar's orders for the construction of this great city included nobles' dwellings, a great mosque, imperial palaces, baths, serais, a bazaar, gardens, schools, a khanqah and workshops. Thus Fatehpur Sikri was more than a royal residence; it had an economic, administrative and residential base. Contemporary accounts stress that the city was finished quickly. Work was ceaseless. One European visitor stated that because the work was done a short distance away and then assembled at the site, the inhabitants were spared from the stone masons' constant noise. The city, however, was only inhabited by Akbar for about fifteen years. Then in 1585 he assumed residence in Lahore to be closer to the less stable part of his empire.

Situated on the highest place on the ridge, the khanqah is the site's focal point. Within this religious compound, 111 by 139 meters, is an enormous Jamic mosque (Plate 25), its cloistered enclosure walls, three entrance gates, and the tomb of Shaikh Salim Chishti (Plate 26). Beneath the courtyard are underground reservoirs, an important consideration for a site which suffers from a poor water supply. The Buland Darwaza (Plate 23), the complex's towering south entrance gate, 54 meters in height, is visible from a considerable distance.

This enormous gate was almost certainly constructed concurrently with the mosque complex. While commonly believed that it was not erected until the early seventeenth century, this gate was certainly designed before 1587, when the calligrapher Ahmad al-Chishti, responsible for its monumental Quranic inscriptions, died. The gate was probably built to commemorate Akbar's successful Gujarat campaign in 1573, when Sikri came to be known as Fatehpur Sikri, the City of Victory. This monumental gate, however, was probably less intended to commemorate a military victory than to underscore Akbar's links with the Chishti order. Its surface is covered by marble slabs inscribed with Quranic verses promising paradise to true believers, appropriate for the entrance into a khanqah, a complex intended for meditation and devotion.

The Jamic mosque (Plates 24-25) is situated on the west side of the complex so that it can face Mecca as required in Islam. An inscription on the mosque's east facade states that it was built in 1571-72 by Shaikh Salim himself, while interior inscriptions are dated 1574, indicating its completion. Textual references also verify that the mosque was finished about this time. Measuring 89 by 20 meters, the mosque was at that time the largest in the Mughal empire. The exterior is marked by a high central pishtaq flanked on either side by delicately arched side wings. In addition to domes a row of small chattris crown the entire eastern edge of the roof.

The mosque's multiple arched openings resting on slender pillars recall pre-Mughal Jamic mosques at Chanderi and Mandu. The superstructure also appears to be modeled on the type seen in the Mandu Jamic mosque; however, at Fatehpur Sikri, chattris are used in lieu of smaller domes. Thus much of the facade's overall appearance derives from an older pre-Mughal Indian tradition, but the high central pishtaq is characteristic of all Mughal Jamic mosques and can be considered a Mughal interpretation of an older Timurid architectural device. Here the Timurid origins of this pishtaq are more apparent than on Babur's or Humayun's mosques, for, like Timurid portals, the recessed portion above the arched entrance is vaulted.

The mosque's interior central bay is a vastly more sophisticated rendition of the type found in the Jamic mosques built under Humayun and Babur. Behind the central pishtaq is the mosque's main prayer chamber magnificently embellished with white marble inlaid into the red stone to form intricate geometric patterns. Painted arabesques and floral motifs are rendered in polychrome and gilt, creating the most impressive Mughal monument of its time. While such patterns were known in the late Lodi and Sur times in India, the sophistication and intricacy of the motifs suggest an awareness of Timurid prototypes.

Side wings flank the mosque's central bay. Each is composed of multi-aisled trabeated bays and a double-aisled pillared veranda. The elegant slender red sandstone pillars of the side wings are surmounted by brackets similar to those on Akbar's Jahangiri Mahal in his Agra fort. This mosque is a unique blend of long-established Indian and Timurid techniques. Akbar himself is said to have humbly swept the floor and called the prayer in this mosque. Yet, ironically, some of Akbar's acts here alienated the orthodox culema, the Islamic scholars and jurists who traditionally have ultimate authority over matters religious. Here in 1579 he himself read the khutba, the prayer legitimizing an Islamic ruler's sovereignty. Although this had been done by his Timurid ancestors, in India the culema interpreted this as an attempt by Akbar to declare himself the arbitrator of religious affairs and thus a radical move.

Then two months later Akbar issued the declaration (mabzar) which assigned to himself limited power in deciding religious matters. This declaration was approved unwillingly by the leading religious arbitrators and further alienated the orthodox culema. In fact, the mahzar was more a political document than a religious one, for it allowed Akbar control over secular and administrative affairs; his authority over religious matters was limited to instances when the leading religious figures failed to agree.

Shaikh Salim, Akbar's spiritual adviser who had predicted the birth of his son, died in 1572. His tomb (Plate 26) was completed almost a decade later, in 15 80-81, as indicated by inscriptions on its inner walls, even though it probably was commenced much earlier. This white marble single-domed building measuring 15 meters square is rightfully considered a masterpiece. The interior square chamber is surrounded by an enclosed corridor to facilitate circumambulation of the tomb. This tomb-type was known earlier in Gujarat, the source of this plan. The outer walls are composed of intricately carved white marble screens (jalis).

Although less intricate, pierced screens are on the exterior of Shaikh Ahmad Khattu's tomb at Sarkhej, Gujarat's premier shrine. Exquisitely carved serpentine brackets belonging to the Indo-Islamic architectural traditions of Mandu, Chanderi and Gujarat support deep eaves (cbajja) that encircle the entire tomb and its projecting south entrance porch. These screens and the multi-colored stone flooring, similar to that at Sarkhej, were donated by a noble, Qutb al-Din Muhammad Khan, at his own expense; he had served in Gujarat and was buried in Baroda in 1583.

Artisans trained in Gujarat and brought to Fatehpur Sikri by Qutb al-Din Muhammad Khan worked on Shaikh Salim's tomb. However, the features derived from the tomb of Shaikh Ahmad Khattu may have been used intentionally, for this shrine had been built by the sultans of Gujarat, and like the shrine of Shaikh Salim Chishti at Fatehpur Sikri was at the site of their palace. Hence the sultans of Gujarat are linked with Shaikh Ahmad Khattu, much as Akbar sought to link his rule with the Chishti saint. Akbar's association with the Chishti saint explains the reason behind the tomb's extraordinary workmanship.

Even its fabric, white marble, links it with the Chishti order. Twenty years earlier the tomb of the Chishti saint Nizam al-Din in Delhi had been renewed in white marble. It is ironic, however, that Shaikh Salim's tomb was not completed until Akbar began to break with the Chishti, in fact, with all saint veneration. After 1579, Akbar no longer made his annual pilgrimage on foot to the shrine of Mucin al-Din Chishti. Stopping this practice of long standing, he stated that saint worship was a shallow preoccupation, not a profound religious one.

Akbar probably commenced the tomb as a means of exerting authority over this popular Islamic order. He also denied the shaikh's descendants hereditary custodianship of the tomb, by now a popular site of pilgrimage. Instead, Akbar himself appointed the shrine's supervisor. The emperor had assumed similar control over the premier dargah of Mucin al-Din Chishti in Ajmer in 1570, when he resolved a dispute regarding the shrine's successorship by appointing his own candidate. Thus, at both important Chishti sites, Akbar himself held the reins on matters elsewhere left to a saint's spiritual heirs.

Chishti descendants, instead of serving these dargahs, were encouraged to enter imperial service, suggesting that Akbar's association with this mystic order served himself in political ways as well as spiritual ones. Akbar's palace complex at Fatehpur Sikri lies to the southeast of the mosque. This complex was clearly planned, for the palace buildings are axially and geometrically related to the khanqah. Abu al-Fazl described Akbar's architects and designers as "lofty-minded mathematicians"; even the emperor, one chronicler stated, had a "geometry decoding mind," and his architecture was described by the court biographer as understandable to "the minds of the mathematical." Geometry here serves as a metaphor for Akbar's control and power.

The Hathiya Pol, or Elephant gate, situated at the southern end of the palace complex, was probably the imperial entrance. Here there was a naqqar khana, or chamber where ceremonial drums were played. The view toward this southern entrance is imposing, almost as spectacular as that toward the powerful Buland Darwaza on the north. In front of the Hathiya Pol is a large serai. Beyond the gate, the chattris and roofs of the palaces are visible. Once one enters the gate, there is access to both the mosque complex (Plate 25) and the palace structures, including the Daulat Khana-i Khass o Amm, or Public Audience Hall (Plate 28), one of the most important administrative units. All Indian forts have an entrance associated with elephants.

They probably were intended for the entry of palanquined elephants, in India long considered the imperial mount. For Akbar, moreover, elephants appear to have had a special importance. His reverence for these animals is discussed by Abu al-Fazl, who notes that they can only be controlled by wise and intelligent men. In the illustrated Akbar Nama in the Victoria and Albert Museum, generally believed to have been Akbar's personal copy, elephants are frequently depicted, and on several pages there are illustrations of Akbar controlling mad elephants - elephants that no other mortal could ride. As the emperor indicated to Abu al-Fazl, successfully riding such a beast without being killed should be taken as a sign of God's contentment with him.

At the foot of the rampart leading to the Hathiya Pol is a minaret spiked with stone projections resembling elephant tusks (Plate 27). Popularly known as the Hiran Minar and considered a hunting tower, it is not mentioned in any contemporary text. This tower, derived from Iranian prototypes, was probably used to indicate the starting point for subsequent mile posts (kos minar). In Mughal India, such mile posts were conical-shaped smooth-faced minarets; many remain between Agra and Delhi as well as in other areas of northwestern India and Pakistan. The tusk-like shape of the protruding stones appears appropriate for this tower's location near the Elephant gate, and may be yet another reference to Akbar as controller of elephants and ultimately of the well-run state.

To the east of the Elephant gate is a large quadrangular courtyard known as the Public Audience Hall. It is one of the few areas within the palace whose function is certain. The road leading from the city walls to this audience hall was lined with shops and markets that were commenced in 1576-77. It is a focal point of the palace, a secular one complementing the mosque complex. The rest of the palace lay between the mosque and audience hall, pivotal points which reflect Akbar's concerns with religion and the welfare of the state. The structure enclosing the courtyard is simple given the nature of its importance, for here the emperor presented himself to all levels of the nobility and to others who wanted recourse to the king. This structure is essentially a pillared flat-roofed veranda, called an aiwan. In the center of the west wall is a projection where Akbar sat enthroned (Plate 28). His subjects, when confronting him, faced the qibla or direction of prayer, perhaps suggesting the metaphor of Akbar as the qibla of the state. This imperial chamber was even used as a mosque.

Due west of the Public Audience Hall is an area which appears to have been reserved for the emperor's private administrative and personal matters. Only a few structures in this area can be identified with much certainty. One of these is the Anup Talao, a square pool in whose center was a pavilion. Its base still remains connected to each of the pool's four edges by stone planks. Here, Akbar engaged in serious discussion regarding Islamic law with leading Muslim theologians, as several contemporary writers describe. They also note that he filled this tank with gold coins and distributed them to shaikhs and amirs.

Surrounding the tank are trabeated structures, most of them a single story high. One, known as the Turkish Sultana's House, is completely covered with carvings of geometric patterns, trees, flowering vines, birds and animals. Although some of this ornamentation draws upon earlier Indian imagery, the decor of this palace, more than that of any other residential or civic structure here, is based on Timurid tradition. The richly carved ornamentation (Plate 29) situated at floor level indicates that here inhabitants were intended to sit on silk and cotton cushions, not stand as in a public audience hall. The ceiling and walls, too, were often covered with luxurious fabrics. Thus we must recall that these buildings were not simply red sandstone, but decked, as contemporary accounts remind us, with rich textile trappings.

On the south edge of the Anup Talao is a multi-storied building, traditionally known as the Khwabgah, or Akbar's sleeping chamber. Its plain architectural members bear traces of figural painting and calligraphy, suggesting that structures not carved were polychromed. The painted verses make direct reference to Akbar, calling him "the adorner of the realm of Hindustan," 35 and so suggesting that this palace was intended for imperial use. Further underscoring this is the plan of the top story, consisting of a central rectangular pavilion with a flat interior roof surrounded by a pillared veranda, a type identified at Akbar's Allahabad fort as one intended for imperial use. On the southernmost side of a courtyard aligned with the Khwabgah and immediately to its south is the so-called Daftar Khana, or records office (Plate 30). It consists of a small room with a large open window that overlooks the terrain below. This was Akbar's jharoka, the window at which daily he displayed himself to his subjects. Although this ritual was derived from a custom of Hindu kings, the Mughals earlier had adopted it. For example, after Humayun's death, a man resembling the deceased ruler was displayed at a similar window in the Delhi citadel until the young Prince Akbar could be crowned. Such regular appearances reassured the population that all was well in the state.

Of all the buildings at Fatehpur Sikri, a small square building commonly known as the Diwan-i Khass (Plate 31) has been the subject of greatest speculation. Its location, situated just behind the Public Audience Hall and aligned with the jharoka, indicates that this was the Private Audience Hall. The exterior fits well with the other trabeated palace pavilions at Fatehpur Sikri. Its interior, however, is unique. There in the center of the building's single chamber is an elaborately carved faceted pillar reaching about half of the building's total height (Plate 32). Its capital is composed of serpentine brackets, reminiscent of those appearing in the Sultanate architecture of Gujarat, Mandu and Lodi Delhi.

These brackets, fuller at the top than at the bottom, support a circular platform. It is connected to each corner of the building by stone slab walkways attached to the building's corners. A narrow path circumscribes the structure connecting the walkways. Akbar probably sat upon this central platform. Thus some believe that here he projected himself as a chakravartin, or universal ruler, following the indigenous Indian notions of kingship;38 however, since Akbar's deep interest in Hinduism and other non-Islamic traditions developed after much of Fatehpur Sikri was well under construction, this theory must be viewed as tentative.

More likely, Akbar sat on this central platform to project himself as the dominant figure in the Mughal state, its axis and the pillar of its support. West of this area is a number of small palace complexes. Nearly all of them are multi-storied trabeated buildings. Often they are assumed to be the residences of Akbar's queens and nobles. More probably they housed only princes and women of the household, for all of them were linked to the Khwabgah, or imperial chamber, by covered screened passageways.

The tallest of these is the so-called Panch Mahal (Plate 33). The name derives from its five tiers, the final one consisting of a large single chattri. Suggestions that this was a pleasure pavilion are stimulated by its elevation and design, assumed to take advantage of cooling breezes. Because this tall building provided a view of the areas reserved for the emperor and the royal household, only the most trusted would have had access to it. Pierced stone screens faced the facade and probably sub-divided the interior as well, suggesting that it was used by the women of the imperial harem.

The largest among these small palace complexes is today called Jodh Bai's palace. This may have been the first palace constructed at Fatehpur Sikri since it leads most directly, via a passage that once was covered, to the Hathiya Pol. This palace's scale has prompted suggestions that it was the principal residence of Akbar's harem. The building, enclosing a square courtyard, is entered by an arched gate recalling the one at Akbar's Ajmer palace. The rooms of the interior are trabeated. Their carved ornamentation derives more than that of any other palace from the traditions of Gujarat. The sinuous brackets atop recessed niches on the palace's interior recall similar ornamentation on both mosques and Hindu temples of Gujarat. Likewise, the hanging chain-and-bell motif carved on many of the pillars has precedents in the Hindu and Muslim architecture of pre-Mughal Gujarat and Bengal. The so-called House of Raja Birbal, one of Akbar's principal courtiers, is inscribed with a date corresponding to 1572.

A phrase following this date, "royal mansion of initiation," suggests that its purpose was not residential, but ceremonial or even administrative. It emphasizes how little we know about the function of Fatehpur Sikri's buildings. The carved ornamentation of this palace, like that of most of the others, is deeply rooted in the decor of both Hindu and Muslim Indian architecture. For example, the palace's frequent chandrashala motifs were long used in pre- Islamic Indian architecture, as well as on Sultanate buildings. The ornate brackets, too, while much earlier seen on Hindu buildings, long had been incorporated into the basic vocabulary of Sultanate architecture. Buildings that would appeal to both Hindus and Muslims were important since these forts and palaces were recognized as vital in the maintenance of Akbar's wellbalanced state.

Akbar's choice of a style that appealed to all subjects regardless of sectarian affiliation is better understood if we consider certain imperial policies promulgated while Fatehpur Sikri and the Agra and Ajmer forts were built. Abu al- Fazl clearly indicates that Akbar, adhering to well-established Perso-Islamic concepts of sovereignty, believed that the ultimate justification for the Mughal empire was the propagation of justice. Under Akbar, Abu al-Fazl reports, the canopy of justice was extended officially to all subjects regardless of religious affiliation. This is his policy of sulh-i kul, or universal toleration. The policy was evolving at the very time Fatehpur Sikri was under construction. In other words, the inclusion of styles appropriate to all groups of the nobility - that is, the political strength of the empire - was truly in keeping with Akbar's nascent policy of universal toleration.

In the early 1560s, prior to the construction of his palaces, Akbar instituted liberal treatment of Hindus, for example, forbidding the forced conversion of prisoners to Islam and renouncing the jiziya, the tax on non-Muslims. Political, not personal, considerations probably stimulated these measures and suggested the styles adopted for his palaces. It was not until much later, in the 1580s and 1590s, that Akbar began personally to adopt indigenous Indian customs and practices. However, when these palaces were erected, Akbar equally was as concerned with winning over the sympathy of the orthodox Indian Muslims. For example, the reorganization of the Sadarat (chief religious and legal office) probably was aimed specifically at gaining favor with the Indian Muslims, a group that in the previous Mughal rulers' administration held no power. Akbar's goal in doing this was to reduce the influence of the dominant Iranian nobles, that is, Central Asian and Persian nobles, by including Indian Muslims and even Hindus in his administration.

In other words, what we see in these nascent stages of Akbar's policy of sulh-i kul is an attempt to place the indigenous elements of Indian society, be they Hindu or Muslim, on an equal footing with the traditionally more favored and powerful Central Asian and Persian nobility.

Once Akbar left Fatehpur Sikri, he built little. In the emperor's stead, his amirs served as architectural patrons, particularly in the developing Mughal hinterlands. Some nobles had provided buildings long before Akbar's departure from Fatehpur Sikri, in part to gain imperial favor. But especially in the later phases of Akbar's reign, patronage by nobles became increasingly significant. Much of this reflected the complex relationship between the emperor and his nobility. While the Mughal emperor was the highest authority, his power depended on carefully balanced and constantly fluctuating relationships with his own nobles and local rulers, be they Hindu or Muslim. By extension, these non-imperial works often aided the spread of styles favored by the center.

Raja Man Singh, Hindu Patron and Mughal Agent

Raja Man Singh was a Hindu in the court of the Muslim Akbar and one of his highest ranking amirs. Although his landholdings shifted as his appointments changed, he was a prince with stable ancestral lands {watan jagir) as well. The buildings that he constructed on these lands provide insight into the relationship between the emperor and his nobles as well as into the extension of Mughal architecture in the hinterlands.

Raja Man Singh's prolific patronage throughout the Mughal domain may in part reflect his special status. His family, the Kachhwahas, was the first princely house of Rajasthan to join the Mughal ranks and give their daughters in marriage to Mughal princes and emperors. As a result, Man Singh and his father, Raja Bhagwant Das, were constant companions of Akbar. Akbar developed deep affection for Man Singh. As prince, Man Singh served Akbar well, leading major military campaigns. In 1589, after the death of Man Singh's father, Akbar awarded Man Singh the title raja as well as the highest rank (mansab) awarded at that time. Raja Man Singh's architecture includes palaces and gardens, temples and even mosques. Among temples are the Govind Deva temple in Brindavan (Plate 34), not far from Agra, and the Jagat Shiromani temple in Amber (Plate 35), the seat of Raja Man Singh's ancestral land. Inscriptions on the Govind Deva temple, dated 1590, suggest it was built to commemorate his recently deceased father.

The Jagat Shiromani temple, too, was built to honor a recently deceased relative, Raja Man Singh's eldest son and heir apparent who died in 1599. Other temples he built also memorialized recently deceased family members. Raja Man Singh's temples reflect contemporary Mughal taste. The Govind Deva temple (Plate 34), nearly 80 meters in length, is by far the largest temple constructed in north India since the thirteenth century. In plan, the temple is cruciform, recalling many similar temple plans. Continuous horizontal moldings cover the entire elevation of the temple's exterior, broken only by pillared apertures on the ground floor and bracketed and pillared oriel windows on the upper level. The aniconic nature of the temple's exterior is in keeping with others, such as his father's slightly earlier temple at nearby Govardhan. While the Govind Deva temple's Sikri sandstone exterior, particularly in its brackets and pillars, reflects pan-Indian trends, its arcuated, vaulted and domed interior corridors flanked by elaborate bracketed pillars are very specifically Mughal in appearance.

Temples exhibiting features commonly associated with Muslim constructed architecture did not originate with Man Singh. For example, temples with domes are depicted in paintings executed about 1570, such as those illustrating the Tuti Nama. On Man Singh's Govind Deva temple, however, net pendentives, domes and lengthy barrel-vaults are used to create a sense of open longitudinal and vertical space unprecedented in Akbari architecture.

Thus the Govind Deva temple does not merely reflect existing Mughal building, but in many ways anticipates trends yet to develop in imperial Mughal architecture. The Jagat Shiromani temple in Amber (Plate 35), built about a decade later, is based on artistic traditions established in Akbar's capital, Fatehpur Sikri; it is even more ornate than buildings of the capital. In this manner, Raja Man Singh can be said to be an innovator of Mughal taste, not simply an imitator. Raja Man Singh, one of Akbar's most successful administrators, governed first the province (suba) of Bihar and then Bengal from 1578 through the early years of Jahangir's reign, a period of nearly twenty years. In the hill fort of Rohtas and at Rajmahal, Raja Man Singh's capitals respectively of Bihar and Bengal, he provided buildings that furthered his own image yet represented Mughal presence. At Rohtas, Man Singh built by far the most impressive palace for any governor in the Mughal empire. It was also the largest non-imperial palace in the entire Mughal empire.

Man Singh's palace, completed in 1596 according to an inscription over the main entrance, served both himself and the Mughal empire. The palace, measuring 200 by 18 5 meters, is modeled closely on the plan of Fatehpur Sikri. Like the Fatehpur Sikri palace (Plate 22), Man Singh's palace at Rohtas can be divided into administrative and domestic sections. The domestic portions included hammams, latrines and residential quarters for Man Singh and his zenana. The administrative section had areas intended for public and private purposes. The public area included a viewing window for public audience (jharoka) (Plate 36) that faces an open quadrangle.

This quadrangle for public audience is a large rectangular area in front of the palace that until now has been identified as a serai. An elaborate set of buildings, including one traditionally called a baradari, were probably in the private administrative area of the palace. Also in this area is a building known as the Private Audience Hall, situated just behind the public viewing balcony. Both a Public and Private Audience Hall were necessary so that a governor could enact the sort of court ritual that was maintained at the distant imperial seat.

Not only does the Rohtas palace recall the general plan and arrangement of Fatehpur Sikri, but also the style of the palace is very much in keeping with imperial Mughal architecture. The carved brackets on the Private Audience Hall, for example, recall those of several buildings at Fatehpur Sikri (Plates 28 and 31), and the arcuated forms of the Shish Mahal, part of the zenana, resemble those of the Fatehpur Sikri hammams. In these ways and others, the palace is the first structure to introduce the courtly style of architecture to eastern India. Man Singh's palace thus provides a powerful statement of Mughal presence, especially effective in showing Mughal authority over local recalcitrant zamindars, whose forts were crudely constructed. This imposing site projected more than an image of Mughal presence. It also projected that of Man Singh himself.

He was fully aware of his dual role as Mughal governor and rank holder {mansabdar) on one hand and as raja or prince in his own right. This we may glean from a large stone slab at the palace entrance gate. It bears two inscriptions, one in Persian and one in Sanskrit. The one in Persian suggests that Raja Man Singh primarily built the palace as a servant of Akbar, for it first and most extensively addresses the emperor Akbar with only brief reference to Raja Man Singh, the actual patron. But in the longer Sanskrit inscription on the same slab, Akbar's name is omitted altogether. Instead the raja is mentioned twice, once even as king of kings, overlord, suggesting that he, the governor, was supreme monarch.

The grandiloquent title on a palace intended to serve both the governor's needs as well as those of the state underscores the dual nature of the relationship between the raja and the Mughal emperor. Under the Mughal state system, serving the emperor included defending one's own religion, honor and even patrimony if necessary. Thus evoking a title which may have symbolized Rajput ideals and aspirations in itself did not conflict with Man Singh's role as Akbar's governor, for both were part of the integral success of the functioning Mughal empire. Similarly, the resemblance of the Rohtas palace to Fatehpur Sikri both recalls the emperor and permits Man Singh to assume the guise of the ruler that in fact he was.

He thus played out his dual role as the emperor's agent and raja in his own right, a duality characteristic of the relationship between Akbar and his lesser authorities. Even after Man Singh was transferred from the governorship of Bihar he continued to hold Rohtas and maintained his building program there. Thus his tenure over Rohtas lasted nearly twenty years, a remarkable span when most jagirs were changed every few years so that a power base could not be established. Man Singh's long-term tenure at Rohtas reflected his willingness to invest personal resources in a palace that far surpassed that of any other Mughal governor.

After rapidly consolidating Mughal authority in Bihar, Raja Man Singh was transferred to Bengal in 1594 to assume the governorship there. Akbar hoped that Man Singh's success in subduing rebels in Bihar might be repeated against the rebel Afghans, such as the Qaqshal, and zamindars who continued to challenge Mughal authority in Bengal. In 1595 Man Singh built a new capital at a site known today as Rajmahal. The selection of this site for the capital of Bengal had significance, since here Akbar's army in 1576 had defeated the last legitimate Afghan ruler of Bengal, ending over 200 years of independent rule there. Thus the site of Mughal victory - and Afghan defeat was memorialized by a permanent Mughal presence and, as if taking power from victory, the seat of its government.

Abu al-Fazl reports that in a short time Raja Man Singh constructed "a choice city" to which the "glorious name" Akbarnagar was given. However, this name was not so harmoniously bestowed, for originally Man Singh had named it Rajanagar, after himself and in recognition of his own patronage. Later, however, he acceded to Akbar's objection and called it Akbarnagar. This recalls the tension seen in the Rohtas palace inscriptions, suggesting that while the new capital was intended to serve the needs of the Mughal empire, the individuality of the governor, Raja Man Singh, was not to be sublimated in the process.

Among Man Singh's structures in Rajmahal are a small temple, a bridge and an enormous Jamic mosque (Plates 37 and 38). The construction of a temple and utilitarian bridge is not surprising; his patronage of a mosque, too, is not unusual, for earlier he had built a mosque in Lahore and since 1590 had maintained the shrine of a saint in Hajipur. But none of this would explain the tremendous size of the Rajmahal Jamic mosque, 77 by 65 meters. This mosque, today partially ruined, is notably not designed in the style standard since the mid-sixteenth century in eastern India, that is, a single-aisled three-bayed type. Rather, in plan the Rajmahal Jamic mosque resembles earlier Mughal Jamic mosques, for example, Babur's mosque at Panipat (Plate 7).

In each, a central corridor is flanked on either side by multi-aisled side wings. Furthermore, the arrangement of the Rajmahal mosque's end chambers, otherwise unknown in Bengal, resembles that of Akbar's Jamic mosque at Fatehpur Sikri (Plate 24). Other features of the Rajmahal Jamic mosque also recall the Fatehpur Sikri Jamic mosque (Plate 25), although they are no longer apparent, but recognizable from an early nineteenth-century drawing. It indicates that the central barrel-vault was concealed by a high rectangular pishtaq, faced with bands of contrasting material, following the imperial model. Thus this imposing mosque, built not in the Bengal tradition but that of the great Mughal Jamic mosques, was intended as a statement of Mughal presence in Bengal. Certainly in no other Mughal provincial seat of government during this period was such an extraordinarily large mosque built, especially remarkable in this case since Man Singh was a Hindu.

In fact, local tradition holds that Raja Man Singh did not originally intend to construct a mosque, but a temple; Akbar, however, ordered that a mosque be built since such a structure would better suit the needs at hand. Man Singh seems to have accepted this order with enthusiasm, for the size of this mosque is unparalleled in the works of nonimperial patrons. Its size further may be explained by the chronic difficulties the Mughals had in subduing Bengal. Using the

Rajmahal Jamic mosque as a symbol of imperial presence in the newly established capital doubtless would have had effect since many of the rebels, themselves ex-Mughal amirs, would have recognized the allusion to the great mosque at Fatehpur Sikri.

Throughout Raja Man Singh's career, architectural patronage served varied and at times even seemingly conflicting purposes. Palaces such as the one at Rohtas were constructed for his own dwelling, administration and image, but inevitably they also represented Mughal presence and were built with this in mind. Similarly, the mosques this Hindu constructed to serve Muslim subjects represented a visual reminder of imperial presence. Temples were built as personal gestures in part to commemorate his family and in part to secure religious merit. It might be argued that the construction of temples elevated only the patron's prestige.

Nevertheless, the temples, like most architecture provided by Akbar's nobles, utilized styles that originated with Akbar's court and in essence underscored Akbar's presence. These buildings further promulgated a uniform aesthetic throughout north India. Thus ultimately even the construction of temples served the state. Just as Akbar was the ultimate head of state whose authority was diffused through his nobles and others, so artistic and architectural styles used in the center were disseminated throughout the domain by these officials, both Hindu and Muslim. The degree of imperial intervention in construction remains unclear, but such enterprise certainly served the state and was valued by the emperor. This is apparent from the second of twelve orders issued upon the accession of Akbar's successor, Jahangir. It states that it is the duty oi jagirdars (amirs assigned land revenues in lieu of salary) to provide religious and secular buildings in the hinterlands to encourage population and stability throughout their domain. This nobles such as Man Singh already had done - to such an extent and so successfully that his building activity may have stimulated the order.

No Mughal noble built as widely as did Man Singh. But others built, and did so with similar motivation. They, too, bolstered their status while at the same time serving the emperor and through their building activity extended the Mughal aesthetic into the provinces.

Western India

Nagaur

Akbar realized that subjugation of the princely states in western India was in the Mughals' best interests. To do this, the Rajput princes had to be made Mughal vassals. First, Ajmer and Nagaur, part of the traditional area known as Marwar, fell to the Mughals shortly after Akbar's accession. Then major headway toward consolidation was achieved when Raja Baramal Kachhwaha of Amber, until recently the princely family of Jaipur, agreed to give his daughter in marriage to Akbar in 1562, commencing a long-standing relationship of mutual benefit between these families. By 1570, all the major princely states of Rajasthan, with the exception of Mewar, acknowledged the Mughals as overlord. At the same time, order had to be imposed even on some Mughal nobles. Such was the case with the landholder of Nagaur, Muhammad Sharaf al-Din Husain Mirza, who rebelled for reasons never fully explained. He was replaced in the same year, 1562, by Husain Quli Khan, already a greatly trusted noble, who later was appointed governor of the Punjab and awarded the prestigious title Khan-i Jahan, or Noble of the World.

Husain Quli Khan built in areas where he was posted. His patronage of a mosque in front of the local raja's house in the Punjab is known only from texts. His patronage of a mosque in Nagaur, locally called the Jamic mosque, is confirmed by an inscription dated 1564-65, some two years after his appointment there. This mosque suggests that structures patronized by the Mughal nobility in the early stages of Akbar's reign were constructed with some awareness of the imperial tradition, but largely in local idioms and, in all probability, by local artisans. The mosque, dominating Nagaur's numerous religious monuments, is a single-aisled three-bayed structure surmounted by a single central dome. Towering minarets flanking either end of the east facade make the structure visible for a considerable distance. While certain features, such as the mosque's plan and the deeply recessed tri-partite mihrab, reflect an awareness of architectural forms in contemporary Delhi, then the capital, the mosque draws heavily on the local architectural traditions of Marwar. For example, the facade recalls that of the fifteenth-century Shamsi mosque in Nagaur, and the stone canopied minbar inside this Jamic mosque (Plate 39) recalls those seen in the Jamic mosques of Mandu and Chanderi, but not on any imperially sponsored Mughal mosques.

The mosque's inscription suggests that the building was intended to represent Mughal authority. It is not on the facade where historical inscriptions are generally placed, but embedded into the qibla wall, within the minbar. Here the khutba was delivered, that is, the Friday prayer in which the ruling monarch's name was read. This inscription states that the mosque was constructed in the "reign of the ruler of the age, Akbar," and likens the building to "the qibla of deductions and principles." Thus Husain Quli Khan used the structure as well as the words of the inscription and its unique location to underscore the image Akbar had sought to project of himself: the qibla of the state. The inscription's verses were carved by Darwish Muhammad al-Hajji, whose pen name was Ramzi; he executed several other inscriptions on monuments in this region.

Ajmer

Ajmer especially benefited from imperial interest and intervention. By 1579 Akbar had come on pilgrimage to the dargah of Mucin al-Din Chishti in Ajmer fourteen times. During this period, he repaired and enlarged the fort of Ajmer. Following his lead, nobles built gardens and dwellings for themselves in Ajmer. They also may have been responsible for the gates of the walled city, including one embellished with glazed tiles in its spandrels. The construction of religious structures was encouraged by the new status that Akbar's interest in the Chishti sect conferred upon the city; this was enhanced by imperial decree. Annoyed that Khwaja Husain, the chief attendant of the Chishti shrine there, was improperly distributing its income, Akbar issued orders that mosques and khanqahs should be constructed in the territory, presumably with these funds as well as private ones. The mosque (Plate

40) situated immediately to the west of the dargah's south entrance is almost certainly a product of this order. It probably dates to the early 1570s, shortly after the order was issued. Called the Akbari mosque, the courtyard is entered through a large gate. The interior walls of the compound today are used as a madrasa, probably a continuation of their original function.

The mosque is not simply a regional expression; it clearly manifests an awareness of Timurid-inspired architecture at the center. In fact many believe the mosque was provided by Akbar himself. Colored stone bands frame the recessed large entrance arch and its spandrels, recalling Humayun's near-contemporary tomb (Plate 18). A high-arched pishtaq dominates the facade of the mosque's prayer chamber and appears a more refined version of the entrance to Humayun's Jamic mosque at Kachpura (Plate 12).

The prayer chamber's plan, too, is based on the Kachpura mosque's. The east facade bears white marble inlaid in geometric patterns recalling designs on the Fatehpur Sikri Jamic mosque. The interior of the mosque, too, reveals an awareness of imperial trends, for example, the net pendentives that appeared on Humayun's Kachpura mosque and the Fatehpur Sikri hammams.

During the years that Akbar made pilgrimage to the shrine of Mucin al-Din Chishti, nobles also invested in the city. An inscription dating 1568-69 refers to the construction of a reservoir by Gesu Khan, in charge of the imperial kitchens and an officer in nearby Merta. The reservoir, however, cannot be identified, since the epigraph is no longer in situ. This inscription was designed by Darwish Muhammad al-Hajji al-Ramzi, the same calligrapher who designed the inscription on Husain Quli Khan's mosque in Nagaur.

He also designed the next known inscription from Ajmer. This epigraph is located on a towering gateway (Plate 41) marking the entrance to the shrine of Sayyid Husain Khing Sawar, situated on the fortified hill known as Taragarh above Mucin al-Din's dargah. It attributes the gate's construction to Ismacil Quli Khan in 15 70-71. He was the younger brother of Husain Quli Khan, who had built the

Nagaur Jamic mosque some four years earlier. Sayyid Husain Khing Sawar had been the presiding officer of Ajmer under Aibek, the first Delhi sultan. He probably was martyred defending the fort in the early thirteenth century. Contemporary with the great saint, Mucin al-Din, Sayyid Husain appears to have become his disciple. But it is only in the Mughal period that the religious status of Sayyid Husain was enhanced as was that of Mucin al-Din. Ismacil Quli Khan's gate at the foot of this hill, 19. meters high and 5 meters wide, remains the dargah's dominant feature. Looming above the architecturally undistinguished structures there, this red sandstone gate, now whitewashed, serves as an entrance to the large interior courtyard that contains the saint's tomb. The gate itself is austere; its height, disproportionate to the narrow width, dominates the shrine. Surmounted by two chattris, the gate is pierced by a single open entrance whose apex terminates in an exaggerated ogee point. The use of the ogee arch appears to be a regional characteristic, recalling similar arches on near-contemporary monuments in nearby Nagaur and Merta. Regional, too, is the exaggerated height and much of the gate's form, similar to the pre-Mughal Buland Darwaza, serving as an entrance to the shrine below. At least one feature, however, recalls monuments in Delhi, the monumental rectangular band of Quranic verse framing the entrance. Similar bands of verse are also on the Sur-period Qalca-i Kuhna mosque (Plate 5) and the madrasa of Maham Anga dated 1561.

After 1579, when Akbar made his last annual pilgrimage to Ajmer, construction there waned. At the dargahs of Mucin al-Din and Sayyid Husain Khing Sawar much had been built during the years of Akbar's pilgrimage. Among these is an enclosure around the graves of early Muslim martyrs at Sayyid Husain's shrine built in 1571-72 by Shah Quli Khan, an officer associated with Ajmer, Narnaul and Nagaur. Also several graves at the shrine of Mucin al-Din bear dates before 1579. Even Khwaja Husain, the very superintendent chastised by Akbar for mismanaging the dargah's income, constructed a dome over the tomb of Mucin al-Din Chishti in 1579. This may have been provided in response to Akbar's orders to build at the shrine and hence an attempt to regain imperial favor. But after 1579 Ajmer was provided with no new Mughal buildings until the reign of Jahangir. He revived the public display of devotion to Mucin al-Din Chishti, and patronage in the city again increased with Jahangir's renewed interest in the shrine.

Baroda and Mandu

Few monuments of Akbar's time survive in his westernmost domain, Gujarat. The octagonal tomb of Qutb al-Din Muhammad Khan(d. 1583), who provided the screens and floor at Shaikh Salim Chishti's tomb (Plate 26), breaks with the local regional style. This tomb, in Baroda, is a larger and less refined version of the type Shah Quli Khan had built about a decade earlier in Narnaul (Plate 43). Closer to central India, the fortified hill, Mandu, had been embellished with palaces, mosques and tombs provided by the fifteenth- and sixteenth-century Khalji sultans. Mandu was the doorway to the Deccan during the reigns of Akbar and Jahangir. Akbar visited it four times, while Jahangir stayed in the fort for about seven months.

The Nil Kanth palace, a pleasure pavilion, was built there in 1574-75 by Budagh Khan, the officer in charge of Mandu under Akbar. Water is channelled through the central chamber of this palace to a pool in the open courtyard below, thus incorporating the landscape as is characteristic of Mughal architecture. One side of the palace is open and overlooks the lush valley below. Inscriptions carved on the palace's walls record Akbar's victories in the Deccan in 1600-01, for Mandu was then used as a camp during Akbar's forays into the Deccan.

North India

In the major Mughal cities of north India - Lahore, Delhi, Agra and Allahabad - mostly imperial monuments remain from Akbar's reign. In a few places, however, there are fine sub-imperial monuments. Those buildings show a degree of independence from imperial forms, even though their architects had absorbed or in some cases anticipated a sense of Akbar's imperial aesthetic. One of these places is Hasan Abdal in Rawalpindi District, Pakistan, where Raja Man Singh built a terraced four-part garden over a waterfall. Not far from Hasan Abdal is the tomb of Khwaja Shams al-Din Khwafi, Akbar's governor there.

The flat-roofed octagonal tomb is pierced by deeply recessed arches and recalls similarly shaped pleasure pavilions such as the Hada Mahal at Fatehpur Sikri. Near the tomb is a deep tank fed by underground springs. In its crystal clear water large fish still swim, suggesting that the tomb building was originally conceived as a pleasure pavilion.

At Gwalior, the tomb of Muhammad Ghaus (Plate 42) is the most notable structure of Akbar's reign. The architecture of this fine stone building anticipates trends yet to become popular in Mughal architecture, especially in eastern India. Muhammad Ghaus, a celebrated saint and well-known writer of the Shattari order, died in 1563. His tomb was constructed sometime afterward.

This impressive tomb is a square structure surmounted by a large squat dome and flanking chattris that give the structure a tiered or multi-storied effect. Around the walls of the tomb's central chamber is a continuous veranda enclosed in turn with screened walls. Such screened verandas derive from the architecture of Gujarat, for example, the tomb of Bai Harir in Ahmadabad. This reflects the considerable time Muhammad Ghaus had spent in Gujarat, a source of importance for Mughal tombs, for example, the tomb of Shaikh Salim Chishti built in 1580-81 at Fatehpur Sikri. Even through the mid-eighteenth century, many Mughal tombs including imperial ones continue to be enclosed by screens, although they often had no roofs.

Narnaul

In Narnaul, today in the state of Haryana, not far from Rajasthan, several Akbari structures are well preserved. During Akbar's time, Narnaul was a district headquarters and mint town in Agra Province. Its location between Delhi and the Rajput state of Marwar made Narnaul strategically important. It was also an important place of pilgrimage for Hindus, and for Muslims, who concluded their sojourn at the shrine of a thirteenth-century pir, Shaikh Muhammad Turk Narnauli. Akbar went to Narnaul to visit the esteemed contemporary Chishti Shaikh Nizam al-Din, one of the learned men of the time. The Shaikh died in 1589 and was buried in a square stucco-covered tomb adhering to the older Lodi style; devotion to the Shaikh's memory was so great that in 1622 Nicmat Allah, otherwise unknown, built a single-aisled threebayed mosque facing the tomb.

It is beautifully covered with polychromed arabesques and Quranic inscriptions. No one constructed more in Narnaul than did Shah Quli Khan. Originally a protege of Bhairam Khan, the powerful guardian of the young Akbar, Shah Quli Khan advanced rapidly in the Mughal court. First he rose in imperial favor when he wounded the Sur general Hemu, preventing the fall of the Mughals just after Akbar's accession. By the end of his life, he had been awarded the highest rank then bestowed on any noble. Renowned for his generosity, Shah Quli Khan gave large salary advances to his retinue and upon his deathbed in 1601-02 bestowed much money to charity. This later act, however, might be considered one of shrewdness, for all the property and money of a noble such as Shah Quli Khan, who had no immediate heirs, returned to the state upon his death. Shah Quli Khan's architecture in Narnaul was of a personal sort, rather different from the enclosure he had built at the Taragarh shrine. His patronage of the Narnaul monuments was considered remarkable enough by his contemporaries that these works are mentioned in Mughal-period texts. Shah Quli Khan's first architectural project in Narnaul, his tomb (Plate 43), is dated 1574-75, three years after his enclosure at the Taragarh shrine. A multi-storied arched gateway, built fourteen years after the tomb, serves as the entrance to the tomb's walled garden compound.

The tomb is a small octagonal structure faced with red and gray contrasting stones and surmounted by a white dome. While the contrasting stones closely resemble those used on the nearby tomb of Sher Shah's grandfather, the tomb's octagonal plan is very different from the octagonal type constructed by the Lodi and Sur kings. That type had consisted of an eight-sided veranda encircling a central chamber. Shah Quli Khan's tomb, however, has no veranda and more closely resembles the cylindrical octagonal pavilion known as the Sher Mandal (Plate 11) in Delhi's Purana Qalca and the so-called Hada Mahal, a pleasure pavilion situated near the lake at Fatehpur Sikri, both inspired by Iranian pleasure pavilions.

That Shah Quli Khan's tomb resembles a pleasure pavilion is appropriate. The building, constructed some twenty-five years before Shah Quli Khan's death, was situated in a large planned garden and was used in his life as part of his residential estate. Variations of this octagonal tomb-type are widely used in north India. For example, Shamsher Khan's elegantly painted tomb in Batala constructed in 1589-90 is similar, as are the undated octagonal tombs in Bahlolpur, said to be those of Bahadur Shah and Husain Shah. A similar structure, the tomb dated 1612-13 built in Nakodar for Mumin Husaini (Plate 78), a musician at the court of the Khan-i Khanan, a high-ranking noble under Akbar and Jahangir, indicates the continuing popularity of this type later in the Mughal period. Some fifteen years after he built his tomb, Shah Quli Khan constructed nearby a second gateway situated on the northern edge of a large square tank. It opens to an arched causeway that leads to a pleasure pavilion (Plate 44) situated in the tank's center. The tank and pavilion were commenced in 1590-91 and completed two years later. Inscriptions here show that paradisical imagery continues to be a trademark of Mughal architecture, for the tank in which the tomb sits is called a "second Kausar" (a pool in paradise) and its water "the water of immortality";53 in addition, both the pavilion itself and Shah Quli's tomb are equated with paradise. While such inscriptions often praise the patron, their flattery is usually very general. Here, however, specific reference is made to the patron's heroism of nearly fifty years earlier, when he defeated the Sur general Hemu, thus saving Mughal hegemony. Shah Quli Khan is called "the honor of the country . . . who carried away the ball of valor from his rivals."

Shah Quli Khan's pavilion, locally known as the Jal Mahal or Water Palace, resembles various imperial structures in its individual parts; in combination, it resembles no single one, but combines these features in an innovative fashion. For example, the pavilion's location in the midst of a tank recalls water pavilions at Fatehpur Sikri that sat on the edge of a lake, although both the Hada Mahal and Qush Khana there are octagonal. The chattris of the superstructure recall another building at Fatehpur Sikri, the so-called Diwan-i Khass. Such multiple chattris on flat roofs were typical of domestic architecture, as contemporary illustrations show. This pavilion, then, probably draws inspiration from buildings at Fatehpur Sikri, and in turn it served as a model for a similar pavilion in Bairat (Jaipur District). That pavilion, dated about a decade later than the Jal Mahal and attributed to Raja Man Singh, was also set in water.

Other tombs constructed by amirs of Akbar's time also adhere to no single architectural form, even though their individual components are commonly rendered in evident Mughal style. That is the case, for example, with the tomb of Mirza Muzaffar Husain (d. 1603) in Delhi, known locally as the Bara Batashewala Mahal. This is a flat-roofed structure once probably surmounted by a textile canopy. Its ground floor, like that of the Jal Mahal and Humayun's tomb, has a central chamber surrounded by eight smaller rooms. This type of plan is derived from Iranian prototypes. Perhaps it is no accident that the Bara Batashewala Mahal is situated just outside the walls of Humayun's tomb. Another type, this one rooted in the earlier Sultanate architectural tradition, simply consists of a single chattri on a raised plinth. At times, this type includes a wall mosque and a small entrance gate, as in the case of the tomb of Miyan Raib, dated 1594, in Jhajjar (Haryana). This is not the first Mughal tomb of this older type; the tomb of Saqi Sultan (Plate 45) in Rohtas fort, Bihar, dated 1579-80, is similar.

Eastern India

Mughal authority was imposed with difficulty on eastern Uttar Pradesh, Bihar, Bengal, and Orissa. When the Mughals were attempting to consolidate their power in areas closer to Delhi and Agra, Afghan clans and nobles reasserted themselves in eastern India. Slowly, however, this region fell to the Mughals. Eastern Uttar Pradesh came under Mughal control early in Akbar's reign; the Gangetic valley of Bihar was tentatively taken by Akbar in 1574. It was secured by him after a serious uprising in 1580 instigated by a number of dissatisfied Mughal amirs and Afghans under the leadership of Macsum Khan Kabuli; then this territory, as well as much of Orissa, was successfully incorporated into the Mughal domain. While Bengal was claimed by

Akbar in 1575, Mughal consolidation there was not fully achieved until Jahangir's reign. This prolonged effort to assert Mughal authority in eastern India was accompanied by vigorous architectural construction on the part of Mughal governors and other officials, an attempt to underscore a permanent Mughal presence there.

Jaunpur and Chunar

Jaunpur, some 40 km north of Benares, also known as Varanasi, had been a leading intellectual center in northern India during the fourteenth and fifteenth centuries. Until Akbar's forces took Patna and other territory in the Bihar Gangetic valley, Jaunpur remained the most important eastern seat of the Mughal empire. In 1567, Akbar appointed Khan-i Khanan Muhammad Muncim Khan, a noble faithful since the days of Humayun, as governor there.

His tenure in Jaunpur and the extensive surrounding territory, including the stronghold of Chunar, lasted until his death in 1575. Instrumental in Mughal expansion to the east, Muncim Khan was considered one of Akbar's most loyal nobles. He extensively refurbished the city of Jaunpur, which had been ravaged by the Lodis. Among his works there is a bridge and additions to the older fort. Tradition records that he also constructed mosques throughout the city. Epigraphic evidence, however, indicates these were built by others, suggesting that Muncim Khan's own patronage served as a stimulus for nobles directly responsible to him.

Muncim Khan's bridge (Plate 46), still used today, is generally recognized as Jaunpur's most significant Mughal structure. One Mughal writer states that although the Khan-i Khanan had no heirs, his descendant, the Jaunpur bridge, "will preserve his name for ages."55 It consists of ten arched openings supported on massive pylons; chattris line either side of the top. The six inscriptions on the bridge indicate that it was commenced in 1564-65 and completed in 1568-69. A Persian history of Jaunpur states that Muncim Khan constructed the bridge in response to a discourse by Akbar in which he, hearing a widow complain about the lack of ferry service across the Gumpti, proclaimed that it is better to provide public works than religious edifices. The story is probably apocryphal, but it suggests that just as amirs in Ajmer built in response to Akbar's decree, so here, too, the Khan-i Khanan's architectural patronage was inspired by the ruler himself. The fort walls were constructed earlier, but the massive eastern gate is generally ascribed to Muncim Khan's patronage. It is embellished with blue and yellow tiles similar to those on contemporary buildings of the independent sultans of Bengal. So also a palace known as the Chehil Sutun was probably his product. While traditionally the palace is said to have been built in the fourteenth century, early nineteenth-century drawings indicate that this administrative or residential structure was constructed in a typical Akbari idiom. These drawings of the now demolished palace suggest the early introduction of an imperial style in these eastern hinterlands. The ground floor of this square double-storied structure is encompassed by a pillared veranda or aiwan; the whole is surmounted by a large pillared chattri. While no specific remaining structure at the Agra fort or Fatehpur Sikri can be cited as the model, the Jaunpur palace captures the flavor of contemporary imperial architecture. In turn, it may have been instrumental in the design of the palace Raja Man Singh constructed in the Rohtas fort about twenty years later, when he served as Akbar's governor of Bihar.

Near the site of the Chehil Sutun is a domed and vaulted multi-chambered hammam (Plate 47) that closely resembles the baths of Fatehpur Sikri. This Jaunpur bath, with its carefully planned arrangements for hot and cold water, is a rare example of an intact provincial bath. Since the hammam appears not to have been introduced to India until the Mughal period, its presence in the easternmost hinterlands early in Akbar's reign is indicative of the rapid spread of technology and style.

Although the Jaunpur fort served as the governor's residence early in Akbar's reign, two forts were defensively more important: the fort of Chunar, acquired by Akbar in 1561, and the fort of Allahabad, constructed in 1580. Eventually as the Mughals increased their landholdings further to the east, as far as modern Bangladesh, Jaunpur's significance was overshadowed. Possession of the Chunar fortress long had been considered pivotal to the ultimate control of eastern

India, for it guarded both the Ganges and the major land routes. Humayun held the fort briefly, but it was recaptured by the Surs. It was ceded to other Afghans, who held it until 1561, when they joined the Mughal ranks. Abu al-Fazl, discussing Chunar's importance, called its acquisition by Akbar one of the important events of that year. In 1566 Akbar visited the fort personally, but in describing that visit Abu al-Fazl neglected to note the fort's appearance. However, its present appearance suggests that much of it was constructed in Akbar's reign. Chunar's stone quarries, famous since Maurya times, provided abundant stone and skilled masons. Thus, the task of rebuilding the fort was relatively simple.

The fort's west gate is its only inscribed structure. It bears four Persian epigraphs indicating that the gate was built during the reign of Akbar in 1573-74 by Muhammad Sharif Khan. His identity has not yet been established, although he may have been the son of Abd al-Samad, the famous painter. Muhammad Sharif probably served under Muncim Khan, who had been granted Chunar and a great deal of surrounding territory as income-yielding land in 1567. Muncim Khan held Chunar until his death in 1575.

This gate bears little ornamentation other than the beautifully executed calligraphic slabs. The fort's other gates, by contrast, have intricately carved panels and brackets (Plate 48). Such carving in general fits well with contemporary trends. For example, the S-shaped brackets of the oriel windows on some of these gates more closely resemble work in Agra than any pre-Mughal monuments in eastern India. However, some of the designs, for example a continuous knot motif, are closer to work on Sur-period architecture in Chainpur and Sher Shah's fortress at Shergarh, both some 60 to 75 km east of Chunar, than they are to the Mughal material. This suggests not only a reliance on local artisans, but also a continuation of some regional traditions.

Bihar

In Bihar province, today roughly corresponding to the northern and central portions of Bihar state, by far the most important work of Akbar's time was in the hill fort of Rohtas. In 1576 Akbar's troops captured Rohtas from rebel Afghan forces and used the hill fort, some 45 km in circumference, as a garrison pivotal in controlling the rest of eastern India. Although Rohtas had served as an important fort under the Sur dynasty, the Mughals developed a different portion of the fort. The palace at Rohtas that Raja Man Singh built was discussed earlier in this chapter, but it was not the first Mughal building in the fort. A mosque (Plate 49) had been built in 1578, only two years after the fort became Mughal. This was the first Mughal monument in all Bihar province.

Built by an Akbar loyalist, Habash Khan, who died defending Rohtas against renegade Mughal amirs and Afghan rebels, the mosque is similar in appearance to the Jamic mosque constructed on the hill thirty-five years earlier by Haibat Khan, one of Sher Shah Sur's leading generals. Both adhere to a single-aisled three-bayed rectangular plan. Differences are slight. The central pishtaq of the Mughal mosque is lower, and its facade bears intricately carved panels, recalling similar work on a gate at the Chunar fort. Although the Mughal mosque resembles the earlier Afghan one, situated about 3 km away, it bears an inscription over the central entrance arch that might be interpreted as a poignant statement of Mughal supremacy. Opening with the Quranic phrase, "With God's help victory is imminent," most of this Persian inscription refers to Akbar's victories and concludes with an appeal, in Arabic, to "deliver this good news to believers."60 Considering the shaky political situation at this time, the inscription can be interpreted as a proclamation of Mughal authority over rebels in Bihar.

A single mosque is not enough to suggest an urban setting. There were, however, other Akbari structures on the hill which indicate the presence of a permanent and continuous large population. By far the largest and most important of these is the palace of Raja Man Singh, discussed earlier. Numerous smaller buildings, mostly tombs, remain in the vicinity of the palace and Habash Khan's mosque. Among these are a chattri and wall mosque serving as the tomb of Saqi Sultan (Plate 45), who died in 1579-80, before he could attain the title khan, which he greatly coveted. Further testimony to the fort's large population is a service town at the foot of the hill. It was - and still is - called

Akbarpur, after the then-ruling monarch. Thus, although relatively inaccessible and strongly fortified, Rohtas appears to have functioned as a major urban center as long as it remained a significant administrative center. During the latter part of Akbar's reign, Rohtas fort operated in much the same manner as his completely planned city-palace of Fatehpur Sikri. That is, it was the symbolic seat of the head of state, here the Mughal governor of Bihar, who was the official representative of Mughal authority. But here, even more than at Fatehpur Sikri, the commercial and agrarian components largely were aimed at serving the immediate city.

While Rohtas was an important military headquarters, it was the cities of Hajipur, Patna and Munger, situated on the Ganges, as well as Bihar Sharif, the traditional administrative center of Bihar and long a site of tremendous religious importance, that were the major urban settlements. Inscriptions indicate Akbar-period building activity in all of them except Patna. This is ironic, for Patna was very large, even containing the mint for Bihar Province, and except during Man Singh's governorship it was the leading administrative center.

Hajipur, situated at the confluence of the Gandak and Ganges, across from Patna, was considered the key to north Bihar. The city had been the landholding of Sacid Khan, who on three separate occasions served as governor of Bihar. Here in 1586-87, during Sacid Khan's first period of governorship, his brother Makhsus Khan built a mosque, the second known Mughal mosque in Bihar. Although the mosque's facade and entrance gate were seriously damaged in the 1934 earthquake, the original layout is intact, and the interior (Plate 50) appears little changed.

The mosque's adherence to older Afghan style mosques as well as its Bengali forms, for example, the minbar and curved cornice of the entrance gate, suggest a reliance on local designers. The link with Bengal in particular is not surprising since Hajipur, often in Bengali hands, was an important naval headquarters under the pre-Mughal Husain Shahi dynasty. Thus in Bihar, except for Raja Man Singh's outstanding patronage, architectural design remained conservative.

Bengal

Until 1575 Bengal was under the control of various Afghan houses. Then Akbar's troops brought Bengal into the Mughal empire. Subsequently several revolts against Akbar's authority were staged by renegade nobles of the Mughal camp. Ironically, during this chaotic period, a Mughal style of architecture was introduced by the rebels. Bengali Islamic architecture had a marked regional character. It was founded on a well-established Islamic style in Bengal illustrated by several monuments constructed on the eve of Mughal authority there. Among these are the doubleaisled six-domed mosque of Kusumba built in 1558-59, and the square-plan single-domed tomb of Pir Bahram in Burdwan dated 1562-63. The former is stone-faced, while the latter is brick-constructed, and both, like most pre- Mughal architecture of Islamic Bengal, have a prominent curved cornice. Their plan and elevation - even the ornamental brick - reflect forms that were at the time several centuries old. From this foundation, the Mughal style of Bengal evolves.

Only five years after the establishment of Mughal authority in Bengal, and before any known Mughal building had been erected there, Afghan chiefs revolted against Mughal authority and assumed power. The Afghan Macsum Khan Kabuli, a renegade Mughal noble, declared himself ruler of Bengal, even though the imperial Mughals maintained nominal control. By 1581 Macsum Khan Kabuli had assumed the title of sultan, as indicated by an inscription on the first surviving Mughal monument in Bengal, the Jamic mosque at Chatmohar (Pabna District). About one year later, in 1582, two mosques were constructed, each reflecting divergent stylistic traditions. The Qutb Shahi mosque of 1582-83 in Pandua, built by Makhdum Shaikh in honor of the longdeceased but deeply revered saint, Nur Qutb Alam, adheres to a plan popular in Bengal since the fourteenth century. This stone-faced mosque is divided into two aisles of five bays each. Not only is it constructed in the traditional Bengali style, but also the inscription is in Arabic, the language of most pre-Mughal inscriptions in Bengal. This is the last stone-faced mosque built in Bengal until the twentieth century, and it is the last small double-aisled rectangular mosque constructed in Bengal until the nineteenth century. A different trend is represented by the single-aisled, three-bayed plan of the Kherua mosque in Sherpur (Bogra District), also built in 1582 (Plate 51). Its patron was Murad Khan, son of Jauhar Ali Khan Qaqshal. The Qaqshal were an Afghan tribe that, along with other Afghan groups who followed Macsum Khan Kabuli, sought to oust the Mughals from Bengal. Sherpur, the city in which the mosque is situated, served as the rebel headquarters. Ironically, however, it was this mosque-type that became standard in Mughal and post-Mughal Bengal.

The Kherua mosque's single-aisled, three-bayed plan recalls not only north Indian types but also that of Habash Khan's mosque of 1578 built in Rohtas (Plate 49). While Bengali features remain, such as the brick construction, curved cornice and engaged ribbed corner turrets, the plan is a departure from that of traditional Bengali mosques. This may be attributed to the fact that the ruler, Macsum Khan Kabuli, and many of his rebel followers who had served earlier in Bihar under the Mughals, were familiar with north Indian forms, as well as with the mosques in the great stronghold of Rohtas. When serving the Mughals they had assisted with the fort's initial takeover and later tried to capture Rohtas for themselves.

Older Hindu sculptures were imbedded in the mosque's east facade, leaving only the back visible; that part was carved with a Persian inscription. Reuse of Hindu materials in such a prominent fashion is rare in Bengal after the fourteenth century; the Qaqshal rebels were probably cut off from sources of freshly quarried stone, which would have been used for an inscription on a brick monument, and so had to rely on available materials. This, as much as desecration of a Hindu shrine, probably explains the images' use. Both epigraphs are written in Persian, the lingua franca of the Mughal court, rather than Arabic, more common in Bengal. This is yet another indication that Bengali architecture was moving closer to a pan-Indian idiom whose standards were established at imperial centers. Because of their former association with the Mughal court, the Qaqshal, now rebels, were nevertheless planting the seeds in Bengal of an architectural vocabulary that would become standard throughout the subcontinent from the seventeenth century on. While the language of the inscriptions is characteristic of Mughal epigraphs, the content of these inscriptions is unusual. However, it is perhaps apt for a mosque constructed by rebels. The inscription, still in situ, recounts the story of two pigeons from Mecca, a metaphor for the rebel Qaqshal, who request from a faqir shelter for themselves and for their friends. The faqir grants the permission but states that the mosque is small and will not shelter them from violence. In response, the pigeons say that God's wrath would be great if the mosque or pigeons were harmed. The second inscription, no longer in situ, also admonishes protection of the mosque. Such a plea for protection is appropriate to the world of rebels and appears to have been taken seriously, for the mosque remains in excellent preservation. The otherwise unknown Nawab Mirza Murad Khan Qaqshal thus should be remembered for erecting the first known Bengali mosque of a type that was to become popular throughout Bengal.

Elsewhere in Bengal, architectural activity in Akbar's time was confined largely to Rajmahal, the capital, where Raja Man Singh was active; his Mughalstyle architecture is discussed earlier in this chapter. However, in Malda, a large trade city that benefited from the prosperity of the important shrines in nearby Pandua, a Jamic mosque (Plate 52) was erected in 1595-96, shortly after Raja Man Singh assumed the governorship of Bengal. This was a period when the Mughals began to have some effect in quelling the dissident rebel forces. In the mosque's inscription, neither the patron nor ruling monarch is recorded. It does, however, identify the mosque's location as in "Hind,"64 an area roughly corresponding with north India. This reveals identity with the territory then ruled by the Mughals, not just Bengal.

The Malda Jamic mosque shows an increasing adoption of north Indian forms. The interior gives a sense of open space rarely seen in Bengali rectangular mosques, but common in north Indian examples. The central vaulted corridor is derived from Bengali prototypes, for example the Adina and Gunmant mosques, while north Indian influence is seen in the single-aisled plan. The mosque's ornamentation, too, shows a heightened awareness of north Indian models, for both the facade and interior are largely plastered with a smooth stucco veneer reminiscent, for example, of Humayun's mosque in Kachpura (Plate 12).

The construction of this large mosque suggests the continued economic importance of Malda, despite political turmoil. This is not surprising, for urban centers not wholly created as political centers tend to survive administrative changes, wars and even natural calamity. The most notable Mughal monument in Malda is a tower known today as the Nim Serai Minar (Plate 53). Located across the river from the mosque, this minaret or tower is aligned with the Jamic mosque's qibla wall, the west-facing one. Its name, meaning half, suggests a location between Gaur and Pandua and indicates that it probably served as a mile marker, as did the similar tower at Fatehpur Sikri (Plate 27). The location of this tower, on a hill overlooking the confluence of two rivers, at that time major transport routes, suggests that it also may have served as a watch tower. The tower's facade is covered with stone projections resembling elephant tusks, similar to those on the tower at Fatehpur Sikri. Overall, the Malda tower's form recalls the earlier Chor Minar in Delhi, used to display the heads of thieves. It is thus possible that the Malda tower was constructed when Mughal governors in Bengal were subduing rebel forces and here displayed rebel heads, a custom earlier practiced by the Mughal forebear, Timur. Later than this, during the rebel prince Shah Jahan's bid for the throne in 1625, the heads of some 430 traitors were reportedly on display at Akbarnagar, that is, Rajmahal. In addition, Peter Mundy, traveling through the Mughal empire in 1631, makes references to numerous minarets or towers displaying the heads of executed thieves, noting that these were to be found near important cities. The location of the Malda tower, aligned with a mosque inscribed as being situated in greater India, not just Bengal, makes the possibility of this tower serving as a symbol of strong Mughal presence in this trade town all the more likely.

CONCLUSION

During Akbar's reign imperially sponsored architecture incorporates Timurid design concepts with forms, motifs and building techniques long indigenous to Indian architecture. Many of the resulting buildings, for example much of the palace at Fatehpur Sikri, are highly refined products of prevailing Indian tastes, although the organization and spatial arrangements owe much to Timurid concepts. Akbar, like Humayun, was little involved with religious architecture with the exception of the great khanqah at Fatehpur Sikri. He built primarily forts and palaces, building types that reflect his concept of the Mughal state. The function of many parts of his palaces is often impossible to determine, reflecting the fluid nature of court ceremony in Akbar's reign. This, as we shall see, contrasts with palaces built under subsequent rulers. Akbar also continued to build char baghs, initially introduced to India by Babur. The tomb he built for his father, Humayun, is the first to be set in such a garden. Such funereal settings, evoking visions of paradise, commences what will become a longstanding Mughal architectural concern. Akbar built primarily at his capitals and also defensively at the major cities on the frontier of his domain, such as Allahabad. But Mughal architecture was not confined to these places; rather, it expanded to the hinterlands. There, though, the architecture was built not by the emperor but by his nobles, whose taste most often echoed that of the center. In this expanding Mughal empire, architecture increasingly served as a symbol of Mughal presence.

5

Jahangir: An Age of Transition

Upon the death of Akbar in 1605, Muhammad Sultan Salim assumed the imperial throne. He took the title Nur al-Din Muhammad Jahangir Badshah Ghazi, hence the name Jahangir by which he is most commonly known. It is generally believed that during Jahangir's 22-year reign, half as long as Akbar's, patronage for buildings declined because of his enthusiasm for painting. Further, common belief credits Jahangir's influential wife, Nur Jahan, a leading taste setter of the time, with stimulating the construction of buildings later in the emperor's reign. Her role as patron cannot be denied, but Jahangir continually refers in his own memoirs to his patronage of tombs, pleasure pavilions, forts and gardens as well as to the restoration of older structures. In fact, Jahangir in his memoirs refers more often to architecture he found pleasing or to buildings he ordered than to paintings he commissioned, even though he is regarded as a great connoisseur of painting. During Jahangir's reign the realm was secure. Thus the nobles were encouraged to embellish cities, construct serais, gardens and dwellings and endow shrines - all concrete manifestations of a prosperous state.

Salim was the name given to Jahangir by his father, Akbar, in honor of Salim, the Chishti saint of Fatehpur Sikri who had predicted his birth. He was Akbar's oldest son and heir-apparent. Akbar gave the young prince an education befitting his rank. The leading nobles and scholars such as the great litterateur, Khan-i Khanan Abd al-Rahim, and the leading theologian, Shaikh Abd al-Nabi, were charged with responsibility for educating the future emperor. Well versed in

Persian and Hindi and with a respectable knowledge of Turki, Prince Salim also possessed a good grounding in history, the natural sciences, geography, martial skills and theology - all part of the traditional Islamic curriculum considered appropriate for a prince. But more than this formal education, his innate sense of observation, inherited from his greatgrandfather, Babur, coupled with his extraordinary taste for the exquisite and the unusual made him a remarkable connoisseur of art, rare animals and birds, as well as jewels. His ability to discern the beauty of objects and animals never waned, while his treatment of fellow humans vacillated between cruelty and sensitive tenderness.

Before Salim ascended the throne and assumed the title Jahangir, his two brothers had died prematurely, reputedly from drink, one in 1599 and the other in 1604. Nevertheless, his accession was not without issue. Eager to obtain the throne, Salim revolted in 1600 and established his own court in Akbar's Allahabad fort. Salim struck coins in his own name and assumed imperial titles. Akbar thus sought to consult his confidant and biographer, Abu al-Fazl, then in the Deccan. Salim, however, had him assassinated in 1602. While Salim's revolt did not shake the stability of Akbar's empire, it did shape future events. Several of the most prominent courtiers urged Akbar to skip a generation by designating Khusrau, Salim's oldest son, as his successor. As a result, a tremendous rift occurred between the two princes, father and son, each aspiring to the throne.

Finally, late in 1604 Akbar marched toward Allahabad, but turned back to Agra upon hearing that his mother, Maryam Makhani, had died. After Akbar's return to Agra, Salim followed, probably eager to curtail the elevation of his son, Khusrau, to heir-apparent. Salim and Akbar were more or less reconciled, and the scheme to designate Khusrau as heir failed. On his death-bed in 1605, Akbar designated Salim as his successor.

Salim, who began 'writing his memoirs at the time of his accession, explains that he took the title Jahangir, or World Seizer, since it was the business of kings to control the world; the title Nur al-Din, or Light of the Faith, was appropriate since his accession "coincided with the rising and shining on the earth of the great light, the Sun."2 The assumption of this title is particularly noteworthy, for it indicates, among much other evidence, that the importance of light and light-imagery under Akbar continued under Jahangir. For example, light imagery is also apparent in painting commissioned by Jahangir, especially in his allegorical portraits, as well as in imperial funereal architecture. Abu al-Fazl had developed the notion of light imagery associated with the emperor's semidivine status. How ironic, then, that Jahangir, responsible for Abu al-Fazl's brutal murder, made extensive use of light imagery in his writing and art. Mughal ties with the Chishti saints, maintained by Akbar until 1579, were revived by Jahangir. The emperor's memoirs open with an account of Akbar's journey on foot to the great Chishti shrine in Ajmer and Shaikh Salim's prophecy of the birth of a son. Subsequently in his memoirs, Jahangir recalls that early in his childhood the dying Shaikh Salim had placed his turban on the young prince's head, saying that the prince would be his spiritual successor. Jahangir enacts this role by endowing the Chishti shrines when on pilgrimage. Such patronage must be viewed as an attempt to link Mughal rule to a spiritual source, specifically the one that once had guided his father. It is also motivated by personal piety, but the renewed Chishti link in no way suggests increased orthodoxy in official policy. Military campaigns were relatively unimportant in the reign of Jahangir. Happy to reside in Akbar's largely consolidated empire, Jahangir waged few offensive campaigns. His major victories included the defeat of Rana Amar Singh of Mewar, a campaign brilliantly conducted by Prince Khurram, the future Shah Jahan. This victory was commemorated by the construction of a palace at Pushkar. Jahangir's troops also captured the Kangra fort, and they consolidated Mughal rule in Bengal and Assam. Other campaigns were less successful. During all of them Jahangir remained far from the action.

The course of Jahangir's reign was changed by his marriage in 1611 to Mehr al-Nisa, the widow of Sher Afghan, a Mughal noble. Although he had other wives, she was brilliant and by far the most powerful of them all. She was first given the title Nur Mahal (Light of the Palace) and later, in 1616, Nur Jahan (Light of the World), the name by which she is best known. Born of Iranian parents, Nur Jahan together with her father, Ictimad al-Daula, and her brother, Asaf Khan, assumed increasing power. By 1622, when Jahangir's poor health, exacerbated by immoderate consumption of wine and opium, rendered him incapable of attending to the affairs of state, Nur Jahan's power was nearly absolute.

Until this time, both Jahangir and Nur Jahan considered Khurram, the future Shah Jahan, to be Jahangir's heir. However, upon the marriage of Nur Jahan's daughter from her first marriage to Prince Shahriyar, Jahangir's son by another wife, the empress no longer supported Khurram, but actively championed Shahriyar's cause. This, in part, led to a rebellion on the part of Khurram, which resulted in his seizure of Bihar and Bengal and ultimately the loss of Qandahar for the Mughals. Jahangir died in 1627. Nur Jahan's schemes failed, and although she survived her husband for eighteen years, she wielded no more power in the Mughal court.

The Establishment of Authority (c. 1600-10)

In 1600, Prince Salim established his own court in Akbar's Allahabad fort. Assuming the title Shah Salim, he operated as an independent ruler but did little to upset Mughal authority much beyond Allahabad. The rebel prince's patronage of painters, especially Aqa Reza, is well known, but there is no evidence that he constructed buildings during this period.

The self-styled king, rather, commissioned smaller objects that he himself might use. In 1602-03 Shah Salim ordered construction of a black throne (Plate 54), essentially a large polished slab whose sides were engraved with verses praising the throne and its occupant, Shah Salim. While no calligrapher's name is given, the lettering and sinuous floral background indicate the work of Mir Abd Allah Mushkin Qalam. Even five years after he became emperor, this throne continued to hold significance for Jahangir; he ordered that it be brought from Allahabad to the Agra fort and then added verses to those already on the throne. These new verses, crowded under the original composition, state Jahangir's rightful claim to the throne. Just after his coronation, Jahangir commissioned a verse in honor of his accession. Composed and designed by Muhammad Macsum of Bakkar, a renowned calligrapher of Akbar's reign, it was carved on the Delhi gate of Akbar's Agra fort. The verse itself is a hopeful portent for Jahangir's long and successful rule; its location, under an inscription of Akbar, links Jahangir to his father and further underscores the concept of his rightful claim to kingship. Like all the Mughal emperors, Jahangir was proud of his Timurid heritage. This is made apparent by a monument that attracted Jahangir's support on the eve of his accession - a Maurya-period (third century B.C.) monolithic column that long had been lying on the ground of Akbar's Allahabad fort.

Jahangir re-erected it, as indicated in a Persian epigraph written on the shaft by Mir Abd Allah Mushkin Qalam, between 15 August and 13 September, 1605, several months before Jahangir's coronation. This inscription gives Jahangir's entire lineage down to Timur; the names of God are interspersed with those of his ancestors, underscoring the Mughal notion that kings are divinely chosen. This text was added to other inscriptions on the column, including edicts of the famous Maurya emperor, Ashoka. Thus, in a sense, he continued his father's long-standing policy of linking Mughal rule to both the Timurid tradition and to deeply rooted Indian traditions. In 1607 Jahangir entered Kabul and there visited Babur's gardens. Between two of the gardens he ordered the erection of a large white stone slab. There he had inscribed his lineage back to Timur and verses linking his name with justice. Jahangir also recorded in his memoirs another garden, known as the Seat of the King, Takht-i Shah, where Babur in 1508-09 had carved a large stone basin and throne inscribed with his name. There Jahangir ordered a twin wine basin and throne inscribed with Timur's name and his own. Thus early in his reign Jahangir used inscriptions on large monuments to link himself with his immediate Mughal predecessors as well as with Timur, the ultimate source of Mughal legitimacy. By the time he was well established, he no longer did this.

A concern with legitimacy was not Jahangir's sole reason for architectural patronage during his initial years as king. His memoirs indicate a lively and varied interest in building. In 1606, he ordered a tower (Plate 68) similar to the Hiran Minar at Fatehpur Sikri (Plate 27), to be built next to the grave of a favorite antelope at Jahangirpur, a place known today as Sheikhupura, near Lahore. Jahangir ordered it be inscribed with a prose eulogy written by Mulla Muhammad Husain, whom Jahangir cites as the "chief of the elegant writers of the day."4 Also in the same year he ordered buildings and a garden at his favorite spring in Kashmir, Vernag (Plate 6y). According to Jahangir's memoirs as well as epigraphical evidence, he continued to develop both Sheikhupura and Vernag during the course of his reign. Jahangir also expressed delight over the small pleasure pavilion in Hasan Abdal, today in Punjab, Pakistan, that had been built by Raja Man Singh. Here Jahangir relaxed for several days in 1607, among other activities putting pearls in the noses of fish. Perhaps out of respect for Man Singh's pavilion at Hasan Abdal and the garden around it, Jahangir later ordered that a sizable sum be given for the construction of a bridge and serai and for restorations to an existing building there. These works at Hasan Abdal were not the only building enterprises of others that he admired. For example, he so liked Hakim Ali's house and underground reservoir that he elevated his rank. He described the quarters of Prince Khurram, the future Shah Jahan, in the Kabul fort as "delightful and well-proportioned."5 On the other hand, Jahangir found his own quarters in this same fort unsuitable and ordered them destroyed to make room for a new palace and royal audience hall. Thus Jahangir's keen aesthetic sense, best recognized in his admiration of painting, extended to architecture as well.

Imperial Terraced Tombs

Jahangir's first wife, Shah Begum, the Rajput mother of Khusrau and sister of Raja Man Singh, poisoned herself in 1604. Jahangir attributed her suicide to Khusrau's quest for the throne; more certainly the public contention between her son and Jahangir were the cause of her unmitigated shame. She was buried in a garden in Allahabad, which came to be called Khusrau Bagh after Khusrau was buried there in 1622, and even today retains that name. Finch, traveling through Allahabad in 1611, called the garden Menepur and observed Shah Begum's sumptuous tomb there. Aqa Reza, the principal artist in Salim

Shah's Allahabad court, was charged with the responsibility for constructing Shah Begum's tomb. The garden's enormous west entrance gate, aligned with Shah Begum's tomb, bears an inscription of 1606-07, stating that "this lofty edifice was completed by Aqa Reza, the painter, a devoted official of the emperor."7 The inscription indicates that Mughal painters were expected to have talent beyond wielding the brush.

Dated 1606-07, Aqa Reza's Chunar sandstone gate is handsome, resembling more the entrance to a fort than to a pleasure garden. The deeply recessed entrance arch is flanked on either side by massive engaged bastions. The top is surmounted with battlements. Little ornamentation is carved on the solid surface. By contrast, Shah Begum's three-tiered tomb (Plate 55) has a lighter, more graceful appearance. The overall conception may have been inspired by the Lodi-period tomb of Darya Khan in Delhi, formed of tiered plinths surmounted by a domed chattri covering a grave. The basic plan of Shah Begum's tomb, in turn, seems to have been a prime source for the design of Akbar's tomb. From the exterior, the ground floor today appears to be an austere platform, although eighteenth-century drawings indicate that here as well as on the next level carved screens surmounted each platform.

The top floor consists of a chattri. Situated centrally is the false cenotaph, common to Islamic tombs. On one end of the cenotaph is a vertical marble slab carved with a Persian epigraph giving the date of Shah Begum's death, 1604. This inscription as well as those on the sides of the cenotaph that describe Shah Begum's qualities were designed by Mir Abd Allah Mushkin Qalam, a major calligrapher for Jahangir. Earlier he designed Shah Salim's inscriptions on his black throne in Allahabad (Plate 54); shortly before Jahangir's accession, he executed the inscription on the Allahabad fort pillar. The calligraphy of these inscriptions, characteristic of Mir Abd Allah's work, is interlaced with delicate floral arabesques. Although the tomb bears no date, it was probably constructed concurrently with Aqa Reza's gate and certainly before 1611, when Finch saw it. The tomb, like the gate, is a relatively plain structure. Possibly, it would have been too plain for

Jahangir's tastes, for he found the initial appearance of his father's tomb unsatisfactory. But given the difficulties during the first several years of his reign, when he had no time even to visit the tomb he was building for Akbar in Sikandra, it seems unlikely that he had much direct role in the design of Shah Begum's tomb.

The construction of Akbar's large multi-storied tomb within a char bagh (Plate 56) was Jahangir's most pressing architectural project. Although completed in Jahangir's reign, many believe that the tomb was commenced in Akbar's lifetime; however, its commencement is not mentioned in any contemporary history of Akbar's reign. The Akbar Nama simply states that the emperor was buried in a sacred garden called Behishtabad, that is, the Abode of Paradise, in Sikandra, a suburb of Agra. Other writers of the time, for example, Muhammad Baqir Najm-i Sani in his literary praise of the tomb, mention only Jahangir as its patron and designer.

Jahangir refers several times to Akbar's tomb. The first and most extensive reference records events of the year 1608, when Jahangir first saw the tomb and expressed great dissatisfaction with its progress. He noted that architects had built the tomb after their own designs, so he ordered that "experienced architects should again lay the foundations, in agreement with men of experience, in several places, on a settled plan. By degrees a lofty building . . . a garden . . . and a large and lofty gateway with minarets of white stone [were] built."9 The complex took several years longer to complete. William Finch, visiting the tomb in 1611, states that it was nowhere near completed. His description, however, suggests that the mausoleum itself was largely finished, while the surrounding gardens and gates were incomplete.

Dated inscriptions on the south gate, the main entrance, indicate that it was completed between 1612 and 1614. The tomb's garden setting follows that same basic format established with Humayun's tomb (Plate 19). That is, the square walled garden was sub-divided into four major sections by watercourses evoking the rivers of paradise. Thus the tomb is situated metaphorically in the center of a paradisical garden located in Behishtabad, the Abode of Paradise.

While the garden setting is modeled on that of Humayun's tomb, Akbar's mausoleum itself has little in common with his father's Timurid-influenced tomb. Akbar's tomb consists of five tiered stories. The top floor has no superstructure but consists of an open-air courtyard enclosed on all four sides by walls of carved "white marble screening. There had been earlier multistoried tombs, such as that of Muhammad Ghaus (Plate 42), and the nearcontemporary tomb of Shah Begum, which influenced the appearance of Akbar's tomb. But the resemblance of this tomb to contemporary palace architecture distinguishes it from its predecessors. The tomb's pillared terraces and the numerous domed chattris of the upper stories yield a delicate silhouette resembling closely the five-tiered structure known as the Panch Mahal at Fatehpur Sikri (Plate 33).

The shift from Humayun's Timurid-inspired building type replete with paradisical imagery to tombs resembling contemporary palaces may appear surprising considering the Mughals' pride in their Timurid heritage. Palace building-types, moreover, are more suggestive of splendor, power and wealth than of paradise, the eternal abode of the just ruler on the Day of Judgment. However, the Quran mentions the "beautiful mansions in the Gardens of everlasting bliss" (9: 72) and more specifically proclaims, "lofty mansions, one above the other, have been built: Beneath them flow Rivers of delight" (39: 20). Hence paradisical imagery in imperial funereal architecture continues; however, it is now modeled upon, yet surpasses, a form of luxurious royal architecture. The tomb's first floor, measuring nearly 105 meters per side, serves as a large square plinth for the top four stories. It houses the sarcophagus in a square central chamber; a continuous domed and vaulted gallery is on the building's perimeter. According to Sebastien Manrique, who visited the tomb in 1641, these chambers were used for the 200 readers of the Quran who maintained the tomb's sanctity. The central bay of each side is marked by a high pishtaq surmounted by a rectangular chattri. White marble inlay is used copiously both to form panels of geometric patterns along the sides of the central pishtaq and arabesques in their spandrels. The red sandstone fabric serves as a backdrop for the white marble. Hence the very materials used on this tomb are suggestive of the opulence promised to the true believer in paradise on the Day of Judgment.

Of the interior vaulted chambers behind the four pishtaqs, the south one, which leads to the central domed chamber via a narrow corridor, is the most elaborate. The lower portions of the walls are inlaid with brown, yellow and black stones, like those on the floor of Shaikh Salim Chishti's tomb at Fatehpur Sikri, while the upper walls and flat domed roof are richly ornamented with incised and polychromed stucco forming floral patterns and arabesques. Gold-painted calligraphy against a deep blue background reproduces chapter 47 of the Quran and several other verses (33: 56; 37: 180-182). They stress God's unique power and glory and describe the gardens of paradise as the just reward for the true believer.

A long narrow corridor leads to an interior domed chamber that contains Akbar's sarcophagus. This square room, about 18 meters high, reaches the level of the tomb's third story. Although this interior was later whitewashed, European visitors report that originally it was painted with Christian subjects including angels and the Virgin Mary. But the presence of such images was a matter of fashion, not a reflection of religious belief. Contemporary accounts describing the tomb's desecration by plundering Jats in the late seventeenth century indicate how sumptuous was the tomb's interior. Gold, silver and precious stones as well as all the carpets were pillaged. Significantly, the attack on Akbar's mausoleum was perceived as a blow to Mughal prestige, suggesting its continuing importance as a dynastic symbol.

Three stories rise above the ground level, each smaller than the previous one. Delicate red sandstone chattris are placed at frequent intervals along the exterior walls. The uppermost story consists of a square high walled enclosure composed entirely of white marble screens used increasingly into the seventeenth century for imperial mausolea (Plate 71).

Since white marble previously had been associated with saints' shrines, the distinction between royalty and saints was now blurred. At each corner is a large domed chattri; the tomb has no other finials.

Above the veranda's arch-shaped entrances are lintels that bear verses eulogizing the deceased emperor. The tomb's upper story remains open to the sky (Plate 57). In the center is a magnificently carved white marble cenotaph; at its north end is a lamp stand (chiraqdan), also rendered in finely carved white marble.

Many believe that such an exquisitely rendered marble cenotaph, carved with the ninety-nine names of God and intricate floral motifs, could not have been intended to remain exposed to the elements and that once there must have been a central dome. Yet an uncovered cenotaph is the grave-type that meets orthodox approval and may have been the reason for the open top story of Akbar's tomb. But that is only a partial explanation. Considering the Mughal fascination with light and light symbolism, the placement of this cenotaph directly under the sun and moon follows especially the interests of Akbar and Jahangir. Under- scoring this interpretation is the final verse of the Persian inscription on the tomb's entrance gate that reads: "May his [Akbar's] soul shine like the rays of the sun and the moon in the light of God."

The imposing gate leading into the complex (Plate 58) bears the dates 1612-13 and 1613-14. It consists of an enormous recessed central arch flanked on either side by double-stacked side arches. Surmounting the gate are four towering white marble minarets, one at each corner. The ornamentation of this gate is more elaborate than that embellishing the tomb. Geometric patterns and large floral motifs formed from inlaid white marble and multi-colored stones stand out against the red sandstone ground.

Continuous inscriptional bands of white marble follow the shape of the recessed arch on both the north and south facades. They were designed and written by Abd al-Haqq Shirazi, later known as Amanat Khan, the designer of inscriptions on several major Mughal monuments including the Taj Mahal. The inscriptions on the north facade, the side facing the tomb itself, appropriately eulogize the deceased emperor. Those on the south facade, however, largely praise the patron, Jahangir, but terminate with a poem confirming that the visual metaphors on the Mughal tombs are indeed references to paradise:

Hail, blessed space happier than the garden of Paradise

Hail lofty buildings higher than the divine throne

A paradise, the garden of which has thousands of Rizwans as servants

A garden of which has thousands of paradises for its land

The pen of the mason of the Divine Decree has written on its court

These are the gardens of Eden, enter them and live forever.

The Past, and Public Works

Jahangir's memoirs are full of details recounting his visits to the buildings of pre-Mughal rulers and the Mughal nobility. He even commented on how to tell if a house would bring prosperity or misfortune, indicating the significance that domestic architecture had for him. Subsequent comments indicate his sense that the structure's success does not depend on the building alone. The garden setting, the role of water and the view become crucial elements in his taste, a notion that had commenced with Babur. This is probably why pre-Mughal dwellings rarely please the emperor. He complains that most pre-Mughal structures in the famous Ranthambor fort were devoid of air and space; by contrast he praises the view, spatial arrangement and airiness of a bath, residence and garden also at Ranthambor built by a noble in Akbar's reign. While most Mughal-period structures seem to gain his favor, some do not. For example, he finds fault with Khwaja Waisi's maintenance of his lands in Sirhind, enjoining him to replant the gardens, to repair the baths and build new structures where necessary.

In spite of Jahangir's general dislike of pre-Mughal houses, he shows much enthusiasm for the great congregational mosques of the provinces, for example, the Jamic mosque of Srinagar or the Jamic mosque of Ahmadabad. However, the mosque he most admires is at Fatehpur Sikri. Due to a serious plague epidemic in Agra, Jahangir halted at Fatehpur Sikri for some time. He took much delight in showing his son, the future Shah Jahan, Akbar's palace there. Among the buildings of Fatehpur Sikri he discussed at length are the khanqah of Shaikh Salim Chishti, including a detailed description with measurements of the Shaikh's tomb and Akbar's great Jamic mosque

(Plates 25 and 26). Jahangir's interest in this architecture of the past takes on special meaning, for he carefully explains that here he was designated by Shaikh Salim himself as his spiritual successor.

The emperor did not neglect the immediate needs of state in spite of this deep interest in the past. In 1611, he issued orders for the establishment of kitchens for the needy (bulghur khanas) in all large cities, and in 1619 he ordered that public wells and towers to mark distances (kos minar) should be erected at frequent, regular intervals between Bengal and the Punjab for the welfare of travelers. A number of kos minar, probably datable to Jahangir's time, still remain between Agra and Lahore. Tall conical structures composed of stone and rubble and covered with a stucco veneer, these dominant towers were possibly painted and covered with information giving distances and popular slogans - as they are today.

Jahangir's Palaces

Agra and Lahore Historians of Shah Jahan's reign make clear that all Jahangir's structures in the Agra fort were destroyed and replaced with Shah Jahan's marble pavilions. Fortunately, however, these sources and others give us some insights into Jahangir's palaces there. In 1611 he entered a palace inside the Agra fort prepared for him by Khwaja Jahan Muhammad Dost, an architect who also built palaces for this emperor at Lahore and elsewhere. This palace, according to Jahangir, was completed in three months, suggesting that it was a fairly small structure, not the full extent of his buildings in the fort. Later historians, in the context of discussing Shah Jahan's renovations, state that Jahangir built three marble pillared chambers, indicating that the use of marble for palace structures pre-dates Shah Jahan's reign. These chambers were in close proximity to an octagonal turret known today as the Musamman Burj, that overlooks the Jumna river. This turret is a product of Shah Jahan's reign, replacing an earlier structure known as the Shah Burj, or King's Tower. To this tower Jahangir attached his famous Chain of Justice leading outside the fort. The bells of this chain permitted subjects to rouse the emperor so that he might hear their grievances, ideally at any time.

Accounts by European visitors to the court, some of whom stayed for considerable periods of time, indicate that Jahangir's viewing balcony (jharoka) from which he daily presented himself to the public was in close proximity to the Shah Burj. Beneath this balcony Jahangir in 1616 erected marble statues of the defeated rana of Mewar, Amar Singh, and his son, Karan. It is generally assumed that these statues of the now-submissive princes were a sign of the emperor's respect. Akbar, however, had placed statues of defeated Rajput foes at the Agra palace's Elephant gate to serve as a reminder of the emperor's strength. Jahangir probably had much the same message in mind.

European visitors, awed by the court and its ceremony, describe gold, silver and rich textiles ornamenting Jahangir's throne in the Public Audience Hall of the Agra fort. William Hawkins, who resided at court from 1609 to 1611, indicates that two red railings separated the most favored members of the nobility from the slightly less favored and then, in turn, from the lower ranks. Jahangir's own description of his Public Audience Hall at this time concurs with Hawkins'. In 1613 Jahangir decided to differentiate the first railing from the second by covering it with silver; he similarly embellished the steps leading to the jharoka and two wooden elephants flanking it, further underscoring the levels of hierarchy within the court.

Persian sources refer to Jahangir's Agra palaces as pillared aiwans, or halls, giving no further indication of their appearance. However, references by several European writers, including the Jesuit Father Jerome Xavier, indicate that Christian subject matter embellished the interior of Jahangir's Agra fort palaces. Small renderings of the Virgin and winged angels appear in an illustration belonging to the Jahangir Nama, the emperor's memoirs, that depicts an audience scene with the emperor seated in his jharoka. These paintings of Christian subjects reflect an awareness of newly arrived western paintings, not any sympathy with Christianity. The Mughal emperors, who fully recognized the significance of these works through close contact with Jesuits and other Europeans, used the imagery to enhance their own semi-divine imperial image. The only remaining addition made by Jahangir to the Agra fort is an enormous stone basin, 1. meters high by 1. meters.

Dated 1611, the same year Jahangir married the formidable Mehr al-Nisa, later entitled Nur Jahan, this cistern may be associated with the nuptial celebrations. It was probably made as a wine basin similar to the one discussed earlier that Jahangir had carved into the hillside in Kabul. In 1612 Jahangir mentions his first additions to Akbar's Lahore fort. They were designed by Khwaja Jahan Muhammad Dost, the architect named only one year earlier as the designer of a palace in the Agra fort. At Lahore, work under Jahangir must have begun much earlier, for William Finch, visiting Jahangir's Lahore palaces in 1610, describes these buildings and their interior decoration in detail. Jahangir refers to work at the fort on several occasions, and in 1620, visiting the fort, praises the "charming residences . . . erected in great beauty . . . and embellished with painting by rare artists."15 One of the buildings to which Jahangir here refers is a small walled courtyard known today as the Maktab Khana, identified as the Daulat Khana-i Jahangiri in its inscription. It was constructed in 1617 under the supervision of Macmur Khan, also known as Abd al-Karim, an architect associated with other projects of Jahangir and Shah Jahan. Composed of arched chambers around a central courtyard, it is situated on the Public Audience Hall's west side; it served as a large passage from the palace buildings on the north to the Audience Hall. To the west of this courtyard is a small white marble mosque known as the Moti mosque. Although some credit Jahangir for its construction, it is probably Shah Jahan's work.

Among other buildings in the fort generally assigned to Jahangir's patronage are several small flat-roofed rectangular chambers supported by red sandstone pillars (Plate 59). These buildings today are in an area known as the Jahangiri Quadrangle. While their format differs little from Akbar's palaces, the intricate, complex carving of elephant brackets, the pillars, and the screened windows of the northernmost pavilion suggest a date in Jahangir's reign. These features compare favorably to those on the Kanch Mahal in Agra, also probably constructed in Jahangir's reign.

The most important remaining Jahangiri structure in the Lahore fort is the Kala Burj (Plate 60). Although undated, the flattened interior of the dome, Plate 59. Detail, pavilion, Jahangiri Quadrangle, Lahore fort, Lahore with a net pattern that converges at a stellate medallion center, resembles other Jahangiri vaulting systems, for example, that of the mosque of Maryam al-Zamani (Plate 62) dated 1611. Conservation on the dome has revealed paintings of European-influenced angels and birds - some mythological, others real. They so closely resemble Finch's descriptions of angels in Jahangir's Lahore palaces that this must have been the one he described when visiting the Lahore fort in 1610. Angels painted in the vaults of the palace's dome represent the heavenly retinue of King Solomon, established in the Quran as an ideal ruler and the mythic kingly figure with whom Islamic rulers frequently associate themselves. Indeed, this association between ruler and Solomon is no accident, for, in his sole inscription at the Lahore fort, Jahangir is described as "a Solomon in dignity,"17 while imagery on the fort's exterior tile work, datable to his reign, alludes to a Solomonic retinue. Included on the tiles are angels, who aid the mythic king Solomon's control of the world by leading jinns, or spirits, on chains; this is imagery appropriate for a king who equates himself with the glory of Solomon.

The other subjects seen by Finch, that is, portraits of the nobility and princes, each of whom he very carefully identifies, jinns, the Virgin Mary and Jesus no longer remain. These were probably similar to illustrations known to us from smaller-scale works on paper. Unlike the Agra and Allahabad forts, whose outer walls are made of red stone, the Lahore fort's walls are brick, a traditional building material of the northwestern area of the subcontinent. The north and west exterior brick walls are divided into vertical blocks of arched and paneled areas. The upper panels are decorated with tile mosaics (Plate 61). Commenced under Jahangir, the west wall may have been completed under Shah Jahan; but if so the mosaics were probably done by the same artists, since there is no change in style or technique. In addition to images of angels, sometimes leading jinns, the tile mosaics on the fort's north and west walls depict a myriad of subjects. Since few tiles remain, it is difficult to determine whether this ornamentation had a specific program. However, it is notable that the large angels either leading jinns or holding a regnal standard, and the Simurgh, a mythical bird long associated with imperial symbolism as well as with Solomonic imagery, are situated in spandrels above arched openings. The city under Jahangir

Lahore

Just outside the fort is the mosque of the queen mother, Maryam al-Zamani, the city's oldest surviving Mughal mosque. Located near the fort's Akbar-period Masti gate, this mosque was probably built as the Jamic mosque for those attending court. It was not provided by the emperor, but its construction doubtless met Jahangir's approval and commenced a Mughal tradition whereby important court ladies provided the major mosques in imperial cities. Known as the Begum Shahi mosque and the mosque of Maryam al-Zamani, it was built in 1611-12. The mosque originally was entered by three handsome gateways, though only two remain, each bearing historical inscriptions. The gates provide access to a large walled courtyard before the prayer chamber, whose east facade is pierced by five arched entrances, the central one within a high pishtaq. Thus the mosque's exterior form belongs to a type long popular in Indo-Islamic architecture. The brick core is covered with a plaster veneer which originally bore painted ornament.

Although the interior of the prayer chamber follows a form once associated with Afghan builders - and now a common Mughal one: a single-aisled rectangular space divided into five bays - the interior decor established trends for the later Mughal buildings of Lahore. At the center of the main dome (Plate 62) is a medallion with radiating stellate and net forms rendered in stucco, completing the exquisite decor of the domes. Similar forms are seen in subsequent Mughal architecture. Also anticipating later works is the treatment of the mosque's vaulting, brilliantly painted as are the walls. Unlike the secular wall painting on Jahangir's palaces and garden pavilions, here, in keeping with the aniconic tendencies of Islamic religious art, the patterns are largely floral and geometric, while the names of God are inscribed within stars on the dome. Cypress trees and wine vessels are the only representational objects depicted, but they are symbols of the divine. They are usually associated with later tombs, but their presence here indicates the adoption of this Iranian motif much earlier than generally assumed. Maryam al-Zamani died in Agra in 1623. There is no mention of the construction of a tomb for her in contemporary texts; however, tradition holds that Jahangir converted for her tomb a baradari in Sikandra not far from Akbar's tomb. It is believed to have been initially constructed in the early sixteenth century by the Lodis. Reusing an older building as a tomb for such an important member of the imperial family is not within Mughal tradition. Thus, if the structure is correctly identified, it was surely newly constructed. Indeed, the tomb adheres to Mughal funereal forms, for its exterior resembles closely the plinth of Humayun's tomb (Plate 18), while the multi-chambered interior is typically Mughal.

About 2. km from the Lahore fort is an octagonal structure known as Anarkali's tomb. She was probably one of Jahangir's wives. Its magnificently carved cenotaph is inscribed with the phrase "the profoundly enamored Salim, son of Akbar" and the dates 1599 and 1612. This probably indicates the year of her death and the tomb's completion. This octagonal mausoleum, originally situated in a four-part garden, has several features that depart from those of other imperial tombs. Among these are the arched opening marking each facade and the semi-engaged octagonal turret at each of the eight junctures. The interior, however, follows the familiar plan used for tombs: a central domed chamber is surrounded by smaller ones. Its marble cenotaph carved with floral arabesques and the ninety-nine names of God inlaid in black stone is close in ornamentation to the near-contemporary cenotaph on the upper story of Akbar's tomb.

Ajmer

In 1613 Jahangir left Agra for Ajmer in order to conduct a vigorous campaign against Rana Amar Singh of Mewar, one of his most formidable opponents. Two events especially pleased Jahangir during his three years in Ajmer. One was visiting the shrine of Mucin al-Din Chishti; the second was the defeat and submission of Rana

Amar Singh in 1615. His resulting enthusiasm for the city appears to have colored favorably much of Jahangir's attitude toward architecture - be it pre-existing or newly created - in the environs of Ajmer.

An auspicious moment was chosen for the emperor's entrance into the city. He immediately proceeded to the Chishti dargah on foot, thus re-enacting the pilgrimage to this esteemed shrine that Akbar had performed annually until 1579. En route money was distributed to the poor and pious. Jahangir writes that, during his nearly three-year stay in Ajmer, he visited the shrine nine times. Four paintings illustrating these visits are known, suggesting the importance that the shrine held for Jahangir. During one visit to this shrine in 1614, Jahangir donated an enormous cauldron (dig), made in Agra, that could feed 5,000 needy people. It no longer remains. Akbar earlier had donated a similar vessel at this shrine,[20] suggesting that this act had dynastic significance. During the course of a worrisome illness later in the same year, the emperor paid homage to the shrine. After his recovery, Jahangir began wearing pearl earrings as a sign of devotion to the Chishti saint. This custom was quickly adopted by his courtiers. In 1615, on the occasion of the saint's cUrs, the annual remembrance of the saint's death, the emperor personally distributed money and other material rewards; this event was illustrated for the Jahangir Nama. His major material donation to the shrine was a "gold railing with lattice work" that was installed around the tomb of Mucin al-Din in 1616,[21] but taken in eighteenth-century raids. Jahangir states that the railing was donated in fulfillment of certain vows, but leaves their exact nature unclear. Another painting for the Jahangir Nama illustrating the railing's installation includes Prince Khurram, the future Shah Jahan, and the military commander in the campaign against the rana of Mewar, standing with Jahangir at the tomb's entrance. Thus one of Jahangir's vows may have been the successful subjugation of Mewar. While this is the emperor's last specific reference to the shrine, in 1623 Jahangir dispatched Habash Khan to repair buildings in Ajmer, possibly including ones at the dargah. With the exception of the gold railing, Jahangir's donations to the shrine consisted of food and alms, items whose value was most immediately felt by the pious and needy. Just as Akbar's interests in the shrine had stimulated increased patronage on a sub-imperial level, so, as we shall see, the same was true during Jahangir's reign.

His sincere devotion to the Chishti saint notwithstanding, Jahangir was in Ajmer to complete successfully the on-going Mughal campaign against the ranas of Mewar. Their unwillingness to submit to Mughal authority had been a source of immense concern. Thus Jahangir celebrated his victory by some harsh acts - generally idolatrous and certainly disrespectful to local tradition - all clearly directed at the ranas of Mewar. For example, Jahangir violated local order by hunting on the banks of the sacred tank at Pushkar, on the outskirts of Ajmer. While at Pushkar, Jahangir visited some of the Hindu temples surrounding the tank, and, upon seeing an image of Varaha, the Boar incarnation of Vishnu, ordered that it be destroyed and thrown into the tank. Worshiping a deity in the form of a pig, considered unclean in Islam, was repulsive to Jahangir. But he desecrated the image because the temple in which it had been installed belonged to an uncle of Rana Amar of Mewar, Jahangir's arch enemy. Later, in 1620, when Jahangir became the first Muslim ruler to conquer the Kangra valley, he did similar things. Again, not out of religious sentiment but for a show of strength, he slaughtered a bullock within the fort's walls and erected a mosque as well as other Mughal-style buildings in the vicinity. Jahangir notes simply that the ruling power was now the Mughals, a Muslim state; Hindu subjects were not in any way persecuted or harassed. In 1615-16 Jahangir constructed a small hunting palace on the banks of the Pushkar tank (Plate 63). The inscription there states that its buildings were erected in celebration of Jahangir's victory over the rana only a short time earlier. Hence imperial Mughal presence was made permanent on the shores of a sacred Hindu spot (tirtha). The impact of Mughal authority on the Hindu devotees coming on pilgrimage to this site, considered one of the holiest of all tirthas, a locale where nothing was to be killed, would have been powerful indeed. Jahangir, who loved hunting on these shores, visited the Pushkar palace fifteen times during his residence at Ajmer.

Situated at the edge of the tank in an area away from the temples that line the water's banks, this hunting pavilion today is largely in ruins.

Even in this condition it is possible to see that the overall appearance of the buildings lacks the refinement and elegance of those in his Jahangiri Quadrangle at the Lahore fort (Plate 59). Only two of the original three small pavilions remain on the elevated rectangular plinth. These nearly identical structures, located at the plinth's east and west ends, face each other. Constructed from a brown-colored stone, each consists of a single flat-roofed chamber surrounded on the front and sides by a deep veranda supported on squat polygonal columns. This trabeated palace, basically modeled on traditional Mughal prototypes, probably relied on local labor, thus explaining its unrefined appearance. In the vicinity of Ajmer, Jahangir most loved a small palace he constructed in 1615. He named it Chesma-i Nur, or Fountain of Light, after himself, Nur al-Din Jahangir. Situated in a picturesque valley on the west side of Taragarh hill, Jahangir visited the Chesma-i Nur thirty-eight times during his three years in Ajmer. He laments that it was far from the city and could only be visited on the weekends. Thomas Roe, at the palace in 1616, recounts the rigorous journey to reach it. Jahangir describes the palace as having a square tank and a high-shooting fountain with lovely buildings situated at the fountain's edge. The chambers were painted by master artists, although Jahangir does not mention any subjects illustrated.

Roe similarly describes the Chesma-i Nur. Today it is sadly ruined, but the tank remains as do some buildings on two levels around it. The upper level of the palace consists of stone pillared pavilions (Plate 64) constructed on either side of a stone stream bed. They face each other as do those at the Pushkar pavilion. The stream cascaded to the lower level, where an arched and vaulted chamber (Plate 65), created in part from the natural rock, was built adjacent to the square tank into which the cooling waters fell. On its arched facade is an inscription designed by the scribe Abd Allah, known earlier for his work on the Allahabad pillar and Shah Begum's tomb. Although these buildings were overall more elegant than those erected concurrently at Pushkar, it is the setting that makes them spectacular. Considering Jahangir's concern with any structure's total environment, it is hardly surprising that this was among his favorite dwellings. Jahangir mentions two large tanks in the city of Ajmer. The Visal Sar, the smaller of the two, had been in a ruined condition, and in 1616 Jahangir repaired it. He especially loved the larger tank, the Ana Sagar, which is nearly 13 km in circumference and with its waves appears like a veritable lake. Jahangir describes how he spent the night with the palace ladies on this tank's lamp-lit banks. He makes no mention of construction on its banks, but an official chronicler of Shah Jahan's reign indicates that Jahangir built marble pavilions there. While the white marble pavilions on the banks of the Ana Sagar (Plate 104) are generally attributed to Shah Jahan, Jahangir's son and successor, they may have been started by Jahangir. The ruins of other structures, still visible at the west end of the adjoining park, are the only remaining part of Daulat Bagh, a garden credited to Jahangir.

Mandu

In 1615 Jahangir moved to Mandu, the major hill fortress in Malwa, an area of west-central India. He wanted to be closer to the Deccan, where Mughal campaigns had been suffering setbacks for some time. Ahead of him he sent Abd al-Karim, later associated with buildings in the Lahore fort. In this hill fort, the capital of the former sultans of Malwa, the architect was charged with repairing old palace buildings and with constructing new ones. Jahangir and the imperial entourage departed from Ajmer in November 1616, reaching Mandu about four months later. During the journey, the emperor hunted daily, taking time to explore and even repair buildings along the way. For example, near Ujjain he restored the mansion of Nasir al-Din Khalji, an earlier sultan of Mandu, piping water into gardens and fountains. Reaching Mandu in early 1617, Jahangir was delighted with the fort, its setting and climate. Abd al-Karim's restorations there as well as his new construction so pleased the emperor that he increased the architect's rank and rewarded him with the title Macmur Khan. Buildings such as the so-called Gada's house in the Mandu fort and the Taweli Mahal appear to be products of Mughal restoration or construction, although they cannot be attributed with certainty to Macmur Khan, since the fort had been used under Akbar and Humayun and was subsequently used by Shah Jahan as well. Probably more restoration than new construction was carried out. For example, Jahangir's description of a banquet at Nur Jahan's palaces indicates that she occupied structures around the so-called Jahaz Mahal and the surrounding tanks, structures built previously by the sultans of Mandu. Further evidence of Jahangir's admiration for the buildings of the Mandu sultans is his favorable descriptions of the Jamic mosque of Mandu, the tombs of the early kings, and their palaces, especially the Haft Manazil. Included in his praise is the Nil-Kanth palace, constructed during Akbar's reign in 1574.

Architecture of Pleasure: Gardens and Hunting Pavilions

In 1619 Jahangir returned to Agra after a five-year absence. There he once again found greatest delight in the mansions and gardens of his highest-ranking nobles and those of his wife, Nur Jahan. Jahangir was highly pleased with his Gul Afshan garden, probably the same garden later owned by Nur Jahan and renamed the Nur Afshan Bagh. But at this time Jahangir clearly regarded it his own project, for he personally rewarded the architect, Khwaja Jahan, by increasing his rank. This is yet another indication of the emperor's regard for architects and garden settings. The Nur Manazil garden, also in Agra, was well under way about the time of the emperor's return to the city and appears to be another of Khwaja Jahan's designs. Delighted with its appearance, Jahangir describes a large walled garden with richly embellished dwellings, water basins, canals and planted plots. The emperor mentions that a large sum had already been expended on the project and more was to be spent. Clearly this was done, for later he mentions this garden as an entertainment site.

In Kashmir's capital city, Srinagar, Akbar had constructed a massive fort on a high hill known as the Koh-i Maran or Hari Parbat overlooking Dal lake. There Jahangir ordered the completion of the unfinished portion of the fortifications and the restoration of the palace buildings in it, especially a garden and Public Audience Hall. Muctamad Khan was charged with this work. He created a three-tiered garden. There he had its pavilion embellished with the work of master painters, as was done at Jahangir's palaces in Ajmer, Agra and Lahore. Again, in keeping with many of his earlier works, Jahangir renamed this garden Nur Afza, Light Increasing, after himself, continuing his long-standing fascination with light imagery. The banks of Srinagar's Dal lake are famed for their magnificent Mughal gardens. Although Jahangir visited Kashmir more times than any other Mughal ruler, his role in the construction of the gardens around Dal lake is less clear. However, in 1620 Jahangir ordered his son, the prince Shah Jahan, to block up the stream in an area known as Shalimar, near the banks of Dal lake. While the choice of the setting was Jahangir's, the garden is Shahjahan's (Plate 129). This world-famous garden will be discussed in the next chapter.

Jahangir gave special attention to gardens in the valley south of Srinagar. He loved the natural streams and springs, and so added to them canals, fountains and buildings to create terraced gardens. At Loka Bhavan, some 40 km south of Srinagar, Jahangir ordered the restoration of the reservoir in front of the springs, indicating that he was not the spring's first patron, and constructed a new building there. In fact, few of these gardens are the result of a single patron. In close proximity to Loka Bhavan are the springs of Macchi Bhavan and Inch. Here the patronage was not imperial but that of high-ranking Hindu nobles; Jahangir describes Ram Das Kachhwaha's Macchi Bhavan garden and spring with crystal clear waters, large fish and splendid trees beautiful beyond words. It seems likely that imperial example stimulated the construction of the numerous gardens through this valley.

About 8 km north of Loka Bhavan are the natural spring and waterfall of Achibal (Plate 66). Jahangir describes its water, magnificent trees and enchanting pavilions. He notes a garden with beautiful flowers, not necessarily one he constructed. Although the garden later was associated with Jahan Ara, Shah Jahan's favorite daughter, its appearance was probably established by Jahangir's time. At the summit of the terraced garden is the natural spring which still today is gathered in a large pool that is dammed so that water pressure produces a powerfully impressive waterfall gushing into lower terraced canals. The water chutes, carved to resemble rushing water, are of Mughal origin as are the pavilion bases; however, the pavilions' superstructures, as in most

Mughal gardens, are more recently constructed. Achibal, more than any other Mughal garden, preserves the natural beauty of the falls and dense foliage, set against the towering hills.

The site in Kashmir most often mentioned by Jahangir is the spring at Vernag (Plate 67), about 10 km north of Achibal. When still a prince Jahangir visited Vernag twice. Then the crystal clear waters of the spring, the source of the powerful Jhelum river, were contained within an octagonal reservoir with cells nearby for recluses. In 1606 Jahangir ordered that the sides of the spring be faced with stone and that a garden, canal and splendid edifices be constructed. However, both epigraphical and literary sources indicate that they were not completed until his fifteenth regnal year, 1619-20. Even then, the canal and its watercourses were not fully finished, for a second inscription, dated 1626-27, describes the construction of a water course and cascade by the architect Haider. While much of the garden and surrounding pavilions have disappeared, the tank, with low walls containing arched apertures and blind arched niches, still exists as do descendants of the large fish that swim in the lucid waters, creating a spectacle of royal splendor.

Jahangir twice mentions a tower, tank and pavilion used as a hunting palace about 29 km from Lahore. Today the site is known as Sheikhupura, but Jahangir in 1606 refers to it as Jahangirpura and then in 1620 calls it Jahangirabad, both meaning City of Jahangir, the latter a more Persianate form. Here the emperor's favorite tame antelope died before 1606; it was buried in a grave above which a sculpted antelope and eulogy written by Mulla Muhammad Husain of Kashmir were placed. Adjacent to this gravestone, a tower was constructed around 1606 (Plate 68) under the supervision of Sikandar Mucin Khan, the landholder of the area. On Jahangir's orders, Sikandar Mucin Khan also built a tank and royal residence. Despite Mucin's death while the work was in progress, the complex was handsomely completed by 1620, the later stages of construction having been supervised by Iradat Khan. The expenses incurred were sufficiently awesome that the emperor recorded the amount in his memoirs. Jahangir considered the site a "kingly hunting place,"25 although his successor found the place inadequate and in 1634 spent another sizable sum rebuilding the pavilion.

The tank, tower and pavilion are well preserved. Situated to the west of the tank, the tower resembles closely the plan and elevation the so-called Hiran Minar at Fatehpur Sikri and the Nim Serai Minar at Malda, both datable to Akbar's reign (Plates 27 and 53). Built about 1606, the Sheikhupura tower belongs to the very early part of Jahangir's reign; hence, the close resemblance to Akbari prototypes is not surprising. Missing are the tusk-like projections around the sides, but holes that would have accommodated them remain. The tower's brick fabric was originally covered with a thick stucco veneer which retained traces of red, yellow and green polychrome until recently, when it was plastered anew. The tower sits on an octagonal base and was possibly used as an observation post for hunting. Aligned with the tower is a three-storied octagonal pavilion situated in the center of a large square tank. The tank was constructed in Jahangir's reign, but the three-storied octagonal pavilion in its current state is a product of Shah Jahan's patronage (Plate 128).

Nurjahan 's Patronage

Jahangir married the widow Nurjahan in 1611, although his writings do not mention her until 1614. She quickly overshadowed Jahangir's other wives and assumed an unprecedented role in courtly and political life. Nur Jahan, her father, Ictimad al-Daula, and her brother, Asaf Khan, formed a powerful triumvirate and essentially controlled the state. By the end of Jahangir's reign, when the emperor was incapacitated by failing health, Nur Jahan was the virtual ruler. Jahangir himself acknowledged her ability and legitimized her power. He made her Finance Minister after the death of the previous minister, her father. Coins were even minted in her name, an honor otherwise reserved for the emperor. While the powerful queen was deeply appreciated by Jahangir, other factions viewed her less favorably, ultimately creating schisms within the state. Much of this factionalism was contained until late 1621, when Ictimad al-Daula, a stabilizing force, died. Because Nur Jahan championed her son-inlaw, Shahriyar, as Jahangir's heir apparent, the eldest prince, Shah Jahan, revolted. She nevertheless maintained control until Jahangir's death in 1627, thereafter residing quietly in Lahore until her death in 1645.

Not only interested in politics, Nur Jahan is famed for her impact on culture. She invented a rose perfume, fashioned clothing styles, created new carpet designs, and wrote poetry. Her patronage of architecture is well established although rarely mentioned in contemporary texts. It is better known from inscriptions and the writings of European travelers. According to Francisco Pelsaert, a European residing in India during the height of Nur Jahan's power, the queen constructed pleasure gardens, palaces and serais throughout the land in order to enhance her image and reputation. He further indicates that she built for financial gain. For example, her serai just outside of Agra, situated at the end of the lucrative Patna-Agra trade route, gave the queen complete control over tariffs levied on goods coming from eastern India into Agra and further north. Without these goods, he notes, the country soon would starve. The serai, no longer extant, covered a large area on the east bank of the Jumna; on its outskirts were the tomb of Ictimad al-Daula and several gardens, including the Nur Afshan garden, both products of the queen's patronage. Thus most of the river frontage on the Jumna's east bank probably was under the empress' control. Peter Mundy, who stayed twice in this serai, describes it as a handsome stone structure with arched and domed chambers capable of housing 2,000 to 3,000 people and 500 horses. Although the Agra serai no longer exists, another constructed by her, known as Serai Nur Mahal (Plate 69), stands in a town of the same name in Jalandhar District, Punjab. Inscriptions on the serai indicate that it was commenced in 1618-19 and completed two years later. Jahangir records that he stayed in this serai in 1621 and was splendidly entertained by his queen there. Serai Nur Mahal was commenced about the time that Jahangir had issued orders for kos minar to be constructed from Agra through the Punjab and for the repair of the road between Kashmir and Agra. One of many serais along this road, Serai Nur Mahal with its carved red sandstone gates was especially impressive. Its enclosure walls contained 124 chambers and a mosque. In the center of the south wall was a three-storied royal apartment, originally painted, probably with motifs similar to those in Jahangir's Lahore fort (Plate 60) and the queen's Nur Afshan garden in Agra. Among Mughal serais this one is unusually handsome, not surprising considering Nur Jahan's resources and taste.

Among the many gardens credited to Nur Jahan is her Bagh-i Nur Afshan in Agra, known today as the Ram Bagh. It was probably constructed on the site of Babur's Gul Afshan, or Flower Scattering Garden. By 1621 the name apparently had been changed to Bagh-i Nur Afshan, Light-Scattering Garden, once again using light imagery while playing upon the imperial names. This char bagh is terraced and laid out with stone water courses. Originally the garden, like all Mughal gardens, was planted with cypress trees, small groves of fruit trees and flowers. Although the current planting of the Bagh-i Nur Afshan little resembles the original layout, portions of the channels, tanks and pavilions remain.

At the top of the terrace overlooking the river Jumna are two similar pavilions that face one another (Plate 70), an arrangement seen earlier at Pushkar and Chesma-i Nur. Between them is a large sunken tank and stairs leading to vaulted chambers below. Each rectangular pavilion is composed of three sections of pillared aiwans that alternate with two flat-roofed enclosed chambers. Although largely white-washed, portions of the interior painted vaulting have been restored. Within net vault forms are painted birds, angels, a Simurgh and floral designs, all related to Solomonic imagery appropriate for royalty and similar to that within Jahangir's Kala Burj in the Lahore fort (Plate 60). Traces of paintings, including one of a courtly lady that is Europeaninfluenced, also remain on the exterior walls. According to Mundy and others, European-influenced painting was common on the walls of similar pavilions. Today the best preserved of all Nur Jahan's architectural projects is the tomb she constructed for her parents in Agra (Plate 71). This white marble mausoleum is known as the tomb of Ictimad al-Daula, although both Nur Jahan's mother, Asmat Begum, who died in 1621, and her father, who died in the same year, are buried there. Nur Jahan, who genuinely was devoted to her parents, spent vast sums on its construction. The tomb was completed about six years after their death as indicated by inscriptions dated 1626-27 and 1627-28 that were written by the scribe Abd al-Nabi al-Quraishi.

Situated on the river bank, the tomb is a small two-storied marble structure in the center of a char bagh about 165 meters square. It is approached by road from the east through a red sandstone gate; a gate on the west serves as the river entrance. This multi-storied western entrance is conceived as a pleasure pavilion with spacious interior chambers and arched openings overlooking the river. Similar sandstone structures, not actual entrances, are on the north and south sides. On all four, the red stone is inlaid with white marble, a typical Mughal device. The white marble tomb, about 7 meters per side, is magnificently crafted and profusely inlaid with semi-precious stones. Resting on a low red sandstone plinth, the tomb's first story is marked at each corner by an engaged octagonal turret. On each side is a single arched portal flanked by screened openings for illumination. The interior is divided into nine bays, recalling in concept the arrangement of Humayun's tomb. However, unlike the radial plan based on an octagon found at Humayun's tomb, here eight rooms, two on each side, hug the central vaulted chamber. This plan is seen earlier at Akbar's Ajmer palace, and derives in its Indo-Islamic context from palace structures. The walls of all these rooms are richly painted with flowers, vases, cypresses and wine vessels, but the central chamber, containing two stone cenotaphs, is the most lavishly embellished. The ceiling's richly polychromed net vaulting and stellate forms are a more refined version of those at Maryam al-Zamani's mosque (Plate 62), built early in Jahangir's reign.

The second or top story is marked at each corner by a chattri-topped turret. In the center is a single chamber, surmounted by a truncated pyramidal vault. Intricately carved pierced screens, modeled on those at Shaikh Salim Chishti's tomb, essentially form the walls. Semi-precious stones are profusely inlaid into the white marble of the tomb's exterior as well as in the interior of the second story. Most believe that this pietra dura technique - that is, design rendered by the inlay of hard precious stones into marble - was introduced from

Europe in the seventeenth century; others maintain that this technique developed independently without western stimulation. Regardless of the technique's origin, in India only on Mughal architecture is it used as a major source of decoration. Inlay forming designs similar to those on the gateway to Akbar's tomb, where they are executed in less precious stones, cover the first story's exterior. On the upper story there are wine vessels, fruit and cypress trees (Plate 72). These forms, drawn from Persian poetry, were long known in Indo-Islamic culture, but their depiction on Mughal architecture probably derives from Safavid sources. For example, there are wine vessels in the ceiling of the Ali Kapu, the entrance to Shah Abbas' palace in Isfahan built about the turn of the seventeenth century. Such motifs appear in India first on Jahangir-period architecture, for example on the mosque of Maryam al-Zamani in Lahore. Since Ictimad al-Daula and his family come from Safavid Iran, the use of these motifs is particularly appropriate. At this time, many artists from the Safavid court immigrated to Mughal India.

While Safavid in origin, these forms serve as symbols of paradise and the divine. For example, fruit is a promised commodity of paradise in numerous Quranic verses, thus appropriate for funereal imagery. Although the consumption of wine is forbidden in Islam, the promised nectar in paradise according to the Quran will be a pure wine that gives neither inebriation nor headache. In addition, wine and the consumption of wine in Persian mystical poetry is used as a metaphor for spiritual intoxication resulting from the intense feeling of love for the beloved, who on the most profound level is God. The cypress tree in mystical poetry is yet another reference to God. In lieu of literary inscriptions inviting one to paradise, as on the entrance to Akbar's tomb, here the concept of paradise is enhanced by using expensive materials and visual devices to suggest that the heavenly abode of the deceàsed royal noble will surpass even his earthly abode.

Although the tomb is commonly described as Safavid influenced, this only pertains to the choice of decorative motifs. The overall appearance of the tomb is wholly Indian, recalling, for example, the exterior of Akbar's Diwan-i Khass at Fatehpur Sikri (Plate 31). Ictimad al-Daula's tomb, like Akbar's (Plate 56), belongs to the type based on contemporary palace pavilions. The intricately carved marble screens of the top floor (Plate 73), similar to those on Shaikh Salim Chishti's tomb (Plate 26), allow light to flood the room, making it appear to dissolve. Given the imperial Mughal fascination with light and in particular Nur Jahan's and Jahangir's obsession with light imagery, the manipulation of light here seems intentional. Light was more than an imperial symbol. For the Mughals, it also served as a metaphor for Divine Light, symbolizing the very presence of God. This play of light upon the solid marble of the room may be intended as a reminder that only God, here symbolized by light, is real - all other is illusion. In contrast to the chamber's light-flooded elevation are the sinuous arabesques and floral motifs formed from yellow and brown semi-precious stones inlaid into the white marble floor. This recalls the design of expensive carpets, such as those depicted in contemporary court paintings, for example, one at Mucin al-Din's shrine in Ajmer illustrated for the Jahangir Nama. Here again is an instance where the most coveted forms from temporal life are used to depict the luxury anticipated in paradise.

Western India

Ajmer and Vicinity

Roe, writing in January 1616, noted that in Ajmer the nobility resided in tents since there was only one stone-constructed residence there - that of the king - all others being mud-built. Not much later, however, the nobility must have built stone dwellings, for Mundy, who visited Ajmer in 1633, states that the housing constructed by Jahangir's court was already in ruins. In Ajmer, as elsewhere, Jahangir's presence stimulated building by others. This is particularly so at the Chishti shrines of Mucin al-Din and Khwaja Sayyid Husain Khing Sawar. Concurrent with Jahangir's presence in Ajmer inscribed gates, graves and ancillary buildings were constructed at each shrine. The most significant material contribution was Ictibar Khan's lattice railing provided in 1615 around the grave of Husain Khing Sawar. It was given in celebration of Jahangir's victory over the rana of Mewar. Jahangir a year later donated a gold railing to the Chishti shrine below, almost certainly for this same reason, perhaps in a curious reversal deriving his inspiration from sub-imperial patronage. Patronage in Rajasthan was not limited to shrines. For example, in 1615 Gajhast Khan, Jahangir's supervisor of elephant stables, constructed a step-well in Gangwana, close to Ajmer. Carved at the bottom of the inscriptional slab is an elephant and prodding implements, emblems appropriate for his position. In the same year Nawab Daulat Khan provided additions to a palace he had commenced during Akbar's reign in Fatehpur, Shekhawati District. Jahangir's mother, Maryam al-Zamani, built a serai and well near Bayana in 1613-14. Lying on the Fatehpur Sikri-Ajmer route in an important indigo growing center, it accommodated both Jahangir and the traveler Finch. Nobles built mosques during this period at Merta, Hindaun and Jalor, and an cIdgah (a mosque intended especially for the annual cId celebrations) was constructed in 1613 at Bairat, in the ancestral lands of Raja Man Singh. With the exception of Jalor, situated on the Surat-Ajmer trade route, all these works were constructed in a region between Agra and Ajmer, then under firm control of the Mughals.

Ahmadabad

Ahmadabad remained the primary city of Gujarat under the Mughals just as it had been under the independent sultans of Gujarat. During Jahangir's reign, both gardens and mansions were built, although few of these survive in their original condition. The garden and palace (Plates 74-75) that the prince Shah Jahan constructed for himself is today used as a museum and known as the Moti Bagh. Built during the prince's tenure as governor there between 1616 and 1623, it was known then as Shahi Bagh (Princely Garden). Jahangir, who admired this residence, had a marble seat built in its garden. A European visiting Ahmadabad in 1638 praised the gardens, its reservoirs and the palace as unusually lovely. This is not surprising, for its patron, Shah Jahan, would become the greatest Mughal patron of architecture. Shah Jahan's palace is characteristic of contemporary Mughal architecture. The exterior is a twostoried trabeated structure with a delicate pillared entrance, essentially a more refined version of Akbar's Ajmer palace (Plate 20). It contains vaulted subterranean rooms with water cascades for protection from the summer's heat. The ground floor is similar in plan to many Mughal-period mansions. There is a large square central chamber surrounded by eight smaller ones. These rooms are covered by stucco vaulted ceilings embellished with delicate net patterning. According to an eighteenth-century visitor, the rooms were finished with a highly burnished chuna and tastefully painted. Although other gardens and palaces were built by nobles in Ahmadabad, hardly any survive. Rather, religious structures are best preserved because they had a popular and continuing base of support. This may be seen with the architecture of Shaikh Farid Bukhari, entitled Murtaza Khan, who was Jahangir's governor of Gujarat from 1606 to 1609. Known for his patronage throughout the Mughal domain, he established in Ahmadabad a quarter known as Bukhari, after himself, and built administrative buildings in the city; none of these remains. Still standing, however, is the tomb he constructed for Shaikh Wajih al-Din (Plate j6), who had died in 1598. Shaikh Wajih al-Din was a disciple of Muhammad Ghaus, who had resided in Gujarat and whose tomb in Gwalior was discussed in the previous chapter. When governor, Shaikh Farid Bukhari built Wajih al-Din's tomb. It is a large stone structure whose interior is divided into eighteen bays. Small domes surmount the roof; over the saint's grave is a bulbous dome resting on a high constricted neck, recalling the shape of the dome on Ataga Khan's tomb in Delhi (Plate 16). The screens that comprise the walls are small square panels emulating those at the nearby shrine of Sarkhej that later Jahangir greatly admired. Thus the tomb reflects pan- Mughal and regional traditions.

North India

Lahore and the Road to Delhi

During Jahangir's reign, Lahore, Delhi and Agra remained the primary cities in north India. They lay along the route to Kashmir, the imperial pleasure grounds, as well as on the road to Kabul and Qandahar further to the northwest. This was territory that Jahangir, because of his Timurid heritage, believed was rightfully his, even though by the end of his reign it was no longer Mughal. Just as Jahangir and Nur

Jahan built in cities along these routes, so did other members of the Mughal house and the nobility. Under Jahangir, Lahore gained increasing prominence. European visitors describe Lahore as one of the great cities of the east. Included among the subimperial structures they mention are the char bagh of Asaf Khan, the mosque of Shaikh Farid Bukhari, a serai and a great bazaar, none of them surviving. On the road from Lahore to Kashmir, Jahangir ordered his nobles to build serais because it was too cold to stay in tents. Similarly, the road from Lahore to Agra was lined with serais. Many of them were constructed in response to Jahangir's accession orders demanding that serais and wells be constructed in the hinterlands. Beside the empress' Serai Nur Mahal (Plate 69), already discussed, others were in regular use. Finch, writing in 1610, mentions many serais, including one at Sirhind with a tank and pleasure pavilion in the middle and another under construction by Jahangir at Fatehpur to celebrate his defeat of Khusrau. Others traveling later in the century state that beautiful serais were built about every 20 km by great men or the king to enhance the road, to glorify the patron's name and to ensure the safety of travelers. One of the best preserved serais of Jahangir's time on the Lahore-Delhi route is Serai Doraha (Plate 77) in the Punjab between Serai Nur Mahal and Sirhind. Constructed of brick, a medium typical of this region, the serai covers a square of about 168 meters. Within the walls are the remains of a hammam. A domed mosque, originally covered with paintings, is situated in the serai's center. The north and south brick entrance gates remain the most striking portions of the serai. Each facade is pierced with a large recessed entrance arch that is framed with a rectangular band of glazed tile-work, also typical of this region.

The Doraha serai bears no inscription, but on the basis of stylistic and literary evidence it is datable to about 1610. The gates' geometric tile decoration resembles closely that on the nearby octagonal tomb built in 1612-13 at Nakodar. Moreover, in 1611 and 1615 travelers mention Doraha as a halting place, suggesting that it was ready for use as early as 1611. Later it was known as Ictimad al-Daula serai, indicating that this powerful figure may have been the patron. Doraha was part of his landholding. Although serais directly facilitated trade and travel and so were a highly significant architectural form, many other structures in the area between Delhi and Lahore result from sub-imperial patronage. At Nakodar, for example, is a tomb consistent with contemporary courtly taste (Plate 78). Dated 1612-13, this octagonal tomb was built for Muhammad Mumin Husaini, a musician in the court of Abd al-Rahim Khan-i Khanan, who was a very high-ranking noble under Akbar and Jahangir. It is constructed of brick and embellished with glazed tiles inlaid in geometric patterns, materials and designs typical of Mughal architecture of this region. Even the plan anticipates evolving Mughal taste, for it is not a regular octagon but a type known as Baghdadi octagon, that is, with four sides longer than the intermediate ones. Here the larger sides bear deeply recessed arches flanked by shallow arched niches, while the alternating smaller ones are marked by two vertically arranged arches. A Timund building type, the Baghdadi octagon had been used in the early Mughal period, for example at the Delhi Sabz Burj. It is seen increasingly in Jahangir's, but especially in Shah Jahan's reign. Some structures, however, continue to follow older patterns, but generally they were constructed by little-known subjects, not high-ranking nobles, who more often than not followed and perpetuated contemporary Mughal taste. At Jhajjar, for example, several tombs built between 1611 and 1625 are in the form of pillared chattris similar to ones built here in Akbar's time. Others are small square tombs reminiscent of even older structures, those built commonly during the pre-Mughal Lodi period.

Delhi

Delhi remained a city of major importance during Jahangir's time and architecture there tended to be innovative. Here, for example, notables such as Shaikh Farid Bukhari built their own tombs; nearby Shaikh Farid Bukhari established the town of Faridabad, providing a serai and mosque. Visits by the emperor to Delhi inevitably included hunting in the environs, attending to administrative concerns and visits to Humayun's tomb and the adjacent Chishti dargah of Nizam al-Din. The dargah was particularly revitalized through architectural patronage during the Mughal period. In it, the tomb of the fourteenth-century poet Amir Khusrau, considered by many the greatest writer of Indian

Persian, had been embellished during the reigns of Babur, Humayun and Akbar. The tomb as it presently appears, however, was constructed in 1605-06 by Khwaja Tahir Muhammad Imad al-Din Hasan during Jahangir's reign. Within a Humayun-period rectangular enclosure composed of red sandstone latticed walls (Plate 13) is the Jahangir-period tomb (Plate 194). It is constructed of white marble lattice screen walls continuing a tradition established in Akbar's reign (cf. Plate 26). There screens are surmounted by a pyramidal vault. The white marble provides a subtle visual link between the poet, long revered as a saint, and Nizam al-Din himself, also enshrined in a tomb of this material.

Nizam al-Din's own tomb, reconstructed during Akbar's reign, was further embellished by Shaikh Farid Bukhari. In 1608-09, he provided a canopy for the tomb's interior. Constructed of wood exquisitely inlaid with mother-of-pearl, this canopy is a rare example of dated Mughal woodwork. Four bracketed pillars support the canopy's vaulted roof, reflecting the inscription here that describes the sky as supported on four pillars. The inscription further states that the canopy was donated to honor the saint, but also to increase the honor of the builder. Concurrently with the provision of this canopy, Shaikh Farid Bukhari built the tomb of another Chishti saint, Wajih al-Din, in Ahmadabad, and several other religious buildings in the eastern Indian city of Bihar Sharif (Plates y6 and 94).

While these two structures in the dargah date to the initial period of Jahangir's reign, the next monument, containing a grave inscribed 1623-24, belongs to his final years. This is the tomb of Mirza Aziz Koka Khan-i Aczam, the son of Ataga Khan (Plate 79). He built this, his own mausoleum, during his lifetime, but earlier, in Akbar's reign, he had constructed a tomb for his father in this dargah. Mirza Aziz Koka obviously favored beautiful buildings. For example, his house in the Agra fort was painted by the head of Akbar's painting atelier, Abd al-Samad,30 and his tomb remains the finest Jahangir-period building in Delhi today. Constructed wholly of white marble, the tomb is known popularly as the Chausath Khamba after the sixty-four pillars that divide it internally into twenty-five bays. Each bay is surmounted by a dome; nevertheless, externally the tomb appears flat-roofed. Each facade contains five arches supported by square pilasters. Between each pilaster is a screen recalling those at the tomb of Sarkhej in Gujarat. The links with Sarkhej are not accidental, for Mirza Aziz Koka served several times as Jahangir's governor of Gujarat. He died there and was temporarily buried at Sarkhej. With the exception of the marble screens, the tomb bears very little ornamentation; its forms instead emphasized by uncluttered lines of the white marble surface serve as the main architectural vocabulary. Thus this tomb, perhaps more than any other surviving example of late Jahangir-period architecture, serves as a transition to the style associated with Shah Jahan's period.

Yet not all work in Delhi reflects current trends. Situated roughly between the dargah and Humayun's tomb is the tomb of Abd al-Rahim Khan-i Khanan, who died in 1626, a great general under both Akbar and Jahangir. Modeled on Humayun's tomb, the Khan-i Khanan's tomb is a large square domed structure that probably once stood in a four-quartered garden. This tomb was originally embellished with red sandstone and narrow strips of white marble trim as at Humayun's tomb. Most of the facing, however, was stripped in the eighteenth century and used on the tomb of Safdar Jang in south Delhi. The tomb appears remarkably conservative for a structure built at the time of the Khan-i Khanan's death. It may, in fact, be an earlier work, for, despite its half-dome and the net squinches within recessed entrance arches, one Mughal source states that the Khan-i Khanan was buried in the tomb of his wife, who had died in 1598.

The Road from Delhi to Allahabad

The road between Delhi and Agra was marked during Jahangir's reign by kos minar, many of them still extant. Along this road, the highest-ranking nobles built magnificent serais - at Faridabad, Hodal, Palwal, Chatta and Mathura. This construction was intended in part to protect their own investments; for example, Maryam al-Zamani, the queen mother, invested heavily in trade. It also responded to Jahangir's accession order that serais be built, earning these nobles greater favor with the king, while at the same time serving as a manifestation of their own power and wealth. Although most of these serais have disappeared, at least the entrance gate of one, at Chatta, about 60 km north of Agra, is well preserved (Plate 80). The red sandstone gate, flanked on either side by oriel windows, is entered through a deeply recessed arch. Although the gate is uninscribed, the carved wine vessels and elaborate battlement that embellish it reflect current Mughal taste. That date is also supported by literary evidence. Finch, traveling in 1611, omits Chatta from his extensive list of serais, but Steel and Crowther, traveling in 1615, mention it, suggesting that the Chatta serai was constructed between 1611 and 1615.

Beyond Chatta lay Agra, Jahangir's paramount city, then known as Akbarabad. Contemporary texts refer to the splendid structures built by the nobility there. Few of these remain, however, except the mosque of Muctamad Khan and two buildings known as the Kanch Mahal and the Suraj Bhan-ka Bagh, both constructed of red sandstone that bears elaborate carved ornament.

The Kanch Mahal (Plate 81), a gateway to a tomb, is situated east of Akbar's tomb. Its proximity to this imperial tomb suggests that the structure was built by a member of the royal household; the elaborate screens in its windows, areas that otherwise are left open, indicate it was used by women. A two-storied structure, this entrance gate opens onto a rectangular courtyard containing an octagonal tomb. Several features of the Kanch Mahal confirm its Jahangirperiod date. Its interior plan with a central chamber surrounded by eight smaller ones follows that of other buildings of the time, for example, the prince Shah Jahan's Shahi Bagh in Ahmadabad (Plate 74). Its elaborately carved red sandstone facade is magnificently trimmed with white marble inlay, an elaboration of the surface that evolves from such earlier buildings as Akbar's so-called Sultana's House at Fatehpur Sikri and the Jahangiri Mahal at Agra fort (Plate 21). Here, however, the surface of the Kanch Mahal is even more complex. Motifs such as the wine vessels, not seen in Akbar-period buildings, and the dominant arabesque of the spandrels recalling those on the gateway of Akbar's tomb, confirm the Kanch Mahal's Jahangir-period date.

In the heart of Agra city is a well-preserved red sandstone mosque attributed to Muctamad Khan (Plate 82). He was responsible for Jahangir's officers serving in the Deccan. The emperor was very fond of Muctamad Khan and entrusted him with writing his memoirs when he himself was no longer able to do so, stating that Muctamad Khan "is a servant who knows my temperament and understands my words." Perhaps inspired by this trust, he wrote his own history of Jahangir's reign, the Iqbal Nama. As at the Kanch Mahal and Suraj Bhan-ka Bagh, the red sandstone surface of this rectangular mosque is divided into square and rectangular panels carved with wine vessels and geometric patterns (Plate 83). The engaged exterior turrets, similar to those on Ictimad al-Daula's tomb (Plate 71), may suggest a date toward the end of Jahangir's reign. The placement of the decoration in panels that cover the surface in a grid plan is characteristic of later Jahangiri ornamentation, seen, for example, on the Serai Nur Mahal dated 1618-20 (Plate 69). Thus, in the Agra region, close to the Fatehpur Sikri quarries, nobles favored construction in red sandstone carved with elaborate decoration.

A number of serais marked the road between Agra and Allahabad but few remain. The largest monument in Allahabad remained Akbar's fort that had been seized by Jahangir in his days as Shah Salim. But he appears to have made no subsequent additions there. Rather it was the four-part garden containing the tomb of his first wife, Shah Begum (Plate 55), that was embellished later in his reign. It became the site of two more princely tombs. In the center of this garden, aligned with the queen's tomb, is that of her daughter, Sultan Nisar Begum, while the more distant from the queen's tomb but still aligned with it is the tomb of her son, Khusrau. Behind Sultan Nisar Begum's tomb is a large baoli, praised by Mundy, that provided water for the four-part garden. In 1621 Jahangir delivered his ill-fated son, Khusrau, into the hands of Prince Shah Jahan; a year later Khusrau was dead. Many believe that Shah Jahan murdered his elder brother, seeing him as a potential rival for the throne. Khusrau's body, according to the European Manrique, was taken first to Agra, but at Nur Jahan's insistence was removed from the imperial capital to Allahabad. During the journey, shrines honoring him as a saint were erected, but quickly dismantled under imperial order.

A verse inside the Chunar sandstone tomb bears the date 1622, recording the year of Khusrau's demise, not the tomb's construction. It was probably commenced by Sultan Nisar Begum, Khusrau's sister, when she constructed her own tomb. This square-plan tomb appears two-storied from the exterior, even though it consists of a single chamber (Plate 84). A single dome surmounts it, and a chattri is placed at each corner. Above the tomb's arched entrance is a recessed demi-dome in whose kite-shaped pedentives are painted floral patterns and an angel.

On the interior of the tomb's dome is a central medallion with radiating stellate and net patterning; it is similar to the one at Ictimad al-Daula's nearcontemporary tomb. The walls are painted with cypress, floral and other motifs, but it is the Persian verses, whose message reflects the sorrow of Khusrau's own life, that dominate the interior. Next to the cenotaph, Mundy observed in 1632, was Khusrau's own copy of the Quran. Then, too, a wooden canopy, probably similar to that in Shaikh Nizam al-Din's tomb, was over the grave. Thus despite imperial injunction, the deceased Khusrau was given saintly status.

The tomb Sultan Nisar Begum built for herself in 1624-25 but never used is the most impressive. Similar to Khusrau's tomb, this one sits on a very high plinth, dominating the garden. Its Chunar sandstone fabric is more elaborate than Khusrau's, embellished with panels of carved scalloped arches. Within the crypt in the plinth's interior is a small chamber whose ceiling is conceived as a series of concentric stars within a net-like vault. Here the original polychrome of yellows, blues and reds is beautifully preserved. The dome of the tomb's main chamber (Plate 85) is similar in conception; its walls (Plate 86) bear paintings of wine vessels, geometric dadoes, cypresses and flowering plants of the type derived from European herbals popular in the late Jahangir period. Persian verses evoking God as the sole refuge also embellish the walls. These are the best preserved examples of painting in any Mughal tomb. The motifs, borrowed from the vocabulary of mystical poetry, are similar to those found on the interior of Ictimad al-Daula's tomb. While Sultan Nisar Begum embellished this garden site ostensibly to honor her ill-fated brother, in truth, the central position and beauty of her own tomb suggest that her own glorification was also intended.

Eastern India

Chunar

Akbar's fortress at Chunar, the gateway to eastern India, remained a Mughal garrison, though no significant buildings were added there during Jahangir's reign. Elsewhere in Chunar, however, are two fine Jahangir-period buildings constructed of stone from the Chunar quarries that had provided building materials since the third century B.C. One, Shah Qasim Sulaiman's dargab, not far from the fort, was admired by British travelers and artists, although it is rarely noticed today. The second, the tomb of Iftikhar Khan, is located several kilometers from the town.

Shah Qasim Sulaiman, also known as Shaikh Qasim Qadiri, had attracted a considerable following in Lahore, but supported Khusrau and as a result was imprisoned in the Chunar fort. A year after his death in 1606, his followers reputedly constructed his simple unadorned tomb. Its entrance gate (Plates 87 and 88), unusually refined and elegant, is far more impressive than the tomb itself. This is, in part, due to the emphasis on height achieved by the balance between the proportionately small entrance arch and the soaring pishtaq. The screened walls surmounting the roof, the projecting battlement, and the corner finials (guldasta) further accentuate the sense of height. The entire facade is covered with superb carving that further enhances the structure's refinement. The jewel-like work, one of the best examples of Mughal carving in all eastern India, is reminiscent of that on Sultan Nisar Begum's tomb, although here there is considerably more detail. Clearly a patron of considerable taste must have constructed the dargah gate. In fact, it may have been the emperor himself, for tradition claims that Jahangir eventually recognized the sanctity of Shah Sulaiman's dargah and endowed land for its support. Considering Khusrau's popularity, Jahangir's provision of funds for this gate at the shrine of the deceased prince's supporter would have been one way for the emperor to absolve his role in Khusrau's death and at the same time maintain popular support. On the outskirts of Chunar, in a village known as Serai Sikandarpur, is the Chunar sandstone tomb of Iftikhar Khan, known locally as the Tahsildar Daftar, or the Tahsildar's Office (Plates 89 and 90). It is a striking monument, though it lacks the prolific carving of the nearby dargah gate that was built about the same time. In 1612 Iftikhar Khan, noted for his bravery in warfare, died in Bengal. His association with Chunar remains unclear, although he probably had a landholding there. The tomb is not dated, but an inscription of 1613-14 in a well just outside the compound's sole entrance gate records the construction of a building, almost surely the tomb, by Sikandar. Nothing is known about Sikandar, even though his name is memorialized by the site's current name. The well served as the water source for the garden in which the tomb is set.

Iftikhar Khan's tomb establishes a type that quickly becomes popular across eastern India. Its entrance gate, similar in form to the one at the nearby dargah of Shah Qasim Sulaiman, leads to the square-plan tomb situated on a high plinth in the middle of the garden. Its central chamber is surrounded by a veranda. In lieu of screened walls, as seen at the Akbar-period tombs of Muhammad Ghaus in Gwalior or Salim Chishti at Fatehpur Sikri (Plates 16 and 42), here the veranda is left open. The tomb is surmounted by a single dome that sits on a high square base; a chattri marks each corner of the roof. All these features are adopted for a tomb-type that becomes especially popular in eastern India.

Bihar: Tombs at Maner and Champanagar

The second and most magnificent tomb of this type is at Maner, in Mughal times at the confluence of the Son and Ganges rivers, about 25 km west of Patna. There an important shrine known as the Bari Dargah had developed around the grave of Yahya Manen, the father of Sharaf al-Din Manen, a fourteenth-century mystic. Pre-Mughal sultans as well as Humayun and Akbar had visited this shrine. Then, between 1605 and 1619, Ibrahim Khan Kakar, whose title was Dilawar Khan, methodically enhanced this shrine and built other structures in Maner, for example, an extensive khanqah. Tradition holds that he was the disciple of Shah Daulat, a descendent and spiritual heir of Yahya Maneri. His wealth probably came from landholdings, among them Jaunpur, which was granted as his jagir in 1607, two years after he had constructed a mosque in the Bari Dargah.

Ibrahim Khan Kakar's most ambitious architectural endeavor was a second shrine, the Chotti Dargah, built around the grave of his spiritual master (pir), Shah Daulat, and housing a large tomb that follows the type established by Iftikhar Khan's tomb at Chunar (Plate 90). The Chunar sandstone complex is the most magnificent Mughal mausoleum in eastern India. The compound's north entrance gate was built in 1613-14; three years later, in 1616-17, the main tomb was finished; and the mosque and enclosure walls (actually never completed) were constructed in 1618-19. Linking this dargah to the Bari Dargah is a large tank whose ghats (stepped embankments) are embellished with chattris. The overall appearance of the elevated two-storied gate is fortress-like, but its individual features are finely carved. So, too, is the three-bayed single-aisled mosque, surmounted by a single truncated cloistered vault. Its east facade is highly articulated by numerous arched niches, although it is less ornate than the entrance gate at Shah Qasim Sulaiman's dargab.

Shah Daulat's tomb (Plates 91 and 92), the first of its type in Bihar, is a refined version of Iftikhar Khan's tomb in Chunar, built three years earlier. It is, moreover, taller and better proportioned. Like Iftikhar Khan's tomb, this one consists of a central square chamber surrounded by a continuous veranda. It is also crowned by a single central dome and flanked at each corner by a domed chattri. Overall, the tomb is embellished with well-executed inscriptions and exquisitely carved floral and geometric patterns as well as fine stone screens. This is the last major monument in all eastern India to be constructed wholly in ashlar masonry; however, the tomb-type will be seen again in slightly variant forms in both Bihar and Bengal, for example, in the tomb of Bibi Maryam in Narayanganj (Dhaka District) and the tomb of Shamsher Khan in Shamshernagar (Aurangabad District) (Plate 220). This tomb-type, like the sandstone from which Shah Daulat's mausoleum was constructed, was carried eastward along the Ganges.

By contrast to the standard eastern Indian tomb-type established at Chunar and enhanced at Maner, one tomb is different in its obvious use of pre-Mughal Bengali features. This is the tomb of Makhdum Sahib at Champanagar, just outside of Bhagalpur (Plate 93). This tomb, known as the Maskan-i Barari and dated to 1622-23, w a s constructed by Khwaja Ahmad Samarqandi, a recently appointed Mughal administrator. Characteristic of its pre-Mughal Bengali style are the simple square form, the austere brick facade, and the curved cornice. While the impact of pre-Mughal Bengali architecture is seen on buildings of Bihar well into the late sixteenth century, for example the 1587 Jamic mosque at Hajipur, the lack of Mughal traits on the tomb of Makhdum Sahib is unusual considering the fact that there was a well-established Mughal tomb-type in eastern India. That it was not used here is surprising because by now the Mughals had long ruled Bihar. In fact, the very name of Prince Parviz appears on this tomb's inscription.

Bihar: Bihar Sharif

Bihar Sharif, the capital of pre-Mughal Bihar, remains today a site of considerable importance, since the saint Sharaf al-Din Maneri (d. 1381) is buried here. Even though the town had diminished in administrative significance, Mughal nobles continued to build there. Among them was Shaikh Farid Bukhari, known for his patronage in Delhi, Lahore and Ahmadabad (Plate 76), who, with his wife, provided the most notable Mughal building in Bihar Sharif. This is the Bukhari mosque (Plate 94), completed on November 20,1608. Epigraphs indicate that Shaikh Lad, otherwise unknown, was responsible for the procurement of the materials as well as for the supervision of the work. More important, they relate that the mosque was designed by Shaikh Farid himself, noteworthy since he was not in Bihar when it was built. However, during Akbar's reign his family must have been associated with Bihar, for his brother is buried in a grave dated 1583-

84 close to Maner. Although the mosque form derives in large part from that of the 1587 Jamic mosque in Hajipur, at that time a highly localized type, it becomes the standard for subsequent mosques across eastern India. This Bihar Sharif mosque is a large single-aisled three-bayed rectangular structure surmounted by three domes and marked at each corner by semi-engaged octagonal turrets. For more than a century it served as the standard for mosques in Bihar and Bengal, for example Mirza Macsum's mosque (1614-16) in Patna and the mosque of Raja Bahroz (1656-57) in Kharagpur (Plate 152).

The mosque's patron, Shaikh Farid, is noted in Mughal texts for his generous patronage of architecture throughout north India. His buildings, however, were constructed during the few years between 1606 and 1609, perhaps in thanksgiving for his newly bestowed title, Nawab Murtaza Khan, invariably mentioned in the building's inscriptions. Possibly, then, grateful for his increased prestige under Jahangir, he took seriously the emperor's accession orders to build both serais and religious structures. Although the role of construction by highly placed nobles such as Shaikh Farid is mentioned in Mughal histories and biographies, much of the work in the Mughal hinterlands remains unnoticed. Such is the case with an entire town named Khurramabad, in honor of the then heir apparent, Prince Khurram, the future Shah Jahan. According to an inscription on the east face of the town's Jamic mosque, Ali Akbar constructed here a bridge, mosque, serai, fort and baths between 1612-13 and 1617. The Khurramabad bridge (Plate 95), used until recently, is a smaller version of Raja Man Singh's bridge in Rajmahal and an eleven-arched bridge in Delhi dated 1612. Of Akbar Ali's other buildings only the largely ruined mosque remains. It was a single-aisled three-bayed structure whose central pishtaq, some 12 meters high, was flanked on either side by bays with narrow arched entrances, revealing the influence of north Indian Mughal buildings. The date of Khurramabad's commencement, 1612, suggests that the town, near the notorious dacoit-ridden Kaimar hills on the main road from Benares to Sasaram and Rohtas, was built in response to Jahangir's accession order issued some five years earlier. Peter Mundy, traveling through eastern India in 1632, twice mentions

Khurramabad as a flourishing settlement constructed as a residential headquarters for the landholder of Sasaram, situated about 20 km to the east.

At Sasaram is a mansion, or Qalca as it is known today, a rare example of Mughal residential architecture in the hinterlands. It is attributed to Ali Akbar, who according to local tradition was also known as Safdar Khan, the landholder of Sasaram in Jahangir's period. The main building is three stories high. The interior consists of a high central chamber almost certainly used as the Diwan Khana, or main reception room. Surrounding this on all the floors were ancillary chambers, many of which overlooked the central room. On the west exterior facade is a large pishtaq, whose recessed arch is ornamented with patterns on burnished stucco recalling Mughal decor elsewhere, for example, Narnaul's Jal Mahal. Surrounding this three-storied building are traces of a single-storied flat-roofed gallery similar to the contemporary galleries of the Chotti Dargah in Maner. This complex matches well the descriptions written by European visitors of the housing for Mughal nobility in Agra or Delhi during Shah Jahan's reign and later. It thus suggests that the housing type of the Mughal nobility was established before Shah Jahan's reign and that this particular dwelling was modeled on those constructed at the major centers.

Patna

In Patna, as in many cities that still retain their importance, very few buildings of early Mughal date remain. The continuous process of urbanization has replaced them. Only two early Mughal monuments in Patna are worthy of comment, both characteristic of styles more widely seen in Bihar. The first is Mirza Macsum's mosque, inscribed as a Jamic mosque and constructed between 1614-15 and 1616-17. Mirza Macsum entered imperial service during Akbar's reign and then served in Bengal under Jahangir's governor, Islam Khan. Evidently Mirza Macsum left Bengal after Islam Khan's death in 1613 and retired to Patna, where he constructed a mosque and also a market. Mirza Macsum's mosque is a less refined version of Shaikh Farid Bukhari's mosque built in Bihar Sharif in 1608 (Plate 94). The engaged columns flanking the central bay rise above the central pishtaq, a feature characteristic of many mosques in Patna and elsewhere in eastern India. Net patterns rendered in stucco appear in the central mihrab's soffit (Plate 96) and again in the vaulting. This is the earliest known use of net patterning in stucco on an eastern Indian mosque, although the technique is seen earlier in parts of the Rohtas palace. The second surviving Mughal monument in Patna is the Patthar-ki Masjid, built by Nazar Khwishgi in 1626-27. Nazar Khwishgi is best known for his stellar career under Shah Jahan, but during Jahangir's reign he was a close attendant of Prince Parviz, one of Jahangir's sons. Parviz was governor of Bihar, but never actually went there; probably Nazar Khwishgi served as his deputy.

The mosque's east facade is stucco faced and adheres to the formula already seen in all Mughal mosques in Bihar. The other three sides, however, are stonefaced, nearly the last use of stone for a building's facade in either Bengal or Bihar. The stone is carved with small floral medallions and slender-necked wine flasks, a motif seen on contemporary monuments at the center (Plates 72 and 83), but rarely in eastern India.

Bengal

Islam Khan, Jahangir's governor of Bengal from 1609 to 1613, finally terminated rebel activities that had plagued the Mughals in Bengal since Akbar's time. He moved the capital from Akbarnagar (Rajmahal) to Dhaka, then named Jahangirnagar. Little remains of early seventeenth-century Dhaka except some small river forts used against pirates, a constant threat to Mughal authority. Outside of Dhaka, the Jamic mosque at Atiya (Plate 97) in Tangail District, Bangladesh, constructed in 1609, is the sole dated monument of Jahangir's era in all Bengal. This is the latest mosque here built in a pre-Mughal regional idiom. It consists of a single-domed square prayer chamber with a tripledomed veranda projecting on the east, suggesting that in areas away from Mughal administrative centers there was little influence from the mainstream Mughal architectural tradition. The rebel prince Shah Jahan, in his quest for the Mughal throne, was well aware of the continued weakness of imperial authority in Bengal. He marched to Bengal in 1624, defeated Jahangir's governor, and gained control of Akbarnagar, long the key to Bengal. From this strategic vantage, the rebel prince easily gained all Bengal and Bihar. While credit for re-establishing Akbarnagar's pre-eminence generally is given to Shah Shujac, his father Shah Jahan was initially responsible.

The memoirs of Mirza Nathan, a noble posted in Bengal since the early seventeenth century and serving in the rebel prince Shah Jahan's army, give insight into several architectural projects of the time. Among these are a palace at Akbarnagar and a new fort at Garhi. Today known as Teliagarhi, Garhi is just 30 km northeast of Akbarnagar. The fort, situated at the traditional approach to Bengal, was secured with stone walls. Mirza Nathan, charged with erecting this fort, notes that a different officer was responsible for every 20 meters of the fortification walls, thus assuring their speedy completion. In spite of this, the walls, constructed of alternating layers of local brown and black stones, appear uniform. No royal palace, however, was built inside, since the hasty construction of such an edifice, a contemporary stated, would alarm the local population. In any event, all the available workers were already engaged on the walls. John Marshall, an early agent with the East India Company who visited the fort in 1761, reports that it was remarkably strong, adequate for about eighty cannon and twice as many small guns and muskets. Partially still standing, the fortifications remain as testimony to solid workmanship in spite of speedy construction.

While Garhi was being built, the rebel prince Shah Jahan ordered Muhammad Salih to construct a palace at Akbarnagar. Mirza Nathan describes the palace, which no longer survives, as consisting of the following buildings: a Private Audience Hall {Ghusl Khana), a Throne Room (Takht-i Daulat), quarters for the harem, a Public Audience Hall and a bath. They probably were tent-constructed, not built of more durable materials, since he describes them as easily rearranged.

Although Akbar's reign is generally considered the period most tolerant of the Hindu nobility, under Jahangir they also fared well.

Hindu nobles built mansions, palaces and temples. And just as the houses and gardens built by the Muslim nobility were considered state, not private, property, the same held true for the Hindu amirs. For example, the Matiyaburj palace of Ram Das Kachhwaha, a Hindu, was confiscated in 1612 when Jahangir became displeased with his performance in battle, indicating that the dwelling was regarded as state property, not a personal investment to which the patron had absolute right. Construction on a watan jagir, an ancestral landholding of a vassal prince, seems to have been more secure. That land was generally left in the hands of successive rulers, although the Mughal monarch occasionally ignored primogeniture and awarded the title raja if he believed another candidate was more suitable. During Jahangir's reign there is no better example of patronage in a watan jagir than that of Raja Bir Singh Deo in his territory of Orchha in Bundelkhand. Bir Singh's rise commenced in 1602, when at the future Jahangir's request the raja killed Abu al-Fazl. In 1623, after steady advancement, Jahangir awarded him the title maharaja (great prince), the first time this was bestowed as an official Mughal title. The raja died in 1627, the same year as his patron, Jahangir.

Although Jahangir makes no reference to Bir Singh's building activities, chronicles of Shah Jahan's time praise the works he constructed. Among these, the most notable are his palace at Datia and an addition known as the Jahangiri Mandir to the earlier sixteenth-century palaces at Orchha. The Jahangiri Mandir (Plate 98) is a square-plan structure measuring 61 meters per side. Impressively high, it is surmounted by chattris. The interior consists of three stories arranged around a large open courtyard, similar to the zenana at the palace Raja Man Singh built at Rohtas. Many of the interior walls are magnificently painted with scenes from Hindu lore as well as courtly figures based in large measure on Mughal types.

The palace Raja Bir Singh constructed at Datia, about 30 km northeast of Orchha, was built about 1620. This square-plan building, situated on a rocky outcrop, dominates the terrain (Plate 99). The five-storied palace, rising to a height of 40 meters, has a layout similar to that of contemporary Rajput royal dwellings, but many of the motifs that adorn it belong to a characteristic Mughal vocabulary. Its multi-storied chambers are arranged around a central courtyard, a plan like that at the Orchha Jahangiri Mandir. Here, however, a pavilion at the courtyard's center is linked to each wing by double-storied corridors, thus dividing the palace's courtyard into four units, recalling the arrangement of a char bagh.

Most of the palace's chambers are trabeated, although some of the ceilings are vaulted and bear traces in stucco of net patterning typical in Jahangir-period architecture (Plates 60, 61 and 85). Also revealing the influence of imperial Jahangir architecture are the motifs painted on the stucco. These are rendered in a Persianized manner similar to motifs on the walls of Sultan Nisar Begum's tomb dated 1624-2 5 (Plate 85). On the spandrels and sides of a high arched niche that towers over the main entrance are fine paintings (Plate 100).

There, in addition to the centrally placed figure of the elephant-headed god Ganesh, found at the entrance to many Hindu dwellings, are subjects more characteristic of Mughal painting: geometric patterns, horses and riders, wine vessels and nobles. At Orchha Bir Singh constructed an enormous temple, today known as the Chaturbhuj. Although it was partially demolished under Shah Jahan in response to considerable political difficulties the Mughals were having there, it remains well preserved.

The temple's interior is domed and arcuated, possibly inspired by Raja Man Singh's Govind Deva temple of 1590 at Brindavan. Close to Brindavan, at Mathura, Bir Singh built another temple, known as the Keshava Deva temple, dismantled at the beginning of Aurangzeb's reign. It was constructed of red Sikri stone at a cost of 33 million rupees, an enormous sum. The Frenchman Tavernier relates that the temple was very large and sumptuous, visible from a distance of 16 km. The sanctum of this temple, too, was probably influenced by Raja Man Singh's Govind Deva temple at Brindavan. On the temple's walls was a profusion of carved images, a feature lacking at the earlier Govind Deva temple. Under Jahangir, just as under his father, rank and favor appear to have played a much larger role than sectarian affiliation in determining who built major structures. Moreover, building temples in the Mathura-Brindavan region, an area not far from the imperial seat at Agra, appears to have been one way that Hindus who were part of the Mughal administrative system could display their status and owealth.

This did not go unnoticed, for Jahangir comments on the beauty of Brindavan's temples. Moreover, a considerable number of those in Brindavan were the beneficiary of imperial grants. Among those the emperor probably admired were the temple complex of Madan Mohan and the Jugal Kishore temple (Plate 101). Each is constructed of Sikn sandstone and with features adhering to a Mughal idiom. Unlike north Indian temples reflecting current Mughal taste, temples constructed in Bengal assumed an increasingly regional character. Among these is a type known as bangala, probably modeled on the curved roofs of Bengali huts, which is pertinent to the subsequent development of Mughal architecture (Plates 113,119 and 175). Although this building type only survives in Bengal's temples, it was probably used in domestic settings as well.

These temples are rectangular in plan and surmounted by curved roofs described as bangala, for example the Gopinath temple in Pabna, dated 1607. Such temples were not limited to Bengal, but are found also in the eastern portions of Bihar, adjacent to Bengal, for example, the Raja Rani temple (Plate 102) in Kharagpur (Munger District). Built by the Kharagpur rajas before their conversion to Islam in Jahangir's reign,37 temples of this sort would have been known to the rebel prince Shah Jahan from the period that he spent in nearby Rajmahal. Later in Shah Jahan's period, as we shall see, rectangular-plan structures with bangala roofs are adopted in imperial palace structures, especially those associated with public viewing chambers.

CONCLUSION

Jahangir had considerably more interest in architecture than is commonly believed. He constructed extensively - palaces, hunting lodges and tombs - although hardly any religious buildings, despite his devotion to Mucin al-Din. Under Jahangir, Mughal architecture shows considerable continuity as the concepts mature. Thus, for example, paradisical imagery associated with funereal settings, first seen in Akbar's architecture, is developed in the tomb Jahangir constructed for his father. Also, like Akbar, Jahangir used architecture to imply the ruler's semi-divine status, foreshadowing developments under his son and successor, Shah Jahan. This we see both in tile and painted ornament on surviving buildings, for example, the Kala Burj in the Lahore fort, as well as in paintings illustrating the emperor enthroned. In addition, Jahangir, like his grandfather, Babur, was concerned not only with the building itself but also with its setting. Buildings such as his Chesma-i Nur are architecturally uninspiring but spectacularly situated.

Many aspects of Jahangir's architectural style have strong roots in the buildings of Akbar. They are not, however, always the roots one might expect. Tombs, for example those Jahangir built for Akbar and Shah Begum, are not based on older Timurid-inspired tomb-types but rather on Akbar's multistoried palace pavilions. The few surviving palaces Jahangir constructed, on the other hand, are modeled on older palace types, such as Akbar's trabeated pavilions at Fatehpur Sikri, even continuing the dominant use of red sandstone. Now though, surfaces are at times more highly articulated, and white marble, previously used only for tombs at the shrines of saints, was introduced for palace architecture. This sets the stage for the substantially more extensive use of white marble under Shah Jahan. Despite the fact that most of Jahangir's residential architecture - his forts, palaces and hunting pavilions - is trabeated, Timurid building techniques were not altogether rejected during his reign. The Kala Burj, for example, reveals an elaborately vaulted interior as does the tomb Sultan Nisar Begum built for herself in Allahabad near the end of Jahangir's reign. Buildings such as those constructed in Jahangir's reign explain the persistence of Timurid forms into the reign of Shah Jahan, where they surface most clearly and magnificently in the world-famous Taj Mahal. The emperor was not the only trend setter, for his favorite wife, Nur Jahan, was a leading arbitrator of taste. She built elegant serais, gardens and an exquisite white marble tomb whose inlay and motifs foreshadow developments in Shah Jahan's reign. Her dynamic interest in construction stimulated a similar interest by court women in subsequent reigns.

Jahangir not only encouraged the nobility to build, especially in the hinterlands, but also often rewarded them by advancement in rank. If in Akbar's period architecture at the frontier was often a symbol of Mughal power, in Jahangir's reign it was an indication of genuine presence, serving permanent populations as well as encouraging trade across the empire. Hindu rajas, also members of the Mughal nobility, built palaces on their ancestral lands that incorporated trends at the Mughal court. The styles of all these structures, as in Akbar's time, introduced new aesthetics to the provinces, ones that usually echoed contemporary tastes in the major cities of Agra and Lahore.

6

Shah Jahan and the Crystallization of Mughal Style

Shah Jahan, Jahangir's third son, emerged victorious in the power struggle that developed after Jahangir's death and assumed the Mughal throne in 1628. His thirty-year reign is dominated by an outward sense of prosperity and stability unmatched even during Akbar's rule. At the same time, almost every aspect of courtly culture became increasingly formalized. Shah Jahan was portrayed as an aloof ideal king. Official histories thus present him as a just leader and staunch upholder of orthodox Islam, but they give little insight into the emperor's personal thoughts. Yet Shah Jahan's unreserved preference for Dara Shukoh, his eldest son, an eclectic mystic thinker, suggests other aspects of this ruler's character never alluded to in court histories.

The painted image of Shah Jahan parallels the literary one. The emperor is portrayed in an idealized manner - while he ages over time, his features remain flawless. His inner character is never revealed. Rather, his role as semi-divine king of the world, a play on his name, is the focus of each portrait.

His face is always surrounded by a halo, as in late representations of Jahangir. In some of these illustrations the metaphoric nature of the king's semi-divine and just quality is taken so far as to show small angels above his head, often crowning him, while at his feet are the lion and the lamb of peace. Even more than light imagery, paradisical imagery now evolves from verbal to visual forms, particularly in Shah Jahan's architecture.

Best known for his construction of the Taj Mahal, Shah Jahan was the greatest patron of Mughal architecture. The sums expended on his tombs, palaces, hunting pavilions, gardens and entire planned cities is extraordinary even by modern standards. Just as the literary and painted image of Shah Jahan became increasingly ceremonial and formal, so his architecture, much of it meant to serve as an imperial setting, assumed an air of formality unprecedented in earlier Mughal structures. The use of white marble inlaid with stones, noted during the later portion of Jahangir's reign, characterizes much of Shah Jahan's architectural production. His buildings appear increasingly refined, establishing a style that became an Indian classic.

SHAH JAHAN'S RULE

The future Shah Jahan, Prince Khurram, was the favorite of his grandfather Akbar and of his own father Jahangir. Schooled by renowned scholars and religious thinkers, Khurram revealed a quick mind and good memory, although both father and grandfather were disappointed in his shallow mastery of Turki, Babur's native tongue. The prince did, however, excel in the martial arts. Unlike his father, Prince Khurram possessed great military prowess and was responsible for the major victories of Jahangir's reign. It was, for example, Khurram who had waged successful campaigns against Rana Amar Singh of Mewar and in the Deccan. In honor of his success in the Deccan, Jahangir bestowed upon the prince the title Shah Jahan (King of the World). Jahangir recognized his son's military and administrative capabilities and so treated Shah Jahan as his heir apparent until about 1622. Then Nur Jahan realized that the prince was too independent to carry out her schemes and so convinced the emperor to support Shahriyar, her own son-in-law. Shah Jahan rebelled, establishing himself as an independent ruler in eastern India with Rajmahal as his headquarters. However, within three years, the prince again acknowledged Jahangir's authority.

At the time of Jahangir's death late in 1627, Shah Jahan had active, powerful supporters at court, most notable among them, Asaf Khan. With his help all rivals for the throne were eliminated and early in 1628

Shah Jahan was crowned emperor in the Agra fort. Adopting lofty titles, he proclaimed himself not only the King of the World, but also the Meteor of the Faith, a role he took seriously. He termed himself the Lord of the Auspicious Conjunctions, a title borrowed from Timur, for, like his predecessors, he was proud of his Timurid heritage. He had genealogies painted illustrating his links with Timurid ancestors, and, as we shall see, the Taj Mahal is modeled on Timurid buildings or at least on structures influenced by Timurid architecture. Under Shah Jahan Islamic orthodoxy increased. For example, like Akbar and Jahangir, Shah Jahan often visited the tomb of Mucin al-Din Chishti in Ajmer. But unlike Akbar, who later abandoned the pilgrimage to Ajmer, and Jahangir, who never returned to the shrine once he left Ajmer as his residence, Shah Jahan paid homage to the saint at Ajmer until the end of his reign. Official histories indicate that the construction of Hindu temples was in some cases forbidden and a few earlier ones were dismantled, leading some to argue that Shah Jahan was intolerant of other religions. Even the percentage of high-ranking Hindu nobles decreased. Thus Islam took on an importance as never before in Mughal India, although it is difficult to say whether Shah Jahan himself was more orthodox than his predecessors.

The empire inherited by Shah Jahan was by early modern standards a stable one; however, unlike his father, Jahangir, Shah Jahan was interested in territorial expansion. The most consuming campaigns were those in the Deccan and in territories to the northwest, including the Timurid homelands of Balkh and beyond. The conquest and consolidation of the Deccan presented problems that continued into the next reign. By the end of his rule, Shah Jahan recognized that the Mughal conquest of Timurid homelands was not feasible. While events in the Deccan, with the exception of his favorite wife's death there in 1631, had little impact on his architectural patronage, Shah Jahan's frequent journeys to the northwest, including Lahore, Kashmir and Kabul, inspired construction. Internal rebellions, largely headed by vassal chieftains who wished to assert their independence from the Mughal empire, also disrupted but did not debilitate Shah Jahan's empire. Among the rebels was the successor of Bir Singh Deo, the raja of Bundelkhand. He was adequately subversive that Prince Aurangzeb was forced to intervene. Aurangzeb wrote his father about the palaces of Datia and Orchha, built during Akbar's and Jahangir's reign, and inspired him to visit them. En route, Shah Jahan stopped at Bari, a hunting resort that he came to love and there constructed a palace. While at Orchha, he ordered the destruction of a temple, not an iconoclastic act, but one intended to demonstrate his authority.

In 1657, Shah Jahan became so ill that those around him believed he had little time to live. His four sons - Murad, Shah Shujac, Aurangzeb and Dara Shukoh, the king's favored heir apparent - vied for the crown. Each proclaimed himself emperor, for in the Timurid tradition succession was not based on primogeniture, but on cunning and strength. Shah Jahan recovered fully within a month, but the war of succession already was well under way. Prince Aurangzeb emerged victorious, and to insure his position he had his brothers and their sons imprisoned or murdered. Proclaiming his father incompetent to rule, Aurangzeb declared himself Mughal emperor in 1658. Shah Jahan survived for another seven years, imprisoned inside the Agra fort in one of his own palaces that overlooked his most famous creation, the Taj Mahal. Dying in 1666, Shah Jahan was buried there next to his wife.

SHAH JAHAN S PATRONAGE

Shah Jahan's Patronage as a Prince

By 1628, when Shah Jahan ascended the throne, he already had shown considerable interest in the construction of architecture and gardens. By the age of sixteen, the future Shah Jahan had built quarters that greatly impressed Jahangir inside Babur's Kabul fort,1 and redesigned buildings inside the Agra fort. Also while a prince, Shah Jahan built the Shahi Bagh in Ahmadabad (Plates 74 and 75), a building characteristic of Jahangir's time. After forcing the Udaipur rana to submit to Mughal authority, he constructed buildings on a hill in Udaipur in 1613. The prince's dwelling was near the summit. Below it the nobles built their own houses, the higher their rank, the closer to the imperial seat. Thus, early in his career, Shah Jahan revealed an interest in the organization of an entire imperial entourage. Near Burhanpur in the Deccan Shah Jahan built a fine hunting resort on an artificial lake he created by adding a second dam to one constructed before his time. Even earlier he had commenced construction of the renowned Shalimar garden in Kashmir. Shah Jahan deeply loved Shalimar garden and in 1634, after his coronation, further embellished the site.

Imperial Tombs in Lahore

Several events that occurred around the time of Shah Jahan's coronation relate directly to his subsequent patronage of architecture. These include the construction of Jahangir's tomb, a vow to construct a mosque at the shrine of Mucin al-Din Chishti in Ajmer, and finally an order to build the Public Audience Halls at the Lahore and Agra forts. Shah Jahan's construction at the Ajmer shrine and at the forts is described in detail by contemporary historians. By contrast, Jahangir's tomb is scarcely mentioned. Lahauri, Shah Jahan's official chronicler during the part of his reign when the tomb was built, does not discuss its construction but only mentions its forecourt, while Kanbo, a contemporary historian, describes the tomb and notes that it took ten years to build. Compared to the lengthy descriptions of other imperial projects, the brief reference to Jahangir's tomb suggests that the tension between father and son was never fully resolved in Shah Jahan's mind. It also suggests that Shah Jahan had little personal involvement in its planning and execution, unlike many of his other architectural projects.

Jahangir died in Rajauri while en route from Lahore to Kashmir. Because the terrain there was unsuitable for a large mausoleum, his body was carried to Lahore and buried in Nur Jahan's garden on the banks of the Ravi. The mausoleum (Plate 103), centered in a char bagh covering 55 acres, is entered through large gates on the north and south. The southern gate, today serving as the tomb's main entrance, is faced with red Sikri sandstone and profusely inlaid with white marble, recalling the less elaborate gates at Ictimad al-Daula's 1626-28 tomb in Agra. The mausoleum today consists of a single-storied platform about 84 meters square. At each corner is a towering minaret.

Like the entrance gates, the tomb's red sandstone surface is decorated with white inlay depicting vessels and flower vases. Chevron patterns in white and pink stone embellish the minarets. The crypt is within the platform, reached by long corridors that extend from each of the four sides. It contains the marble cenotaph inlaid with black in lettering giving the year of Jahangir's death and the ninety-nine names of God. Floral arabesques cover the top of the platform upon which the cenotaph rests. This cenotaph thus is similar to the one at the tomb of Mumtaz Mahal, known as the Taj Mahal and built at the same time. While the tomb today has no second story, originally marble screens enclosed a second cenotaph. The platform atop the large square first story still exists; even in the nineteenth century there were regularly placed oblong indentations for the placement of posts, and marks on the platform indicated that there had been a trellised screen. Some believe that this screened enclosure was surmounted by a roof, like that at Ictimad al-Daula's tomb (Plate 71). However, Jahangir, before dying, had requested a tomb that would be open to the air, like Babur's, so that it could be directly exposed to God's mercy. Kanbo, who lived in Lahore and doubtless had seen the tomb, confirms that the cenotaph was uncovered.

Just west of the char bagh containing the mausoleum is a large rectangular enclosure wall that was completed in 1637. According to Lahauri, this quadrangle, today known as the Akbari Serai, served as a forecourt (chowk-i jilo khana) to the tomb. It was here that horses, weapons and other items were left before their owners went to pay homage to the deceased king. Thus, during the Mughal period, this quadrangle must have served as the main entrance. On the quadrangle's west wall is a single-aisled three-bayed mosque. Its central portal, considerably higher than the flanking ones, as well as the exaggerated height of the three entrance arches, give the mosque an archaic appearance, recalling the Akbar-period mosque at Ajmer (Plate 40) more than contemporary imperial mosques, for example, Shah Jahan's mosque at the Ajmer shrine (Plate 105). No part of this mosque at the tomb shows the elegance generally associated with Shah Jahan's architecture, suggesting that he paid no more personal attention to its form than he did to other parts of Jahangir's tomb. West of the tomb's forecourt a tomb was built on Shah Jahan's order for Nur Jahan's brother, Asaf Khan, who died in 1641. Asaf Khan's lineage was impeccable. Not only was he Nur Jahan's brother and the father of Shah Jahan's favorite wife, but also he was the emperor's closest adviser. Today only the brick shell of his octagonal tomb remains. The white marble that had been ordered for the dome and interior have been stripped away. The recessed entrance arches, however, bear multi-colored glazed tiles. Although not constructed by Shah Jahan, the former empress, Nur Jahan, built her own tomb in close proximity to Jahangir's. She died in 1645, having survived her husband, Jahangir, by eighteen years. Despite the generous yearly allowance Shah Jahan granted to Nur Jahan, the relationship between this once formidable queen and Shah Jahan remained strained. Her tomb was modeled closely on the mausolea of her father and husband. The building is pierced by seven arched openings on each side. Today there is no second story, but it probably consisted of a roofless screened enclosure. Stripped of its original red sandstone and white marble facing, the tomb recently has been restored. Ajmer: dargah and city Ajmer and its premier shrine had special significance for Shah Jahan, as it had for his Mughal predecessors. It was here that the prince Shah Jahan's victory over the rana of Mewar was celebrated. That victory inspired patronage of buildings, including work at the shrine of Mucin al-Din Chishti and the imperial residence.

In January, 1628 Shah Jahan encamped in Jahangir's palace on the Ana Sagar, which then consisted of a garden and a marble building. Shah Jahan then must have ordered extra buildings, for when he visited Ajmer next in December 1636 he saw his own newly constructed additions. Among these was a ceremonial viewing balcony (jharoka-i daulat kbana khass o camm), part of the Public Audience Hall.

While virtually nothing remains of Jahangir's garden and structures on the banks of the Ana Sagar, several white marble pavilions built by Shah Jahan on the lake's stone embankment do survive. These structures, known today as baradaris, were part of Shah Jahan's palace at Ajmer, considerably more refined and elegant than any of Jahangir's buildings there. The buildings represent only a small portion of the original complex. Only four of these white marble pavilions, all trabeated structures, are still standing.

A fifth has been dismantled, but was distinct from the others. These five pavilions almost certainly were intended for imperial use, since Mughal palace buildings overlooking water had an exclusively imperial function, while those structures increasingly distant from the shore - none of which remain at the Ana Sagar palace - were intended for others in the royal retinue. Probably the Private Audience Hall was located in close proximity to the shore, but the Public Audience Hall and its ceremonial viewing balcony, mentioned in contemporary texts, was probably located in a separate quadrangle, away from the structures intended exclusively for imperial use. The two pavilions furthest south (Plate 104), similar in appearance, face each other and were conceived together.

These trabeated structures are supported by faceted columns with multi-lobed brackets all carved in white marble. They are more refined versions of sandstone buildings constructed by Akbar and Jahangir (Plates 28, 59, 63 and 64). The other two pavilions are rather different, for one opens toward the lake and the other onto the embankment. The pillars of the second pavilion divide it into two distinct concentric spaces, recalling the plan of buildings that Akbar had designed specifically for his own use. It was the Jamic mosque (Plate 105), built within the famed Chishti dargah to the west of Mucin al-Din's tomb, that Shah Jahan himself felt to be his most significant act of patronage in Ajmer. Constructed entirely of white marble, quarried in nearby Makrana, this mosque remains even today the finest building at the shrine. A rectangular structure measuring 45 by 7. meters, the mosque is divided into two aisles by slender pillars. The central mihrab (Plate 106) is a deeply recessed tri-partite arched niche with stellate and net vaulting. Its fine appearance inspired later works in the city (Plate 137). The east facade consists of eleven equal-sized arched openings supported on slender piers. These are not true arches, but brackets that meet at the center. This is not a new technique but one seen earlier on Akbar's Jamic mosque at Fatehpur Sikri (Plate 25).

The smooth flowing lines of these entrance arches combined with the white marble give the structure a sophisticated yet pristine appearance often associated with the classicism of Shah Jahan's age. The mosque's appearance foreshadows the Jamic mosque Shah Jahan built in 1653 inside the Agra fort (Plate 115).

Beneath the eaves on the mosque's east facade is a lengthy Persian inscription that gives the date of completion, 1637-38. In addition it states that Shah Jahan, when a prince, had resolved to build a mosque at the shrine of Mucin al-Din Chishti in thanksgiving for his second victory over the rana of Mewar in 1615. Because of his devotion to this esteemed saint, the inscription continues, Shah Jahan ordered the construction of a mosque compatible with the tomb's design. The mosque was built without a dome, insuring that the saint's tomb remained the shrine's dominant building. The inscription further states that Shah Jahan ordered the mosque since there was none aligned with the mausoleum.

The mosque's location thus would allow Shah Jahan during prayer to be positioned auspiciously between the qibla of the mosque and the saint's tomb. Finally, the imagery used throughout the inscription compares the mosque to the Kaaba m Mecca, the most sacred monument in Islam. While such imagery is not innovative, the presence of such a lengthy inscription on a Mughal mosque's facade is unusual and, as we shall see, is the first among several that will become standard on Shah Jahan's religious structures. Like the mosque's appearance, the imagery of its inscription anticipates that used in the epigraph of the Agra fort's Jamic mosque. Although the orders for this mosque were issued in January 1628, shortly before Shah Jahan ascended the throne, it took about nine years to complete. This can be explained by the death of Shah Jahan's favorite wife in 1631 and the subsequent construction of her tomb, the Taj Mahal, which diverted resources and energy. The mosque's inscription is dated 1637-38, but most of the structure must have been completed by the time of the king's visit in December, 1636. At that time, Shah Jahan approached the shrine on foot, as his father and grandfather had done earlier, distributing large sums of money. Shah Jahan visited the shrine two more times. One was in 1643, when he ordered the preparation of food for the poor in the enormous caldrons, or digs, given to the shrine by his father, Jahangir. His last visit was in 1654, when he paid homage to the saint on three separate occasions, always approaching the shrine on foot. In that year, he ordered the construction of a large gateway for the shrine to commemorate his subjugation of a troublesome raja. The gate was completed one year later, in 1655. Visible from the road, it serves as the first entrance into the shrine, in front of the much taller gate built earlier. This gate is marked by a pointed ogee arch in the high central pishtaq, conforming to the gate which looms above.

The Renovation of Palace and City

Shah Jahan constructed and renovated forts throughout his reign. For example, he continued to build at the Agra fort long after he shifted his capital to Delhi. However, most of the construction at his Lahore and Agra forts was done in about the first decade of his rule. By contrast, his entire Delhi (Shahjahanabad) fort was executed after 1639. All three of these major projects have striking similarities reflecting continuing Mughal practice. Perhaps the most notable was placing imperial chambers at the fort's far end overlooking a river. This practice was established certainly by Akbar's reign and probably as early as Babur's. Although the Agra and Lahore forts were constructed concurrently, they each have individual personalities and merit separate discussion. Shortly after his accession, Shah Jahan ordered renovations at the Agra and Lahore forts, then the two most important ones. These are but two examples of Shah Jahan's continual effort to improve existing fortified palaces. In addition new buildings were added to Akbar's and Jahangir's structures in the Gwalior fort,8 but it was little used by the king and served primarily, as it had earlier, as an important prison.

The Kabul fort was Shah Jahan's residence during the unsuccessful campaigns to consolidate territory originally part of the Timurid homeland. The emperor's commitment of a half million rupees for work there in 1646 included the construction of several buildings for ceremonial and administrative use, though none of them remains. An identical amount was expended for strengthening the fort of Qandahar between 1648 and 1653 under the supervision of Ali Mardan Khan. Improvement here was to prevent the fort's capture by the Safavids.

Lahore

Lahore remained the most important Mughal city after Agra until 1648, when the new imperial capital, Shahjahanabad, surpassed them both. Shah Jahan's additions to the Lahore fort commenced in 1628, the year of his coronation, continuing through 1645. Here, as elsewhere, he was personally involved in establishing the forms for his architecture. He first ordered a Chehil Sutun, or forty-pillared Public Audience Hall. Until its construction, cloth canopies had protected courtiers from the elements when paying homage to the emperor. Although this hall is similar to a better preserved one built concurrently at the Agra fort, it is less elaborate.

About the time Shah Jahan built the Lahore fort's Public Audience Hall, he completed the courtyard containing a tower then known as the Shah Burj, today called the Musamman Burj. It had been commenced under Jahangir, but Shah Jahan was dissatisfied with the appearance of this tower, situated at the fort's northwest corner. Asaf Khan, Shah Jahan's father-in-law and the brother of Nur Jahan, was assigned to oversee the reconstruction, for he more than any other noble understood the emperor's taste. Asaf Khan presented the emperor with several plans, and Shah Jahan himself made the final decision, underscoring the personal role that this fifth Mughal emperor usually played in the development of his own architecture.

The entrance to the Shah Burj quadrangle, known today as the Elephant gate, is a large tile-covered brick structure. It was completed in 1631-32 by Abd al-Karim, also known as Macmur Khan, who had designed the Lahore fort's Daulat Khana-i Jahangiri in 1617. The same architect also was probably responsible for the exterior tiled walls built largely in Jahangir's reign adjacent to this gate (Plate 61). This would explain the stylistic homogeneity. The Shah Burj originally overlooked the river, whose course now has changed. Its white marble buildings, like their counterparts at Shah Jahan's palaces elsewhere, overlook the water and were reserved for the emperor and his family. Among the most impressive is the Shish Mahal (Plate 107). This name is a modern one, deriving from the mirrors, known in Mughal texts as Aleppo glass, that are inlaid into the walls and on the ceiling, thus creating a shimmering effect. Such chambers were even more impressive when filled with the lighted lamps so often mentioned in contemporary texts. The central portion of this pavilion's facade is composed of five cusped marble arches supported on faceted double marble pillars whose bases are inlaid with precious stones. This and a similar pavilion erected about the same time in the Agra fort indicates the emperor's predilection for highly ornate personal chambers.

A small rectangular marble pavilion, known today as the Naulakha (Plate 108), is on the west side of the quadrangle. This exquisitely carved marble building inlaid with stones is generally considered Shah Jahan's, but it may be a later addition. Originally it was covered by a deeply curved sloping roof. Such sloping roofs {bangala) were derived in part from the indigenous tradition of Bengal, where Shah Jahan as a rebel prince had spent much time, and in part from the baldachin coverings seen in European illustrations, associated during his reign with religious and royal images. These curved roofs were first used in Mughal architecture by Shah Jahan and are associated with imperial presence. Probably this roof, like similar ones in the Agra fort, was of gilded metal (Plate 113). The west facade, overlooking the fortification walls, bears a central arched bay composed of exquisitely carved marble screens; three rectangular windows in the screen possibly served as the jharoka, the window through which the king daily presented himself to the public. In the Agra fort is a similar structure constructed about the same time; it is designated by Shah Jahan's court historian as the public viewing window. Enhancing the image of the king's daily appearances at the Naulakha are the glazed tiles illustrating angels leading jinns, Solomonic images of kingship, made of tile mosaic on the spandrels of the arches directly below the openings. This marble pavilion is situated close to the Elephant gate, whose inscription commences with lines that describe Shah Jahan as a Solomon in Grandeur.

Later, in 1645, the emperor visited the Lahore fort, inspecting a new palace that overlooked the river, and, as he did frequently, indicated changes to be made. Although this new palace is not further identified, it was probably the white marble structure today known as the Diwan-i Khass, or Private Audience Hall. Its interior consists of two concentric rectangular areas. This plan and the use of white marble, as we have seen at Ajmer, suggest that the building was intended for Shah Jahan's own use. The fort's white marble mosque, known as the Moti or Pearl mosque, is probably the product of Shah Jahan's patronage, although it is not mentioned in any contemporary source. It is less elegant than his mosque at Ajmer, but the cusped arches that meet at acanthus leaf apexes, engaged baluster columns on the east facade, and white marble are all features associated with many of Shah Jahan's buildings. The smooth lines of the interior piers, coupled with the uniformity of the cusped arches, yield a formal crystallized appearance in keeping with the official image of Shah Jahan rendered in imperial chronicles, poetry and paintings.

Agra Fort

Shah Jahan dismantled nearly all the structures that Akbar and Jahangir had built inside the Agra fort. He replaced them with white marble and stuccocovered buildings, all contained in walled quadrangles. With the exception of the mosque known today as the Moti mosque, which was not completed until 1653, Shah Jahan commenced his other structures in the Agra fort as early as 1628, his first regnal year, and completed them by the beginning of 1637, when he first used them for ceremonial purposes. As at Shah Jahan's other palaces, the buildings reserved solely for the emperor are made of white marble and overlook the river, while the others he built, for example the Moti mosque and the Public Audience Hall, are away from the waterfront. Just as at the Lahore fort, so here in the first year of his accession Shah Jahan ordered a Chehil Sutun (Plate 109) to be placed inside the courtyard of the Public Audience Hall. This flat-roofed rectangular structure, today called a Diwan-i Amm, is divided into three aisles of ten bays each. Faceted pillars support cusped arches with acanthus leaves in each apex. This is typical of those on much of Shah Jahan's architecture.

Constructed of red sandstone, this pavilion is covered with a veneer of highly burnished plaster (cbuna), giving it the appearance of white marble.

The east wall of the Audience Hall contains a raised rectangular chamber with three tri-lobed openings (Plate no) that serves as zjharoka from which the emperor presented himself to those assembled in the Chehil Sutun. Unlike the nobles' area, covered with a burnished plaster veneer, this area reserved for the emperor is constructed of marble that in many places is richly inlaid with precious stones. The lower portion of the chamber's walls is carved with a row of baluster columns, that is, bulbous looking columns that appear to grow from a pot. This column type, first used in Mughal architecture during Shah Jahan's period, was inspired by European prints owned by the Mughal emperors; in these prints, kings and religious figures are flanked by this sort of column. Since the Mughal baluster columns derive from illustrations in which they flank both royal and religious subjects, they were intended in Shah Jahan's architecture as a reference to his semi-divine nature. Inside the hall silver balustrades were set up allowing the nobility to stand according to rank. Those who held a rank lower than 200 in the numerical hierarchy designating Mughal nobility stood not in the Chehil Sutun but in the red sandstone arched galleries that lined the perimeter of the huge quadrangle. A European visitor to the Mughal court relates that each noble was ordered to embellish one bay of this surrounding gallery at his own expense. Vying with one another for recognition, they covered the entire gallery with fine brocades and carpets, creating an opulent setting and a lasting memory of the Mughal emperor's power. This, contemporary texts reveal, was the very goal of Shah Jahan, King of the World.

To the east of the Public Audience Hall is a quadrangle now called the Macchi Bhavan, for the storage of treasure. It contains a courtyard lined on three sides by two-storied arched galleries. The upper story's south projecting central bay (Plate 111) was designed as a throne niche whose appearance was enhanced by powerful imagery. It consists of four bulbous baluster columns supporting a rounded baldachin that, like the columns of the nearby Audience Hall, were intended to underscore Shah Jahan's semi-divine character. Beside these structural baluster columns, the baldachin's carving is embellished with relief representations of baluster columns and a sun medallion at the top, thus continuing the long-standing Mughal fascination with sun and light imagery. According to Lahauri, within this pavilion was Shah Jahan's golden throne, which he likens to the seventh heaven.

On the quadrangle's eastern side, overlooking the river, is a raised white marble platform. At its northern and southern ends are marble pavilions facing one another. The northern one, originally faced with a gallery of inlaid marble pillars, is the royal multi-roomed bath, or hammam. Here, in addition to bathing, private conferences were held. The Private Audience Hall (Daulat Khana-i Khass), popularly today called the Diwan-i Khass, is the pavilion at the southern end of the platform. This double-chambered structure is entered through five openings flanked by double pillars supporting cusped arches. Inside is a lengthy Persian inscription dated 1636-37 inlaid in black stone. It compares this room to the highest heavens, while the emperor himself is likened to the sun in the sky. Enhancing this celestial imagery is the ceiling that was once covered with gold and silver like the rays of the sun. Shah Jahan's private residential quarters, inside another quadrangle, stand on a plinth that overlooks the river. On the north is the octagonal tower known today as the Musamman Burj. At this site Shah Jahan demolished Jahangir's palaces, just as he had done at the Lahore fort, and in their place erected this multi-storied tower whose marble fabric is richly inlaid with precious stones. Adjoining the tower to the west is a small pavilion, known as the Shah Burj, with an exquisitely carved sunken tank in its center (Plate 112). This pavilion, decorated with inlay over most of its marble surface, is perhaps the most ornate building in the entire Agra fort. Its materials and design indicate imperial use, as does its location between the Private Audience Hall and the king's sleeping quarters.

The central pavilion on this platform is Shah Jahan's sleeping quarters, known today as the Khass Mahal, but in contemporary texts as the Aramgah, or place of rest. Flanking it on either side are two almost identical rectangular pavilions within screened enclosures. From the north one (Plate 113), Shah Jahan presented himself to the public outside the fort on the terrain below. This pavilion was surmounted by curved sloping eaves and a bangala roof that was gilded. Shah Jahan's official chronicler, Lahauri, notes that when the emperor presented himself to his subjects under this gilt roof, it appeared as if there were two suns. One was light from the morning sun reflected on the roof of this pavilion. The other, Lahauri said, was the emperor himself. Light reflected from the gold roof appeared to crown the king with a halo of the sort often depicted in contemporary paintings and described in literature. The nearly identical pavilion on the other side of the Aramgah was the living quarters of Jahan Ara, Shah Jahan's eldest and most devoted daughter. Known as the Begum Sahib, she assumed the responsibilities of the chief queen after the death of her mother, Mumtaz Mahal, in 1631. There are two small marble mosques inside the fort. Although they are not mentioned in contemporary sources, they were probably completed in the initial phases of Shah Jahan's work there. The more important of them, known today as the Nagina mosque (Plate 114), is approached from the throne chamber of the Public Audience Hall and the Macchi Bhavan, suggesting that it was built as Shah Jahan's personal chapel. Its imperial character is further corroborated by baluster columns, used only on royal buildings at this time. This mosque consists of two aisles divided into six bays by slender piers supporting cusped arches. The parapet and eaves above the central bay are curved, recalling the exterior facade of the pavilion for public presentation near the imperial sleeping chamber and emphasizing its regnal character.

In addition to the small mosques is the fort's Jamic mosque, today known as the Moti or Pearl mosque (Plate 115). It was not completed until October 1653, about five years after the imperial residence had shifted to Delhi. After Shah Jahan saw the mosque in December, 1653, he was so impressed that later he returned to show it to two of his sons. Often considered the most majestic of all Mughal mosques, it is modeled on Shah Jahan's earlier Jamic mosque in Ajmer (Plate 105). Each is constructed entirely of white marble; each is divided internally into multi-bayed aisles; and each bears lengthy Persian inscriptions executed in black marble under the eaves. The Agra mosque is, however, situated in a walled enclosure following the Mughal version of a standard fouraiwan mosque-type, while the Ajmer mosque is not walled, emphasizing direct alignment with the shrine of Mucin al-Din.

The Agra mosque has twelve-sided piers, typical of Shah Jahan's later architecture, that support cusped arches. Three high bulbous domes as well as marble chattris surmount the roof of the Agra Jamic mosque, features not present in the earlier Ajmer mosque, but inspired by Akbar's Jamic mosque at Fatehpur Sikri (Plate 25). Both of these structures reflect the tendency for exquisite yet relatively unembellished marble in Shah Jahan's private religious architecture. The Agra fort mosque, more than any other, is a perfectly balanced marriage of form, mass and scale. The similarity of the inscriptions on the Agra and Ajmer mosques is also striking. Both depict Shah Jahan as a world ruler while at the same time using paradisical and sacral imagery to describe the mosques' features. The imagery of the Agra mosque's inscription, on the other hand, is more complex, a trend that, as we shall see, is evident in other aspects of Shah Jahan's architecture as well. While some have interpreted the use of heightened paradisical imagery as evidence for Shah Jahan's interest in mysticism, it is surely an elaboration of a long-standing motif in Mughal art. Agra, the city As early as 1637 Shah Jahan expressed dissatisfaction with Agra's terrain, hence with its suitability as the imperial capital. Nevertheless, he and his favorite daughter, Jahan Ara, tried to improve the city. Soon after 1637 Shah Jahan constructed a public area (chowk) in the shape of a Baghdadi octagon in front of the fort. Its perimeter consisted of small chambers and pillared arcades. At the same time, Jahan Ara requested permission to endow a Jamic mosque close to the fort. Earlier one had been commenced near the river, but its construction was interrupted so that the Taj Mahal could be completed quickly. Some of the land for Jahan Ara's mosque was crown land, but the rest had to be purchased; in accordance with tradition, it could not be confiscated. The acquisition of this additional land must have taken some time, for, according to inscriptions preserved on the mosque's facade, it was not even commenced until 1643 not completed until 1648.

Jahan Ara's imposing Jamic mosque (Plates 116 and 117) is elevated well above ground level and in Mughal times was visible from a considerable distance. Its large prayer chamber composed mainly of red sandstone and white marble trim is surmounted by three domes embellished with narrow rows of red and white stone. The prayer chamber's east facade is pierced by five entrance arches, the central one within a high pishtaq. It recalls the elevation, although not the ornamentation, of Wazir Khan's mosque in Lahore, built in 1634 (Plate 140). Framing the pishtaq is a rectangular band of black lettering inlaid into the white marble ground, similar to the bands used on the nearby tomb of Mumtaz Mahal (Plate 131). Here the inscriptions are not Quranic but Persian encomiums, largely praising Shah Jahan and his just rule. Quranic inscriptions are inlaid in black stone above a recessed mihrab. The minbar, or pulpit, only found in Jamic mosques, is carved with an illustration of this mosque's east facade, a unique feature. The side wings are divided into double aisles of three bays each following the standard pattern of imperial Mughal congregational mosques.

Shhjahanabad

Shahjahanabad, literally the abode of Shah Jahan, was not simply a fortified palace, but an entire walled city built as the new Mughal capital. It was constructed at Delhi, the capital of many earlier Islamic dynasties in India. North of the older Mughal nucleus of Delhi, the city was built on a bluff overlooking the Jumna river next to a fortified hillock known during Jahangir's time as Nurgarh. As early as 1637 Shah Jahan lamented that Agra and Lahore provided inadequate space for the proper observance of court ceremony and processions. Two years later, in 1639, and at an auspiciously chosen moment, the foundations of Shahjahanabad were commenced. The city and palace plans were designed by Ustad Hamid and Ustad Ahmad, neither of whom lived to see the city's completion. Ghairat Khan, governor of Delhi, was appointed supervisor. Later Makramat Khan superseded Ghairat Khan, and it was under him that the bulk of the project was completed in 1648. As with most of his other architectural projects, Shah Jahan was actively involved. He played a role not only in the approval of the design, but also in the on-going construction. The emperor several times visited the site, ordered suitable changes in the plans, and rewarded the workers for their progress. While visiting the site in 1647, the emperor ordered the fort's completion within the following year. Thus two additional architects, Aqil Khan and Aqa Yusuf, were brought in to assist Makramat Khan.

The Fort and Interior Palaces

The fort was dedicated in April, 1648. Its buildings, especially the Public Audience Hall, where much of the celebration took place, were lavishly embellished with textiles embroidered with gold, silver and pearls. Large sums of money, valuable jeweled swords, elephants and other treasures were distributed to members of the royal family and the nobility; many, including Makramat Khan, the supervisor, were awarded an increase in rank. This fortified palace, today known as Delhi's Red Fort, is irregular in plan, but essentially rectangular in shape (Plate 118). Its red sandstone walls, more than 3 km in circumference, enclose nearly 125 acres of land. The fort was situated on Shahjahanabad's eastern edge, dominating the newly constructed city. On the fort's east, just beyond its walls, lay the Jumna river; beyond the walls on its remaining three sides, the nobles, high-ranking ladies and members of the royal family provided markets, mosques and gardens.

For themselves, the nobles constructed mansions that, while smaller in size, mirrored the form and function of the fort's palaces. Among the fort's gates, the south or Akbarabad gate (today called the Delhi gate) and the Lahore gate, situated centrally on the west, were the most imposing and led to the city's most important areas. The Akbarabad gate led to Shah Jahan's Jamic mosque, situated at the city's highest point, and from a major thoroughfare and market later known as Faiz bazaar. Even more important was the massive red sandstone Lahore gate. It was a focal point, the terminus of Shahjahanabad's main avenue through which a canal ran. On the other side, the Lahore gate was aligned with the palace's Public Audience Hall, in which Shah Jahan's magnificent marble throne was installed. Thus the enthroned emperor faced the heart of his newly established capital, symbolizing his role as a just ruler, who like a father was directly in touch with his subjects. This was a visual manifestation of the Mughal concept of kingship that had been established by Akbar.

Walking through the Lahore gate, one immediately enters a covered twostoried arcade, 70. meters long and 8. meters wide. On each side, it contains thirty-two arched bays that served as shops, just as they do today. The Agra fort had a similar set of shops, though not inside a covered arcade. The notion of a covered bazaar was stimulated by one Shah Jahan saw in 1646 in Peshawar. That one had been constructed by Ali Mardan Khan, then his highest-ranking noble. Impressed with this Iranian-style covered market, the king ordered that its plan be sent to Makramat Khan so that such a structure might be included in his new fort of Shahjahanabad. Although the covered bazaar is well preserved, many other parts of the fort's interior have been altered. Most significantly, walls that divided the fort's interior into a series of quadrangles or courtyards as at the Lahore and Agra forts have been eliminated. Within each of these quadrangles was one of the fort's major marble buildings. Most of these buildings, like the bazaar, remain well preserved.

The covered bazaar leads directly to a building known as the Naqqar Khana, or Drum Room. Here music announcing the arrival of the emperor and other important nobles was played. This two-storied structure in turn leads into the courtyard of the Daulat Khana-i Khass o Amm, or Public Audience Hall. Today this is known as the Diwan-i Amm. Originally both the Drum Room and Public Audience Hall stood within a courtyard enclosed on all four sides by an arcade. The Public Audience Hall closely resembles the pillared Chehil Sutun of Shah Jahan's two earlier forts in Agra and Lahore (Plate 109). Within it is Shah Jahan's jharoka (Jharoka-i Khass o Amm), the one from which he presented himself to his nobles (Plate 119). This marble throne, situated in the central bay of the east wall, is composed of a high plinth upon which are carved floral sprays and baluster columns like those on the throne niche in the Public Audience Hall of the Agra fort. At each corner of the platform is a large baluster column that supports a deeply sloping curved roof (bangala) or baldachin. The baluster columns and bangala covering, inspired by European illustrations of royalty and holy personages, explicitly symbolize Shah Jahan's role as a semi-divine world ruler.

Not only the architectural setting, but also the motifs formed by inlay in the throne itself, underscore this symbolism. The upper portion of the throne, as contemporary chroniclers relate, is "famed for its various colored stones inlaid into the walls . . . and adorned with many rare pictures."24 The emphasis on the word rare here is not hyperbole, for rectangular plaques of black marble are inlaid with rare stones, a technique known as pietra dura. These black marble plaques were imported from Italy, doubtless presented to the emperor as a special gift, while the surrounding white marble inlaid with precious stones forming the birds and flowers was Mughal work. Most of these imported pietra dura panels depict single birds and floral motifs; a few that depict lions are probably Indian works, not imported. Different from all the others, the top central panel, an Italian product, illustrates Orpheus playing his lute and wild animals seated peacefully before him. This panel's central location, directly over the emperor's head, was expressly chosen. Although the Mughals may not have known the meaning of the Orpheus theme, they used it, as earlier they had used other European forms, for their own purposes. Here the combination of Orpheus, the birds, flowers and lions symbolize the throne of Solomon, regarded as the ideal model of just Islamic kingship. The theme is not a new one, for symbols of Solomonic kingship had been seen at the Lahore fort. But here Shah Jahan, King of the World, aligned with his city and subjects, is more specifically than ever before identified as an ideal ruler.

The quadrangle containing the Public Audience Hall is organized much like those in the Lahore and Agra forts. It, too, had a quasi-public function, and was centrally located inside the fort, but away from the river front. Those buildings reserved exclusively for the emperor's private use overlooked the river, as they did at Lahore and Agra. The riverfront pavilions were situated on an elevated plinth and were constructed of white marble. In front of each royal building was a courtyard enclosed by walls on three sides; the building itself served as the courtyard's fourth wall. Thus from within the fort there was no unobstructed view of the buildings reserved for royalty. A similar arrangement earlier was seen in the Agra and Lahore forts, revealing a continuity in the concepts that stand behind the design of Shah Jahan's palace architecture. The white marble pavilions on the riverfront include imperial offices, residences for the king and his family, gardens and viewing towers. The northernmost riverfront building is the Shah Burj, or King's Tower, originally surmounted by a chattri, now missing. This pavilion is south facing and aligned with the other imperial chambers on the riverfront. Its exterior consists of five baluster columns supporting cusped arches. Above the central arch is a curved bangala roof suggesting a baldachin covering. According to contemporary sources, only the king and royal children entered this pavilion, underscoring the imperial connotations of this column and roof type. Within the bay of the central arch is a lotus-shaped pool (Plate 120), from which water flows into a channel that originally ran south through the other marble pavilions on the riverfront. The source of the palace's channel, known as the Canal of Paradise (Nahr-i Behisht), was a larger canal 48 km north on the Jumna, excavated originally in the fourteenth century and then re-opened on Shah Jahan's orders. South of the Shah Burj are two marble buildings, the bath (hammam) and the Private Audience Hall (Daulat Khana-i Khass) that were originally part of a single quadrangle. Like their counterparts at the Agra fort, these structures form a single unit. Here the most important state issues were discussed privately, particularly in the baths, where a select few could hold council in a cool environment during the summer or a heated one in the winter. A threechambered structure, the bath's floors, sunken pools and the walls' dado are made wholly of inlaid marble. The most exquisite room, the central chamber, is marked by a sunken marble tank. This and the entire flooring are inlaid with uncluttered floral and chevron patterns, suggesting a simple yet elegant sophistication of form.

The Private Audience Hall (Plate 121) is south of the bath on the same elevated marble platform. It is a rectangular building measuring 27. by 14. meters. The chaste elegance of this Private Audience Hall's exterior, marked by marble piers supporting cusped arches, stands in contrast to its ornate interior. Here the marble is embellished with gilt and floral sprays rendered in inlaid jewels. The ceiling was silver, removed by marauders in the late eighteenth century. In this hall stood Shah Jahan's famous gem-encrusted Peacock Throne (Takht-i Shahi), completed by Bebadal Khan. On the walls of the central chamber Shah Jahan had inscribed the oft-quoted verse, "If there be a paradise on earth, this is it, this is it, this is it."

Shah Jahan's residential quarters are adjacent to the Private Audience Hall. This follows the arrangement of his quarters in the Agra and Lahore forts. The Khwabgah or place of sleep, today called the Khass Mahal, is divided into three chambers with a projecting engaged octagonal tower (Burj-i Tila) off the east side that overlooks the river. The tower's arched windows served as the jbaroka-i darshan, the one from which he presented himself to the public, similar in appearance to the public viewing balcony at the Agra fort. The Canal of Paradise that commenced at the Shah Burj flows through the Khwabgah's central chamber beneath an elaborately carved marble screen (Plate 122). Above the screen is a large gilt relief representation of the scales of justice, an allusion to Shah Jahan's perception of his rule. A lengthy Persian inscription records the date work on the fort was commenced and the date the fort was formally inaugurated; it cites the cost and praises the patron, Shah Jahan; and it compares his fort to the mansions of heaven. That comparison recalls the inscription on the adjacent Private Audience Hall that relates it to paradise on earth, and it recalls the many visual allusions to paradise in Shah Jahan's buildings. Rarely are the private quarters of other emperors provided such inscriptions, as if Shah Jahan anticipated history looking back on him. South of the imperial sleeping quarter and viewing balcony were quarters reserved for the women. Among these is a pavilion known today as the Rang Mahal, properly called the Imtiyaz Mahal, that is, the Hall of Distinction. The Canal of Paradise flows through the central aisle of this building, too, and is caught in a centrally placed marble pool carved to resemble an open lotus (Plate 123). In the main chamber twelve-sided piers support cusped arches, a form used in most buildings of the Shahjahanabad fort. Inlay, gilt and polychrome originally covered the marble walls of the Rang Mahal. Thus in the Shahjahanabad palace, one of Shah Jahan's latest architectural projects, the imperial chambers, even more than those at Lahore and Agra, are elaborately embellished. This stands in striking contrast to Shah Jahan's private mosque architecture of nearly this same period.

The fort's remaining areas have been altered greatly. However, descriptions by seventeenth-century visitors indicate the functions of some of them. The fort was clearly a city within a city, not just a series of palaces. That is, all manufactured and processed products needed by the king, the court and its entourage were produced within the fort. The Frenchman Bernier relates that inside the fort were many roads that led to large halls or quadrangles containing kar khanas, workshops or centers of production for the goods required within the palace. Here everything was produced from fine paintings, jades, textiles and swords to papers, prepared foods and perfumes. It has been estimated that a total of 57,000 people lived within the walls of this palace fort, the function of each intended to serve the emperor's needs.

Shahjahanabad: the City and its Environs

The original walls of Shahjahanabad were mud. They quickly fell into disrepair, however, and so in 1653 they were replaced with more permanent walls of red sandstone. The new walls were punctuated with twenty-seven towers and eleven gates enclosing some 6,400 acres; about 400,000 people lived within them. Shahjahanabad was divided into sectors. In them leading court figures built mansions containing, like the imperial palace, residential buildings as well as all units of production needed to serve the extensive household inside. Even Dara Shukoh, the heir apparent, lived along the riverbank outside the palace.

Large bazaars further divided the city. One of the most important was situated due west of the fort's Lahore gate, corresponding with an area today known as Chandni Chowk. Texts indicate that it was composed of uniform pillared galleries on either side of a central canal. It was the prerogative of the leading court ladies to build in and around these markets. Just north of this market, Jahan Ara Begum constructed a garden known as Sahibabad, used as a serai for the richest merchants. Manucci and Bernier praised its galleries, gardens and canals as among the city's most beautiful. Along the Chandni Chowk, not far from the city's Lahore gate, Fatehpuri Begum, probably Shah Jahan's third wife, built a mosque similar to Jahan Ara's Jamic mosque in Agra. This large structure, dominating the area, was completed about the same time as most of the palace, around 1650. Nearby Sirhindi Begum, an influential woman of the court, provided a smaller red sandstone mosque. Akbarabadi Mahal, usually identified as Shah Jahan's first wife, provided a serai and an impressive mosque in a second major market in the south part of the city. The emperor used this mosque for prayer until his own was completed in 1656. It no longer exists, but nineteenth-century illustrations indicate that the mosque was similar to contemporary ones built by Fatehpuri Begum and Jahan Ara (Plate 116). This suggests that the uniformity in design for imperially sponsored mosques was intentional, signaling power throughout the city.

The two mosques Shah Jahan provided for the city, similar yet even grander than those of the court ladies, further underscore the notion of a uniform style to represent imperial presence. One was an cIdgah, completed in 1655. It was located outside the city walls, where adequate land was available for the enormous crowd that gathered for the annual celebration of the cId prayers. Today it is known as the Purani cIdgah (Old cIdgah), even though little remains of its once impressive red sandstone facade. The second and more important mosque was the Jamic mosque of Shahjahanabad (Plate 124), located inside the city a short distance from the fort.

It is today still considered the Jamic mosque of Delhi. In September 1650 Shah Jahan issued orders for the commencement of this mosque under the supervision of Allami Sacid Khan and Fazl Khan. It was completed after six years, in 1656. Shah Jahan called it the Masjid-i Jahannuma, or the World Displaying Mosque, and claimed he modeled it on Akbar's mosque at Fatehpur Sikri (Plates 24 and 2 5),34 although the interior is closer to the Agra Jamic mosque's (Plate 117). Years earlier Jahangir had proudly shown the prince Shah Jahan that mosque at Fatehpur Sikri, which clearly remained a symbol of Mughal heritage and pride. Like the Fatehpur Sikri mosque, Shah Jahan's Delhi mosque is appropriately situated on top of a rocky ridge, rendering it visible from a great distance. At the time of its construction, this mosque was the largest in the entire subcontinent; even today it is surpassed in size only by Aurangzeb's Jamic mosque in Lahore (Plate 162). The mosque is approached by steep, high stairs recalling those leading to the Fatehpur Sikri mosque (Plate 23). Its interior court and facade, too, owe considerable debt to the great mosque at Fatehpur Sikri. The prayer chamber, faced with red sandstone and extensive white marble trim, is marked by multiple entrance arches. Three bulbous marble domes crown the mosque and towering minarets flank the south and northeast ends.

Above each entrance to the prayer chamber's side wings are marble panels inlaid with a lengthy black stone Persian inscription written by the calligrapher Nur Allah Ahmad. These verses extol the magnificence of the mosque and lavish praise on Shah Jahan. One interior motif may also serve as a reference to Shah Jahan: the baluster columns that appear in recessed demi-domes on the mosque's side walls (Plate 125) and in the mihrabs. Earlier such columns had been used in places frequented exclusively by the king and his family, but here they appear on the mosque intended for Shahjahanabad's entire population. While Shah Jahan performed his prayers here, others did as well. The pillars then possibly serve as a reference to the emperor, proclaimed in the mosque's inscription as the "strengthener of the pillars of state . . . [and] the promulgator of... faith." Extensive suburbs with magnificent gardens developed outside the city walls; these elicited considerable praise from European travelers. Again the imperial women were responsible for much of this construction. Akbarabadi Mahal, noted for building a mosque and serai within the city, in 1650 also provided a magnificent walled garden, today known as Shalimar Bagh, about 8 km north of the city. Contemporary texts indicate that it was modeled on Shah Jahan's gardens in Lahore and Kashmir that are known today as the Shalimar gardens. Very little remains of this large terraced garden, which Bernier claims was Shah Jahan's country estate.

That is probably true, for the layout and baluster columns of the largest remaining pavilion suggest that it was used as a throne room.

Another outstanding garden was provided north of the walled city by Raushan Ara, Shah Jahan's youngest daughter. Concurrent with prolific building activity in the new city about 1650, she commenced this garden and her own tomb (Plate 126). The garden maintains none of its original appearance, and only the tomb among the several structures once there remains. Approached by causeways, the pavilion containing her grave is in the midst of a small tank. The uncovered central portion of the pavilion contains Raushan Ara's grave; the surrounding flat-roofed galleries have cusped arches supported on bulbous baluster columns, generally an imperial perquisite during Shah Jahan's reign. Paradoxically, however, her simple cenotaph remains open to the air, indicative of her role as God's mere slave.

Palaces for Hunting and Retreat

Hunting was sport, but it was also intended to show the emperor's prowess and skill. While hunting could take place anywhere, certain areas renowned for their excellent game were maintained as imperial reserves. At a number of these, Shah Jahan erected permanent palaces and pavilions. By far the best preserved and largest is the hunting estate at Bari. The Bari palace, not far from Babur's Lotus garden at Dholpur, was completed by 1637. Almost every year thereafter Shah Jahan hunted here for several days. Known in Mughal times as the Lai Mahal, or Red Palace, on account of its red stone fabric, the lodge is situated on the edge of a lake. Two small walled enclosures, one of them a hammam, overlook the lake's north end. A long causeway with chattris links these enclosures with a large pavilion on the lake's east. This pavilion is divided into three courtyards with a small char bagh in the middle of each. The side courtyards were used by men and women separately. The central one clearly was reserved for imperial use, and contained the very components essential to Mughal court ritual. Centrally placed on this courtyard's east wall is the emperor's jharoka or viewing balcony covered with a bangala roof (Plate 127). Surviving palaces at Rupbas and Mahal, not far from Agra, are considerably smaller than the one at Bari, but follow a similar layout, apparently one characteristic of a hunting lodge. Others, however, were less elaborate, for example, one at Sheikhupura (Plate 128) in the Punjab; it was commenced by Jahangir (Plate 68) and in 1634 the complex was partially reconstructed by Shah Jahan. The current appearance of this three-storied octagonal pavilion, situated in the center of a large tank, is the result of Shah Jahan's work. Its overall appearance is one of refined elegance, with the light stucco veneer appearing to emulate the marble surfaces of Shah Jahan's palace buildings. In 1653 Shah Jahan ordered the construction of a summer palace at Mukhlispur, about 120 km north of Delhi on the Jumna. He favored the palace and its pavilions, renaming it Faizabad. There he found respite from Delhi's blistering heat; moreover, toward the end of his reign, the palace served as a refuge when plague and cholera infested the imperial capital. Although but a shadow of its former magnificence, this summer retreat featured all the chambers necessary for Mughal court ceremony, administration and daily life.

Shah Jahan's Gardens

Shah Jahan had a life-long interest in the construction of superbly well-ordered gardens. Many of these served as the setting for major structural works, for example the tomb of Mumtaz Mahal, better known today as the Taj Mahal, or Jahangir's tomb in Lahore. Palaces also incorporated gardens into their layout. Other gardens, however, were developed independently of tombs and palaces. Structures enhanced these gardens, but they were not the reason for the gardens' existence. Most of the gardens Shah Jahan built or renovated were situated between Agra and Kabul. They thus could double as camps or as an imperial serai along the road to Kashmir and further to Kabul. In 1634 when Shah Jahan was en route from Agra to Kashmir via Lahore, he stopped at a number of gardens, including one in Ambala. Shah Jahan had constructed a garden there when he was still a prince. Upon his accession he gave the garden to Jahan Ara, his eldest and favorite daughter, and ordered that suitable buildings be erected there for the women serving as imperial wetnurses. Continuing his travels to Kashmir in 1634, Shah Jahan proceeded from Ambala to Sirhind and there pitched camp in the Bagh-i Hafiz Rakhna. It had been initially constructed by Akbar and later renewed under Jahangir. During this visit Shah Jahan ordered Diyanat Khan, the faujdar (law and order official) of Sirhind, to add several structures including private quarters, an audience hall, a viewing balcony and terraced platforms on the banks of the garden's tank.

These buildings, completed in 1635, were visited by Shah Jahan at that time. The garden, today known as the Amm Khass Bagh, was divided into four sections, one for fruit trees, another for flowers, the third for vegetables and the fourth for the royal palace. Several structures there retain the imprint of Shah Jahan's patronage. The most notable of these is a two-storied building with a curved bangala roof, a type associated with imperial structures. The climate and natural beauty of Kashmir made it the Mughal seat of rest and leisure. Shah Jahan enjoyed the many Mughal gardens there - some imperially sponsored, others built by princes and high-ranking officials. Among those he praised were the one at Avantipur constructed by Dara Shukoh, Asaf Khan's Nishat Bagh, and Nur Jahan's Bagh-i Nur Afza, all located within the Srinagar Valley. But the most impressive of all are Shah Jahan's own gardens in Kashmir, especially the world famous Shalimar garden.

Shalimar garden, situated on the edge of Dal lake in Srinagar and set against the Pir Panjal mountain range, was termed by the Frenchman Bernier the most beautiful of all the gardens. While this site long had served as a garden, its conversion into a terraced Mughal-type garden commenced in 1620, when Jahangir ordered the prince Shah Jahan to dam the stream near Shalimar. In 1634 Shah Jahan further enlarged the garden. It was extended to reach the foot of the mountains, and additional pavilions were then built. Although the older name Shalimar was never abandoned, the Mughals called their new garden the Bagh-i Faiz Bakhsh and Farah Bakhsh, reflecting its division into two parts. The lower terraces, used for imperial audiences, formed the Farah Bakhsh garden (Garden of the Bestower of Pleasure). The higher terraces nearer the mountains, intended for private use, were known as the Faiz Bakhsh (Bestower of Plenty). The garden was approached from Dal lake. According to Bernier, a tree-lined canal led to a small fore-garden that originally fronted Shalimar proper.

The entire garden is divided laterally by a wide stream that commences from the mountains behind and runs the entire length of the garden through the terraced levels. Carved water chutes enhance the effect of rapidly running water. Recessed niches for lamps were carved into the terraced walls over which cascading water fell, illuminating the water at night, for the gardens were used as much then as during the day. Pools with spouting fountains further embellish the garden. In the center of each part of the garden is a black stone pavilion (Plate 129) covered with a tiered roof. Serving as imperial seats, these pavilions stretch across the canal overlooking cascading waterfalls. In the lower garden a centrally placed black platform, serving as the imperial throne, is situated across the water between bracketed pillars. Shah Jahan's Shalimar garden epitomizes the long-standing Mughal love of architectural setting within ordered nature.

Although the most famous Shalimar garden is the one in Kashmir, another Shalimar, also known in contemporary times as the Bagh-i Faiz Bakhsh and Farah Bakhsh, was constructed by Shah Jahan in Lahore. In Mughal times, it was on the city's outskirts, though now it is well within modern Lahore. Modeled generally on Shah Jahan's Kashmir Shalimar, it is a large terraced garden, though not situated on a river bank; instead, its water supply derived from a great canal that originated considerably north of Lahore and brought water to this Mughal city. In 1641, Khalil Allah Khan was ordered to commence the garden. A year and a half later it was completed at considerable time.

This garden consists of three terraces divided laterally by a wide canal. The lowest terrace is essentially a square four-part garden of the standard Mughal type. Marble imperial residences and audience halls are located on the second terrace on the edges of the large central tank filled with spouting fountains (Plate 130). One marble platform is even located in the center of the tank and linked to each of the banks by narrow red stone bridges supported on cusped arches. Included in the garden were seats for public audiences, baths inlaid with stones, and residences for the emperor and his daughter. During Shah Jahan's time there were so many buildings that according to contemporary historians tents were not pitched when the imperial camp was in residence. When Shah Jahan visited Lahore, he often stayed here rather than at the imperial residence in the fort.

The Mausoleum for Mumtaz Mahal (the Taj Mahal)

Of all Mughal monuments, the renowned Taj Mahal (Plate 131) best represents the continuing imperial fascination with paradisical imagery. It was built as the tomb of Shah Jahan's favorite wife, Mumtaz Mahal; after his death Shah Jahan was interred there as well, as probably he had long intended. While it is often said that Shah Jahan planned to construct for himself a structure similar to the Taj Mahal in black stone across the river, there is no evidence to support this. The Taj Mahal has become one of the world's best known monuments. This domed white marble structure is situated on a high plinth at the northern end of a four-quartered garden, evoking the gardens of paradise, enclosed within walls measuring 305 by 549 meters. Outside the walls, in an area known as Mumtazabad, were living quarters for attendants, markets, serais and other structures built by local merchants and nobles.

The tomb complex and the other imperial structures of Mumtazabad were maintained by the income of thirty villages given specifically for the tomb's support. The name Taj Mahal is unknown in Mughal chronicles, but it is used by contemporary Europeans in India, suggesting that this was the tomb's popular name. In contemporary texts, it is generally called simply the Illumined Tomb (Rauza-i Munawara). Mumtaz Mahal died shortly after delivering her fourteenth child in 1631. The Mughal court was then residing in Burhanpur. Her remains were temporarily buried by the grief-stricken emperor in a spacious garden known as Zainabad on the bank of the river Tapti. Six months later her body was transported to Agra, where it was interred in land chosen for the mausoleum. This land, situated south of the Mughal city on the bank of the Jumna, had belonged to the Kachhwaha rajas since the time of Raja Man Singh and was purchased from the then current raja, Jai Singh. Although contemporary chronicles indicate Jai Singh's willing cooperation in this exchange, extant farmans (imperial commands) indicate that the final price was not settled until almost two years after the mausoleum's commencement. Jai Singh's further cooperation was insured by imperial orders issued between 1632 and 1637 demanding that he provide stone masons and carts to transport marble from the mines at Makranaj within his ancestral domain, to Agra where both the Taj Mahal and Shah Jahan's additions to the Agra fort were constructed concurrently.

Work on the mausoleum was commenced early in 1632. Inscriptional evidence indicates much of the tomb was completed by 1636. By 1643, when Shah Jahan most lavishly celebrated the cUrs ceremony for Mumtaz Mahal, the entire complex was virtually complete. Some of the numerous artists who worked on the Taj Mahal are known from contemporary sources. Makramat Khan, later associated with the supervision of Shahjahanabad, and Abd al-Karim, a master architect in Jahangir's reign and subsequently responsible for the Shah Burj in the Lahore fort completed in 1631-32, supervised the project. Amanat Khan was the chief calligrapher. No architect's name is recorded in the contemporary chronicles; however, a work by the poet Lutf Allah identifies the poet's father, Ustad Ahmad, later Shahjahanabad's architect, as the designer of Mumtaz Mahal's tomb. Shah Jahan himself doubtless played a major role in the design and execution of this tomb, as he did in his other architectural enterprises. Possibly the emperor's active role in design explains why Ustad Ahmad's name is omitted in the official chronicle written by Lahauri. The entire complex was proportionally designed according to a series of geometrically related grids, hence explaining not only the tomb's perfect balance but also that of the entire complex. The initial part of the complex is a red sandstone forecourt (chowk-i jilo khana) south of the walled garden. This area, like its counterpart at Jahangir's tomb, was intended for the imperial retinue. A magnificent red sandstone gateway, about 30 meters high and leading into the walled garden, also serves as the northern wall of the forecourt. The entrance is within a deeply recessed central arch that is surmounted by small domed chattris recalling Akbar's ceremonial entrance, the Buland Darwaza, to his Jamic mosque at Fatehpur Sikri (Plate 23). The entire central pishtaq is framed by a rectangular panel composed of black Arabic lettering inlaid into a white marble ground and dated 1647. Four chapters from the Quran comprise this text, including the final verses from a chapter entitled Daybreak that invites the faithful to enter paradise (89: 28-30). This message is similar to that given not in Quranic verse but in a Persian poem on the gateway to Akbar's tomb in nearby Sikandra (Plate j8). This parallel is not fortuitous, for the calligrapher responsible for both these gates was Abd al-Haqq Shirazi, who had been awarded the title Amanat Khan early in Shah Jahan's reign. Although Amanat Khan died about two years before the calligraphy on the gate was completed, the close stylistic similarities and the programmatic unity of all the verses on the complex suggest that his design continued to be followed.

Beyond the forecourt is a four-part garden divided into quadrants by wide waterways that resemble the streams of paradise mentioned in the Quran more than the much narrower courses at earlier Mughal tombs. They meet at a large tank in the garden's center. The garden is clearly modeled on a wellestablished concept, the garden of paradise. At the garden's northern end, not in its center, is the splendid tomb. It is flanked on the west by a red sandstone mosque surmounted by white marble domes and on the east by a nearly identical structure called in contemporary texts a guest house or mehman khana. The mosque's facade is delicately inlaid with white marble and in its spandrels are colored stones, while the interior is richly polychromed.

Mumtaz Mahal's superbly proportioned mausoleum is seated on the center of a high square marble plinth that elevates the tomb above the garden. The plinth is at the river's edge, and to compensate for the effects of flooding it rests on deeply sunk wells. At each corner of the plinth is a four-storied marble minaret recalling those used in earlier Timurid funereal architecture, for example the Gur-i Amir at Samarqand, as well as at Jahangir's tomb (Plate 103) whose construction was commenced by Shah Jahan only a few years before the Taj Mahal. Surmounted by a bulbous white dome, the tomb is essentially square in plan with corners chamfered to form a Baghdadi octagon. Each of the tomb's four faces is marked by a high central pishtaq flanked by deeply recessed arched apertures. The design is controlled and balanced, creating a unique architectural achievement that many consider one of the wonders of the world.

The Taj Mahal has often been likened to Humayun's tomb (Plates 18 and 19), a building essentially Timurid in character and designed by an architect trained in the Timurid homeland. This form, quite different from more nearly contemporary multi-tiered Mughal tombs, was probably adopted because Shah Jahan was immensely proud of his Timurid ancestry (upon his accession, remember, he adopted the very titles used by Timur). The exterior of the mausoleum is primarily white marble. Inlaid colored stones are more sparsely used here than on his palace architecture constructed at the same time. As on the gate facade, rectangular panels with black calligraphy rendering verses from the Quran are inlaid into the tomb's white surface. The play of light, reflected and absorbed by the marble surface, is a dominant decorative device. Light continues to have a metaphoric role, associated with God's presence, as it did in Jahangir's monuments. While Islam teaches that God is everywhere, nowhere would God's presence be more appropriate than in the gardens of paradise, that is, the ultimate abode of the true believer. A series of panels carved with sprays of floral motifs form dadoes along the tomb's base. Although the matching of flowers with the leaves on a single spray defies botanical identification, the flowers depicted - roses, narcissus and tulips among others - came in Persianate culture to be associated with the flowers of paradise; moreover, they are the flowers used to describe the features of the beloved in Persian mystic poetry. The beloved on the most profound level is a metaphor for God and also might refer to the beloved of the emperor, his deceased wife here entombed.

The layout of the tomb's ground floor is similar to that at Humayun's tomb, although here the surrounding chambers are linked in a more fluid fashion. As at Humayun's tomb, they are intended to represent the eight levels of paradise in Islamic cosmology. The central chamber is octagonal. In its center is a magnificent inlaid marble cenotaph marking the placement of Mumtaz Mahal's interred body in the crypt below. Shah Jahan's cenotaph, similarly embellished, is to the west of the deceased queen's. The off-center position of Shah Jahan's cenotaph in no way indicates that it was added as an afterthought. In the tomb of Ictimad al-Daula, built in 1626, his wife's cenotaph, not his, occupies the more prominent central position. Surrounding the cenotaphs of Shah Jahan and Mumtaz Mahal is a carved latticed marble screen that Shah Jahan ordered to replace the gold one designed by Bebadal Khan, his master goldsmith. Shah Jahan became worried that the gold one would be looted.

The interior, like the exterior, bears rectangular bands of Quranic verses, more than on any earlier Mughal building. Quranic passages, many of them entire chapters, are inscribed on the tomb complex. All those chosen for inclusion here have a common theme, the reward promised to believers and the fate of eternal doom that awaits non-believers on the Day of Judgment. This theme is appropriate for funereal architecture. The number of Quranic verses and their emphasis on the Day of Judgment is reinforced by the location of the mausoleum, not only at the end of the paradisical gardens but also on the platform above them.

That position matches the very location of God's throne, which, according to Islamic tradition, will be above the gardens of paradise. This is illustrated in a diagrammatic drawing that Shah Jahan owned depicting the assembled on the Day of Judgment. This drawing possibly served as a model for the design of the Taj Mahal, intended not only as a tomb for his beloved wife and himself, but also as a visual replica of the throne of God on that momentous day. Although such an interpretation may seem radical, in fact, evoking God's throne was not an innovation here.

Earlier it was a common poetic conceit and continued in contemporary writing to be used as an image for tombs, gardens, palaces and mosques. All the designers of this unique tomb were highly educated not only in mathematics, engineering and astrology, but also in literature and, of course, theology. They were thus well prepared to formulate the tomb's symbolic program as the ultimate vision of paradise on earth. That such a program would appeal to Shah

Jahan is not difficult to accept, for paradisical imagery is found in nearly every work he commissioned.

BUILDINGS OF THE CHIEF IMPERIAL PRINCESS AND THE HEIR APPARENT

Nur Jahan's impressive architectural output in Jahangir's reign may have motivated the leading ladies of Shah Jahan's court to endow many of the major buildings within cities. The foremost leading lady was Jahan Ara, entitled Begum Sahib. Although not an architectural patron of Nur Jahan's innovative stature, Jahan Ara, Shah Jahan's oldest surviving daughter and his constant companion after Mumtaz Mahal's death, provided many notable buildings. Among these, the Jamic mosque in Agra (Plate 116) and her serai and garden known as Sahibabad, were discussed earlier in their urban context. These, however, were not the only buildings she constructed.

Deeply religious, Jahan Ara wrote a biography of the Chishti saint Mucin al-Din and reputedly gave large sums to his dargah in Ajmer. She also added the white marble pillared porch before the entrance of Mucin al-Din's tomb in Ajmer. Today it is known as the Begumi Dalan, derived from her title, Begum Sahib. Jahan Ara's devotion to saints of the Chishti order is well known and even recorded on her simple white marble tombstone (Plate 167), situated in close proximity to Nizam al-Din's own tomb in Delhi. Less well known is her admiration for Mulla Shah Badakhshi of the Qadiri order and her subsequent initiation into the order. The princess built a mosque for the mulla (Plate 132) and spacious dwellings for the poor beneath Akbar's Srinagar fort on Hari Parbat hill. Both Shah Jahan, visiting the recently constructed mosque in 1651, and the French traveler Bernier had only praise for this single-aisled three-bayed structure surrounded by high enclosure walls. While the grey stone used in construction was local, the delicately carved and cusped entrance arches recall those on Shah Jahan's contemporary palace architecture. These apertures are actually extended brackets within a trabeated door frame, another feature typical of Shah Jahan's architecture. Jahan Ara was not the only member of the royal family to build for Mulla Shah. The heir apparent, Dara Shukoh, a mystic who drew from both Hindu and Muslim traditions in his quest for spiritual fulfillment, also provided buildings for his spiritual guide, Mulla Shah. On a hillside overlooking Dal lake and set against the lofty mountains, he built a school, known as Pari Mahal. Like the nearby Mughal gardens, the now ruined school is constructed on a series of terraces. It has an austere stone-faced quadrangle enclosing spacious vaulted chambers.

Religious architecture was not Jahan Ara's only concern in Kashmir. The garden and spring at Achibal were also a focus of her attention. Among the works she ordered there in 1640 were a public viewing balcony (jharoka), a bath, and living quarters. Her patronage made such an impact on the site that it came to be known as Sahibabad after Jahan Ara, who was known as the Begum Sahib. Bernier described the rushing spring, its ancillary canals, the fruit trees and the garden's buildings as exceptionally handsome. Achibal remains one of the most impressive of all Mughal sites (Plate 66), even though Jahan Ara's structures no longer survive in their original condition. A contemporary writer listing the garden and estates of Lahore includes one built by Jahan Ara, probably the garden whose gate is known as Chauburji (Plate 133). The enormous gateway, marked by towering minarets at each corner, is brick constructed with elaborate tile facing, a material common in Lahore. This gate bears an inscription dated 1646, stating that Jahan Ara first built the garden's entrance gate, but then bestowed it upon Miyan Bai, probably a high-ranking attendant. Although Miyan Bai's identity is obscure, she possessed adequate wealth to construct a mosque in Ajmer (Plate 137), built only a few years earlier, and to complete the garden herself.

SUB-IMPERIAL PATRONAGE

On the whole we have less insight into Shah Jahan's attitude toward the structures built by others than we do into Jahangir's. This is because Shah Jahan viewed the design and construction of architecture as his own special domain. Even so, Bernier observed that nobles hoping to gain Shah Jahan's favor embellished Shahjahanabad at their own expense. At least they gained the emperor's attention, for he rewarded his nobles for their architectural patronage. For example, Zafar Khan's rank was increased for the construction of a fine garden in Kashmir as well as for his diplomatic dealings with the unruly population.

Western India

Thatta

Nowhere in western India is the debt to Timurid-inspired brick construction and tile-covered surfaces more apparent than in the Jamic mosque in Thatta. This is not surprising since the rulers of Sind whom the Mughals defeated had come from Afghanistan. Persian inscriptions rendered in tile indicate that the mosque was constructed between 1644 and 1647 at Shah Jahan's order. However, since Shah Jahan was nowhere near Thatta at that time, there is little reason to believe he was personally involved in the project. Nevertheless, the unusually careful crafting of this brick structure and its magnificent profuse tilework suggest that the mosque was subsidized by the imperial coffers. The mosque may have been constructed in part to reverse the effects of a devastating storm that had swept through the city in 1637. The mosque's prayer chamber's plan and even elevation derive from older conservative Timurid-influenced structures such as the Kachpura mosque in Agra or the Akbari one in Ajmer (Plates 12 and 40). The surface and its decor, however, are modeled on local brick buildings that in turn were based on Iranian prototypes, for example, the nearby tomb built in 1601 for Mirza Jani Beg, an earlier ruler of Thatta. There are no projecting eaves or other members that articulate the building's surface as characteristic of much Indo-Islamic architecture.

Rather, deeply recessed arches pierce the brick-and-tile covered facade, producing a structure that appears to be composed of two contrasting planes. The placement and color of the inlaid tiles on the facade recall this monument's Iranian ancestry. For example, unlike tiles in contemporary Lahore, where only a single color was glazed on a tile, here multiple colors and patterns appear on a single tile. The interior is a showpiece of glazed tilework (Plate 134). The central dome is embellished with tiles arranged in a stellate pattern designed to symbolize the heavens, while the walls are covered with floral, geometric and calligraphic patterns. The three mihrabs, also unusually designed, are composed of pierced stone screens that allow the entry of light. Thus in an area where often a lamp is carved referring to the Quranic verse that likens God's presence to a lamp within a niche, here actual light enters. The use of pierced screens allowing for the entrance of light was common on Mughal funereal architecture, but unique here to a Mughal mosque. While this mosque reveals a close adherence to forms and techniques used earlier in this region, its plan and design suggest an awareness of architectural traditions beyond these local roots.

Gujarat

Under Shah Jahan, Ahmadabad continued to be the major city of Gujarat. The new buildings, both religious and secular, generally were designed in the current Mughal style, not a local idiom, as we see in monuments provided by Aczam Khan. Among his many works is the serai built in 1637-38. Aczam Khan had been appointed governor of Gujarat in 1636, a position he held for six years. The serai was located conveniently adjacent to the main entrance of the city's citadel. It has undergone alterations, although enough of the seventeenthcentury structure remains to determine its original appearance. This quadrangular building, measuring about 64 by 73 meters, is entered through a high two-storied central portal (Plate 135).

The stellate and net vaulting of the interior chambers is typically Mughal. Neither this serai nor the similar nearby Shahi Bagh palace (Plate 75) belongs to local building traditions, but rather to the Timurid-inspired Mughal tradition. The choice of such a style is hardly surprising since Aczam Khan was not only a high-ranking Mughal amir but also was extremely proud of his Iranian heritage, maintaining the customs of his homeland throughout his life. Aczam Khan was an enthusiastic builder. His structures are noted in Mathura and Jaunpur, among other places, but the greatest number is in Gujarat. These include three forts, one of which, Shahpur fort in Ranpur, still survives, but his mosques, a well and baths are known only from written references.

Rajasthan

At Ajmer during earlier Mughal reigns, building activity was largely concentrated within the dargah of Mucin al-Din Chishti or in its vicinity (Plates 40 and 41). During Shah Jahan's reign, only the emperor and his family provided buildings within the shrine, while structures erected in close proximity, provided by the religious or courtly elite, emulate the imperially sponsored buildings. For example, close to the esteemed shrine is the tomb of Khwaja Husain, the dargah's attendant early in Akbar's reign (Plate 136). The tomb, dated 1637-38, is located west of Shah Jahan's recently completed Jamic mosque, just outside the dargah's compound. Provided by Khwaja Dilawar, this tomb is constructed of a cream-colored stone. It is a less refined version of Mucin al-Din's nearby tomb, perhaps intentional since Khwaja Husain had restored the shrine's dome. In any event, Mucin al-Din's tomb was the monument to emulate, as if to imply a link with the saint. Despite Khwaja Husain's fall from favor in Akbar's reign, it is notable that he - not the many other attendants of the shiine - was honored with a monumental tomb, as if to restore him to favor.

Two mosques were built during Shah Jahan's reign on the main street leading to the dargah's entrance. Each was built by a woman, one the daughter of a renowned musician and the other by Miyan Bai, to whom Jahan Ara had given a garden in Lahore. The more impressive is Miyan Bai's mosque, constructed in 1643-44 a nd closely modeled on Shah Jahan's mosque completed some four years earlier within the nearby shrine. Five entrance arches supported on slender piers, almost identical in appearance to those on the nearby imperial mosque, form the east facade of Miyan Bai's mosque; the central mihrab (Plate 137) closely relates to those on Shah Jahan's larger mosque (Plate 106).

Mucin al-Din's house of meditation {chilla khana), where the saint resided until his death, was also a site of veneration. Located on a hi!! overlooking the Ana Sagar tank, this small dwelling was restored in 1628 by Daulat Khan, the revenue collector under Mahabat Khan, one of Shah Jahan's very highestranking nobles. The chilla khana's inscription suggests that Daulat Khan rebuilt it as a thanksgiving for the advancement he received when Mahabat Khan was appointed governor of Ajmer and given the new title Khan-i Khanan. It has been restored so frequently that its seventeenth-century appearance cannot be determined. This was a period when the relationship between Rajput princes and the Mughal court was generally harmonious. For example, the patrons of an cIdgah (Plate 138) built between December 1655 and January 1656 in Merta (Nagaur District) state that they benefited from the kindness of the Marwar maharaja, Jaswant Singh. These patrons, Farahat Khan and Misri, son of Bahadur Khan, were probably Mughal agents. Their Idgah reflects an interaction of Mughal and Rajput forms.

Mughal architectural forms are apparent in the similarity of this cIdgah to one constructed in 1628 in Patna by Saif Khan, a pre-eminent grandee of Shah Jahan's court. The Merta cIdgah simply consists of a west wall as do most mosques of this type, allowing the entire Muslim community to gather in the open area to its east. Like the Patna cIdgah, this one is marked by shallow arched mihrabs in the west wall, each surmounted by an embattlement with cusped kungura. Reflecting Rajput prototypes, however, are the proportionately large chattris that mark the north and south ends of the structure. They resemble local forms, especially chattris used in this part of India as Hindu memorials for the deceased.

Interaction between Mughals and Rajput princes, however, was not always mutually beneficial. Imperial orders (farmans) indicate that Raja Jai Singh of Amber was prohibited from using the Makrana marble quarries in his own watan jagir. They were utilized almost exclusively during the 1630s for imperial buildings. With the commencement of Shahjahanabad in 1639, the imperial monopoly over the stone quarried here probably continued until the city's inauguration in 1648. While restricting the raja's own building activities, considerable income was generated at the quarries. For example, Pahar Khan was able to found a village, well and marble mosque, now totally ruined, in conjunction with two of the quarries between i65oand 1654. He was probably a Silawat Muslim, the community traditionally associated with the lucrative Makrana marble industry.

Not everything built in Mughal times, even some works constructed in response to imperial order, reflects recent building trends. For example, the Kachehri mosque in Didwana (Nagaur District), built in 1638 by Muhammad Sharif Quraishi following royal command, reveals no awareness of contemporary trends elsewhere (Plate 139). In plan, this structure consists of three aisles of seven bays each. Slender faceted but wholly unembellished pillars, similar to those on Jahangir-period structures, support a flat roof. Generally the mosque's plan and overall appearance adhere to earlier regional types such as Nagaur's Sur-period Chowk-ki Masjid dated 1553.

North India

Lahore to Delhi

Lahore was situated strategically on the way to Kabul, Multan and Kashmir. Thus a strong imperial presence there was vital to holding important territories to the north and west. The city, according to Manrique who visited Lahore in 1641, was embellished with magnificent buildings and gardens. Imperial work at the Lahore fort as well as on the city's outskirts continued into the 1640s and, as at other major cities, stimulated similar activity by the nobility. Wazir Khan, governor of Punjab and a distinguished physician of the Mughal court, was among the active builders in Lahore. He embellished the city with many buildings, among them a residence known as baradari, probably originally within a larger garden complex. This is a two-storied flat-roofed structure surmounted by chattris. Its interior arrangement, typical since Akbar's time, consists of a central chamber surrounded by smaller ones. The baradari was built outside the city walls, in the suburbs of Lahore, though the majority of Wazir Khan's buildings were inside its walls. Wazir Khan held a great deal of land in the city near the Delhi gate. There he provided a magnificent Jamic mosque (Plate 140) as well as shops, a serai, houses and a large hammam whose income supported the mosque. The singleaisled five-bayed mosque was constructed in 1634-35 at the grave-site of an esteemed saint, Miran Badshah, whose tomb is located in the mosque's open courtyard. It is elevated on a plinth and entered through a high portal on the east whose interior chamber is a Baghdadi octagon. The spectacular painted prayer chamber of this mosque is modeled on that of the mosque of Maryam al-Zamani dated 1613, also in Lahore. Other features, however - for example, the high arched galleries surrounding the mosque's deep central courtyard - recall features of Iranian (our-aiwan mosques. Four towering minarets, one in each corner of the interior courtyard, dominate the building, an innovation at this time.

Following regional building techniques, the mosque is brick constructed and faced with tiles depicting floral sprays, arabesques and calligraphic panels, all executed in glazed, cut and inlaid tile. The tiles' colors are distinctive, different for example from the predominant blues and whites used in Multan, another tile-glazing center in the Punjab. The prayer chamber's interior as well as the central pishtaq's recessed arch bear stellate vaulting and are richly polychromed using a technique similar to that on Maryam al-Zamani's mosque (Plate 62). Tile-covered brick structures were the hallmark of sub-imperial Mughal architecture in Lahore during Shah Jahan's period and later, generally distinguishing non-imperial works from most imperial ones.

For example, garden entrances were often tile-covered, including the Gulabi Bagh gate built in 1655-56 by Mirza Sultan Beg, commander of the imperial fleet. Also beautifully tile-faced is a single-aisled three-bayed mosque provided in 1650. Commonly called the mosque of Dai Anga (a wet-nurse), inscriptions on its facade indicate it was built under the supervision of Maqbul, whom some have associated with Khwaja Maqbul, a trusted servant of Dara Shukoh.

The mosque of Maqbul, or Dai Anga as this building is still called, is irregular in plan so that it could be aligned with the pre-existing road and still face Mecca. The facade, adhering to a well-established type, is pierced by three cusped entrance arches, a feature not seen on the earlier tile-covered mosques of Lahore.

The central pishtaq (Plate 141), higher than either flanking bay, is covered with calligraphic panels and bands, floral sprays and arabesques all executed in fine tilework inlaid in mosaic-like fashion. The area between Lahore and Delhi came to be heavily traveled, necessitating the construction at this time of additional serais. Serai Dakhni and Serai Amanat Khan are the two most notable ones provided here by nobles during this period. Although uninscribed, Serai Dakhni (Mahlian Kalan, Jalandhar District) was probably constructed by a noble of considerable status. The tile ornamentation on its monumental entrance arches and the polygonal corner towers is remarkably similar to those features on Wazir Khan's Lahore mosque of 1634 (Plate 140). It suggests that either Wazir Khan, Shah Jahan's governor of the Punjab for seven years beginning in 1632, was the patron, or that the artists responsible for his mosque also designed this serai.

Serai Amanat Khan, completed in 1640-41, was built by the calligrapher of the Taj Mahal. Its tile-covered gateways are more highly refined versions of those on Serai Dakhni. Bold calligraphic bands, rendered in blue and yellow tiles, frame the facade of the serai's main structure, that is, its gates and mosque. According to the dedicatory inscription on the west gate, Amanat Khan founded the serai, designing and writing this epigraph himself. Amanat Khan retired to the serai in 1639 after the death of his brother, Afzal Khan, to whom he was deeply attached. The tomb of the famed calligrapher, who died in 1644 or 1645, is just outside the serai compound. The prime location of buildings on the Lahore-Delhi road probably explains, in part, their reflection of current taste. That is the case even with some buildings whose patrons are unknown, for example, the tomb of Hajji Jamal, known locally as the tomb of the Shagird (student) in Nakodar (Jalandhar District). This brick tomb, dated 1657, is a large square structure with engaged octagonal corner minarets, recalling the general plan of Khusrau's tomb in Allahabad. This type had been well-established earlier in Mughal architecture, but the ornamentation of this brick tomb reveals a close awareness of contemporary buildings in Lahore. For example, the colored tile mosaic (kashi kari), inlaid into patterns representing floral sprays in vases and fruit in bowls, recalls ornament on the mosque of Wazir Khan and Jahan Ara's Chauburji.

More than almost any monument of the Delhi-Lahore road, Shaikh Chilli's madrasa and tomb in Thanesar (Kurukshetra District) reveal an awareness of contemporary Mughal taste. They do not, however, simply imitate earlier buildings or ornamentation, and their refinement suggests a patron of considerable wealth and taste. The madrasa is a quadrangle constructed around an open courtyard. Each interior side of the quadrangle has nine chambers, each entered through a high arch. These deeply recessed entrances emphasize the flatness of the surface, recalling Iranian prototypes.

The quadrangular school is brick-constructed, while the tomb (Plate 142) and mosque, situated in an elevated walled compound to the south, are built of buff stone. In plan and even to some extent in elevation, the octagonal tomb continues a type seen as early as Akbar's period, for example, the tomb of Shah Quli Khan at Narnaul (Plate 43). The differences in detail, however, are considerable. While the earlier Narnaul tomb has an elaborate facade whose surface is articulated by both contrasting colors and a variety of architectural shapes, the Thanesar tomb emphasizes the uniformity of its stone and highly burnished plaster surface. The tomb's style as well as its white bulbous dome resting on an elongated drum are characteristic of Shah Jahan's time.

Muqarrab Khan's renovation at Bu Ali Qalandar's shrine in Panipat was considered sufficiently important that it was mentioned in Mughal texts. The style chosen, however, is decidedly conservative. Muqarrab Khan, a highranking officer under Jahangir, retired to serve in Shah Jahan's reign as the shrine's hereditary custodian and probably had little contact with current architectural trends. Within the shrine Muqarrab Khan built a walled enclosure around the tomb of this fourteenth-century saint. There he also built his own tomb (dated 1643-44) and a mosque.

The central chamber of his tomb is surrounded by a screened veranda (Plate 143). These stone-carved screens recall those at the late Jahangir-period tomb of Mirza Aziz Koka in the dargah of Nizam al-Din in Delhi (Plate 79), reflecting a screening type popular before Muqarrab Khan's retirement. Also conservative in form is his single-aisled mosque built into the massive enclosure walls of the complex. Muqarrab Khan amassed great wealth and is noted for building several other structures in his native town of Kairana (Muzaffarnagar District).

Delhi and the Central Plains

Despite the extensive building campaign that created Shahjahanabad, Delhi retains very few structures resulting from sub-imperial patronage in Shah Jahan's time. Those that do survive were built after Shahjahanabad was founded. Only two merit discussion, one in characteristic Mughal style, the other rather different. The Daiwali mosque, built in 1653-54, although heavily rebuilt, retains many features typical of Shah Jahan-period structures, for example, its single-aisled three-bayed plan and the entranceway crowned by cusped arches. By contrast a mosque provided by Khwaja Turab in 1652-53 was built not in a style currently in favor but in an older mode, surprising in the capital. This red sandstone mosque, no longer standing but known from old descriptions, was situated close to the Ajmer gate.

According to one European traveler, the area around Nizam al-Din's dargah infrequently was visited by members of the Mughal court during Shah Jahan's reign. Nevertheless travel near the shrine was sufficient to support the construction there of a new serai, built in 1642-43 by a daughter of Zain Khan, a high-ranking noble. The dargah figures little in contemporary writing, but Shah Jahan did visit the shrine occasionally. When there in 1634 and again in 1638 he gave large sums to the tomb and shrine. The shrine was enhanced in 1652-53 by the emperor's governor of Shahjahanabad, Khalil Allah Khan, who constructed a new veranda of red sandstone pillars around Nizam al-Din's Akbar-period tomb. These red pillars were replaced in the nineteenth century by the marble baluster-type columns that are still present. European travelers make clear that even after Shah Jahan shifted his capital to Delhi, Agra still remained the largest city in all Hindustan. They comment on the numerous serais and road markers (kos minar) seen on the journey between Delhi and Agra, but according to these travelers the road provided little else of interest. Agra, by contrast, was a splendid city, although many of the roads were too narrow and irregular. Every European comments on the magnificent mausolea of Agra, most notably the tombs of Mumtaz Mahal and Akbar (Plates 131 and 56). The Frenchman Tavernier observed that the court eunuchs (khwajasera) in particular wanted similar tombs for themselves. He noted that these wealthy eunuchs had been denied permission to go on the Hajj, so that funds could be maintained within the confines of the Mughal empire. They thus lavished expenses on themselves, among other things constructing their own fine tombs. They did this since all unexpended monies reverted to the state, thus ultimately encouraging a constant cash flow. The mausoleum of the eunuch Firuz Khan (Plate 144), located just south of Agra on the Dholpur road, is a splendid example. Firuz Khan first served under Jahangir, and under Shah Jahan was responsible for the imperial harem until his death in 1647 or 1648. While contemporary texts praise a garden he constructed on the banks of the Jhelum, today he is remembered for his red sandstone tomb situated in a walled enclosure west of a large tank. A double-storied gate leads to the domed octagonal tomb, whose shape is similar to the contemporary tomb of Shaikh Chilli in Thanesar (Plate 142). However, in contrast to the uniform, largely unembellished surface on the Thanesar tomb, the surface of Firuz Khan's tomb is covered with exquisitely carved panels of contrasting colored stones. The entrance gate also is composed of red sandstone whose surface is carved prolifically (Plate 145).

Possibly Firuz Khan's tomb was built in the 1640s, when he was at the height of his career and had amassed great wealth. But the gate's profuse ornamentation is reminiscent of that on the Kanch Mahal or the mosque of Muctamad Khan, both structures of Jahangir's reign (Plates 81-83). 1° Shah Jahan's time, there is an increasing tendency toward sleek uncluttered lines. However, as head of the harem, Firuz Khan would have had access to Shah Jahan's private quarters. There he might have seen buildings such as the Agra fort's Shah Burj, whose interiors were more profusely ornamented, though by inlaid stones, not carving. Possibly then he was inspired by the private imperial quarters familiar to him rather than by any older aesthetic. Not only eunuchs but other courtiers, too, built tombs in Agra. One tomb, known as the Chini-ka Rauza or the Tomb of China, after the profusion of tilework on its exterior, is believed to be the grave of Afzal Khan, Shah Jahan's finance minister (diwan-i kull). He died at the end of 1638. Contemporary texts note that his tomb was across the Jumna from the city of Agra. This corresponds with the location of the Chini-ka Rauza, on the banks of the Jumna between Nur Jahan's Nur Afshan garden and Ictimad al-Daula's tomb. The tomb was originally within a garden. The exterior tilework of this squareplan tomb is badly damaged, but enough remains to indicate its original character. Covering the facade are panels of floral patterns within niches that recall the color, technique and patterns of designs on the near-contemporary mosque of Wazir Khan in Lahore dated 1634. No other contemporary structure in the Agra region is embellished with tile, suggesting a link between the tomb's designer and Lahore.

Inside the tomb is a central octagonal chamber with interlinking ancillary chambers at each of the corners. The interior is magnificently painted, although it has been severely damaged (Plate 146). Quranic verses are carved in stucco along the top of the tomb's central chamber. Although no calligrapher's name is recorded, these verses were clearly executed by a master artist, probably Amanat Khan, the calligrapher of the Taj Mahal, for the interred is Amanat Khan's brother, to whom he was devoted.

Amanat Khan's name is inscribed on Agra's Shahi Madrasa mosque (Plate 147), built in 1636. He designed and signed the Quranic inscriptions on the three interior white marble mihrabs. The small single-aisled three-bayed mosque is strikingly simple in appearance. A panel of cartouche and lozenge medallions rendered in stucco frame the arched entrances in a manner similar to Humayun's Jamic mosque at Kachpura constructed over a century earlier (Plate 12).

The very high and wide entrance arches open directly to the austere interior, allowing for excellent illumination. The only ornamentation is the three marble mihrabs. The attention given to these mihrabs suggests that perhaps Amanat Khan not only designed its calligraphy but also constructed the mosque. The content of the inscriptions here, like those Amanat Khan designed for the Taj Mahal and Akbar's tomb, are cogently ordered. That is, the outer band of verses on the central mihrab are ones that invite the faithful to pray and to avoid outside temptations.

The inner verses proclaim the victory of Islam against unbelievers. Despite the common belief that Shah Jahan built the enormous red sandstone cIdgah in Agra (Plate 148), it is more likely a sub-imperial product and possibly not even of Shah Jahan's time. Little wonder that it is commonly attributed to Shah Jahan, for several features of this cIdgah are characteristic of his architecture. For example, it does not consist simply of the qibla or west wall, but has an interior chamber resembling the cIdgah that Shah Jahan erected outside the walled city of Shahjahanabad in 165 5. The cusped entrance, beneath a high cusped arch, stands within a tall central pishtaq. In the apex of the central mihrab is a radiating sun whose rays lead to delicate scrolled intersecting tracery.

This recalls similar patterns found on the vault of the Macchi Bhavan's baldachin in the nearby Agra fort and in the mihrabs of Shah Jahan's Jamic mosques in Shahjahanabad and the Agra fort. Despite these features - unique in Shah Jahan's period to imperial patronage - this building is mentioned in no text; moreover, the structure lacks epigraphs found on all of Shah Jahan's large mosques. In fact, it is possible that this cIdgah was built later, in Aurangzeb's reign, when motifs formerly used exclusively by imperial patrons became common. That possibility is further suggested by the overall sense of height, often associated with Aurangzeb's period. About 1632, the noble Rustam Khan was awarded Sambhal, the site of the earliest Mughal mosque, as his landholding.

Although he served in many regions, he continued to hold land in that vicinity for a considerable period. Most landholdings were changed about every two years. But just as earlier Raja Man Singh had held Rohtas for an extended time due to construction there, Rustam Khan's tenure of Sambhal may have been a reward for founding a new city and fort known as Moradabad, about 25 km from Sambhal.

He named this new city Rustamabad, after himself, a name Shah Jahan did not sanction. He then changed the name to Moradabad, after Prince Murad Bakhsh, one of Shah Jahan's sons. This recalls Raja Man Singh's unsuccessful attempt to name his new city in Bengal after himself. More significantly, it suggests that the founding of cities by the nobility still was subject to imperial scrutiny.

The inscription on the Moradabad Jamic mosque indicates that a noble entitled Rustam Khan built it in 1636-37 on orders from Shah Jahan. The mosque overlooks the Ganges river. It is a very large structure on a high mound where, as the inscription notes, only infidels had resided. The Moradabad Jamic mosque has undergone considerable renovation. Only by examining the original east facade beneath the extensive modern veranda are its seventeenthcentury features recognizable. The central bay appears to have been higher than the flanking side wings, typical of mosques at this time. In its original condition, the mosque was double aisled.

Moradabad soon replaced nearby Sambhal as the area's primary city. However, Sambhal remained adequately important for Rustam Khan that in 1655 he provided an Idgah there. The following year he repaired the Baburperiod Jamic mosque at Sambhal. Only twenty-five years earlier the mosque had been repaired, suggesting the continued importance of this earliest Mughal mosque.

Eastern India

Bihar

When the prince Shah Jahan rebelled against Jahangir in 1623, he eventually took Burdwan in Bengal and then established a counter-court in Rajmahal. Subsequently he spent time at Rohtas, where his son Murad Bakhsh was born. After his accession in 1628, however, he never returned to the eastern hinterlands. Instead, powerful and effective agents such as his son Prince Shah Shujac, Shaista Khan and Saif Khan were entrusted with their administration. During Shah Jahan's reign, Patna remained the primary city in Bihar Province. Saif Khan, governor there from 1628 until 1632, did much to enhance the city, paralleling his earlier largess when he was Jahangir's governor of Gujarat. He built grand mansions, though they no longer survive, and at least two religious structures. One is an cIdgah that he provided in 1628, his first year as governor of Bihar. The central bay of its qibla wall, the only wall of this cIdgah, is higher than the successively lower flanking ones. It contains a deeply recessed tri-partite mihrab (Plate 149) whose demi-dome is marked by net vaulting. Each side of the wall has an engaged octagonal turret. This feature, seen earlier in Mughal architecture of Bihar and Bengal, such as Farid Bukhari's Bihar Sharif mosque (Plate 94) and the Hajipur Jamic mosque, is derived from the region's pre-Mughal Islamic buildings.

Saif Khan also provided a theological school (madrasa) on the banks of the Ganges. Peter Mundy when visiting the school considered it a magnificent structure, apparently recognizing it as a product of the pan-Indian Mughal aesthetic. Since Saif Khan was related to the queen, Mumtaz Mahal, this building's imperial appearance is not surprising. Today, however, the complex is sadly ruined. The large five-bayed mosque mentioned by Mundy is now faced with a newer veranda, concealing its seventeenth-century character. Originally built to house over a hundred students, the madrasa complex was lined with large vaulted buildings, including a hammam. On the north side, overlooking the river, are chattris to provide shade. Next to the mosque on the west was a large double-storied entrance portal that Mundy describes as stately. Despite its date of 1629, it was still not completed in 1632, Mundy observed, although he indicates it was nevertheless in use. Foreign traders, for a fee, used the school for lodging.

Several mosques were constructed at this time along Patna's main city street paralleling the Ganges, though only a few still remain. The best preserved is the mosque of Hajji Tatar. Exquisitely carved black stone frames the three arched entrances on the east facade (Plate 150). Such black stone is used at times on Mughal structures in Bihar and Bengal, but was commonly found on the mosques of Bengal before Mughal times. It is never used on structures outside of eastern India. The arched niches flanking the entrances and the facade's ribbed engaged columns are typical of mid-seventeenth-century buildings in eastern India, for example on Habib Khan Sur's mosque built in 1638 at nearby Bihar Sharif.

The mosque's ties with local buildings are thus evident, despite its overall conformity with the prevailing Mughal aesthetic. Habib

Khan Sur held a position of great responsibility in Bihar, especially during the frequent absences of the governor. He provided several works in Bihar Sharif, all in proximity to the dargah of Sharaf al-Din Maneri (d. 1381), one of the subcontinent's most esteemed sufi saints. Among these is a refined mosque dated 1638 (Plate 151). This single-aisled three-domed mosque is modeled closely on Shaikh Farid Bukhari's nearby Jahangir-period mosque (Plate 94). It was thus almost certainly the product of a local but skilled architect. Several years later, in 1646, Habib Khan Sur constructed a tank and cIdgah near the shrine of the saint. The cIdgah is crudely constructed, revealing none of the refinements of the patron's earlier mosque, suggesting he had little role in its design. Yet another structure influenced by those in Bihar Sharif is the mosque Raja Bahroz built in Kharagpur in 1656-57. Kharagpur, today in Munger District, long had been the seat of a prominent Hindu family in Bihar. Although initially allied with the Mughals, the Kharagpur rajas were defeated by them in the late sixteenth century. One member of the family acknowledged Mughal authority and converted to Islam. He was then reinstated on the Kharagpur throne. There his successors built several mosques and many more tombs, suggesting that the newly converted Kharagpur rajas consciously attempted to create a seat that proclaimed their new religious affiliation.

The most magnificent of these is Raja Bahroz's single-aisled three-domed mosque (Plate 152). Situated just north of the raja's palace on the bank of the river Man, the mosque is elevated on a high plinth, an increasingly common feature of later Mughal mosques. Visible from a great distance, this imposing mosque is the largest one built in eastern India since Raja Man Singh's Jamic mosque of c. 1600 in Rajmahal (Plate 37). The facade of Raja Bahroz's mosque, now obscured by a modern veranda, adhered closely to the form of contemporary mosques in Bihar Sharif. Because of the sanctity held by Bihar Sharif, those mosques doubtless were known to the converted family. Yet, as if to outshine the mosques of this esteemed city, Raja Bahroz's is even more elegantly ornamented than the ones that serve as its models. Its polychromed stucco relief is more profuse than the ornamentation of any other contemporary structure in eastern India.

This is perhaps one way that these new converts manifest their enthusiasm for Islam.

While the Gangetic valley including Bihar Sharif and Patna was completely under Mughal control, the whole of south Bihar, especially the area around Rohtas, remained semi-independent until Aurangzeb's reign. Shortly after the rebel prince Shah Jahan stayed at Rohtas, this hill fort fell into the hands of an independent Hindu raja. In 1632 the Mughals regained the fort. Just four years later, in 1636, a Mughal official at the fort, Malik Wisal, indicated considerable confidence in long-term Mughal authority there by commencing his own tomb at the base of the hill, in Akbarpur (Plate 153). There he also provided a step well and garden. The tomb's inscriptions tell us that Malik Wisal undertook the construction at a time of deep sorrow in his life, although he found solace in his relationship with Ikhlas Khan, the fort's superintendent, which the inscription compares to the relationship between a son and his father. This probably reflects their difference in rank, not age. Ikhlas Khan, higher ranking, would have treated his subordinate as a son, reflecting the Mughal emperor's relation with his nobles. The tomb is a simple structure consisting of a walled rectangular enclosure entered on the north. In the center of this open courtyard is a raised platform upon which are seven graves. A stone-faced wall mosque punctuated by three mihrabs is attached to its western end. Just outside the tomb is a massive step well, rare so far east in India. Since Mughal authorities commonly were transferred from one part of the realm to another, they served as vehicles for the movement not only of style, but also, as in this case, whole new forms.

Bengal

The lasting impact of Mughal architecture was felt late in Bengal. Little had been built here in Jahangir's reign. Even at the beginning of Shah Jahan's reign, the pan-Indian Mughal aesthetic had not yet penetrated Bengal. For in the first year of Shah Jahan's reign, 1628-29, the Khondokar Tola mosque at Sherpur was completed, a building clearly inspired by the nearby Kherua mosque of 1582 (Plate 51), indicating a reliance on local building traditions. This singleaisled brick-constructed mosque was provided by Sadr Jahan, a local religious official.

Shortly after this, however, building styles began to reflect those at Mughal centers throughout India. Several monuments of this period remain in Dhaka, an important mercantile center and military outpost. An cIdgah of 1640-41 and a serai known as the Bara Katra, dated between 1643 anc^ 1646, were provided by Abd al-Qasim, the administrator there. Little remains today of his oncesplendid serai. Its multi-storied entrance gate, however, still stands and is similar to Aczam Khan's serai entrance in Ahmadabad built less than a decade earlier (Plate 135). The cIdgah was modeled closely on Saif Khan's Patna cIdgah of 1628.

The mosque inside Dhaka's Lalbagh fort, dated 1649, is typical of Shah Jahan-period architecture in Bengal (Plate 154). For example, the faceted recessed arches of the central entrance are also seen on the nearby Bara Katra and the contemporary mosques of Rajmahal. Its cusped arches and rows of recessed niches give this single-aisled three-bayed mosque a more refined quality than those in contemporary Rajmahal. In spite of its fluted domes, an eighteenth-century restoration, it remains the best example of the fully mature Mughal mosque-type of this period in Bengal. Rajmahal (Akbarnagar), not Dhaka, was the capital of Bengal between 1639 and 1659. Shah Shujac, one of Shah Jahan's sons, resided there as governor. A great deal was built at Rajmahal during his governorship. Although Shah Shujac was a prince, he was not in Shah Jahan's eyes a serious contender for the throne. He, however, aspired to kingship and was the first of Shah Jahan's sons to declare himself emperor when he believed his father was dying in 1657. His buildings in Rajmahal and elsewhere in Bengal reflect his imperial aspirations. He provided Rajmahal with a palace, although only a small portion of it remains. Europeans who visited it describe a splendid complex whose grounds were divided into a series of symmetrically arranged quadrangles, suggesting that the palace plan was similar to the design of imperial palaces at Agra and Lahore. The best preserved surviving palace building, known as the Sangi Dalan (Plate 155), has a curved bangala roof on the side that overlooks the

Ganges, recalling those at Shah Jahan's Lai Mahal in Bari and the Agra fort's windows at which the emperor presented himself to the public (Plates 113 and 127). Polished black stone pillars, essentially simple versions of those on Shah Jahan's Shalimar garden pavilion in Kashmir, support three cusped arches. Overlooking the river, this chamber was used by the prince, possibly as his private quarters or perhaps as a public viewing balcony, functions also suggested by notations on early plans made by European visitors.

Lining the main road between the palace and Raja Man Singh's earlier Jamic mosque are several mosques apparently built during this time. Above the central doorway of these brick buildings are recessed panels that once held dedicatory slabs, all of them now lost. Nevertheless, the Sirsi mosque, the Raushan mosque, and the Mahagan Toli mosque, among others, probably date to the time Shah Shujac was governor. They all bear features similar to those on the mosque Shah Shujac built immediately across from his palace. Among these features are the four corner turrets, an established Bengali form, and engaged columns flanking the central entrance. While the patrons of these Rajmahal mosques remain unknown, probably none of these small structures was built by the governor himself. Just as Bernier observed that Shah Jahan's nobles at their own expense embellished much of Shahjahanabad to gain favor with the emperor, so, too, in Rajmahal, we may imagine nobles and wealthy merchants, eager to curry favor with Shah Shujac, the governor, took upon themselves the responsibility of embellishing his capital city.

Shah Shujac not only built at his city of Rajmahal, he also capitalized on the religious significance of Gaur, the ancient citadel of the independent Bengal sultans. Even in a city such as this, with its own established architectural tradition, the Mughal style now prevailed. The focus of Gaur's sacral significance long had been the Qadam Rasul, a domed square-plan structure that had been built in 1530, well before the Mughal conquest of Bengal. Housing an impression said to be the Prophet Muhammad's footprint, the shrine's importance continued into Mughal times. Shah Shujac embellished the grounds of the Qadam Rasul. He built rest houses and a monumental gate known as the Plate 156. Lukochori Darwaza, Gaur Lukochori Darwaza (Plate 156), a three-storied gateway rendered entirely in the imperial Mughal manner, radically different from the earlier architecture of Gaur. In addition, Shah Shujac granted his spiritual mentor, Shah Nicmat Allah, funds to construct a mosque, khanqah and other buildings in Gaur's southern suburb. This area, known as Firuzpur, is today just inside the Bangladesh border. The tomb appears to be modeled on the ground floor of Ictimad al-Daula's tomb in Agra (Plate 71). The mosque is the single-aisled three-bayed type so popular in Rajmahal during this time. The proportionately small entrance arch lends a weighty quality to the mosque, reminiscent of the older Gaur style. While the mosque's exterior has no net patterning in stucco, it does appear in the central mihrab and pedentives of the interior, recalling the Raushan mosque in Rajmahal datable to the mid-seventeenth century. By providing these buildings in Gaur, Shah Shujac attempted to revive the status of the former Bengal capital and to associate his name with this revival.

BUILDINGS UNDER THE NON-MUSLIM NOBILITY

Shah Jahan, more orthodox than his predecessors, is generally depicted as considerably less tolerant of non-Muslims. His destruction of Hindu temples, for example, is often cited. However, he did so only near the beginning of his reign and then largely for political purposes, not iconoclastic ones. His destruction of the enormous temple at Orchha in 1635, for example, was an imperial response to long-term rebellion on the part of the raja Jhajar Singh. Similarly, some believe that Shah Jahan's demolition of the Mewar raja's renovations of the Chitor fort was intended as an anti-Hindu expression. It was, however, a tactical measure. The raja's renovations had not been authorized, thus breaking an older agreement. Moreover, Shah Jahan wished to insure that his long-time Mughal opponent, recently turned unwilling ally, did not develop a secure base for attack.

All the same it is notable that few significant or large-scale temples in north India date to this period, except in Bengal, an area of considerable distance from the center. Instead, most structures erected by non-Muslims are secular. They are either palaces or fortified structures built by vassal princes, largely Rajput, or they are domestic and public structures built by non-Muslim Mughal nobles in their landholdings and ancestral homes.

Among the most notable examples of the latter type are the mansion and serai of Rai Mukand Das in Narnaul. Mukand Das, a native of Narnaul, served as Shah Jahan's superintendent of grants. His multi-storied mansion is a rare example of a nobleman's house that maintains its original design without subsequent modernization. The general layout of the multi-storied interior, as well as many of the design elements, reveal an awareness of contemporary trends. The mansion is essentially organized around two small open courtyards (Plate 157).

The rooms around one were probably intended for men, those around the other for women, following a model of larger Rajput palaces in Rajasthan. Many Rajasthani princes extended older palaces or built new ones during this period. Particularly interesting are Mirza Raja Jai Singh's additions to the Kachhwaha palace at Amber. This house, more than any other in Rajasthan, continued to serve the Mughals loyally and was highly valued by them. Jai Singh ascended the throne of Amber in 1622, near the end of Jahangir's reign, and died in 1667, ten years into Aurangzeb's reign. Like his great-grandfather, Raja Man Singh, he was the most powerful non-Muslim noble in the Mughal empire. Unlike his great-grandfather, however, Jai Singh invested little money in architecture outside his ancestral domain, but built lavish additions to the Amber palace.

Work on Mirza Jai Singh's Amber palace was underway by 1637, for in that year Shah Jahan issued a decree (farman) ordering Jai Singh to cease work on his buildings there since all the marble cutters were needed for work at Agra, the imperial capital. The Amber palace probably was completed considerably later, near the end of Shah Jahan's reign or even at the beginning of Aurangzeb's reign, after the imperial demand for Makrana marble lessened. The most notable structures added by Jai Singh include the white marble temple constructed to house an image of Shila Mata brought from Bengal by Man Singh and the buildings around two courtyards north of Man Singh's zenana.

The northernmost of these two courtyards is situated on an elevated terrace above the palace's large entrance court. In its northeast corner is a pillared Audience Hall. The style of this hall makes it difficult to date. Either it was built by Raja Man Singh before his death in 1614, or early in Jai Singh's reign. Constructed of pink and cream stone, the Public Audience Hall is a rectangular pavilion supported on all four sides by two rows of columns. The resulting plan is similar to buildings constructed since Akbar's time and associated with imperial presence. The faceted pillars on the exterior have bases that recall the carving on those at the Private Audience Hall at Fatehpur Sikri, as do the brackets (Plate 32).

At the southern end of this courtyard is the Ganesh Pol, or Elephant gate (Plate 15 8), named for its painted depiction of the Hindu elephant-headed deity of auspicious beginnings on its central entrance. It serves as a monumental gateway into the palace's private quarters. This gate, with its high entrance arch, is derived in general plan and elevation from Mughal gates. However, the overall appearance is considerably lighter and more delicate than any imperial project. Further contributing to his delicate appearance are the floral sprays and arabesques painted over the entire facade. The emphasis on the structure's height, characteristic of late seventeenth-century architecture, suggests that it was built late in Jai Singh's reign. The Ganesh Pol leads to a magnificent quadrangle which more than any other part of this palace is based on Shah Jahan's palace pavilions (Plate 113). The most impressive building here is the double-storied Jai Mandir, also called the Shish Mahal (Plate 159). It is centrally positioned on the east overlooking the lake below. Its second story is covered with a curved bangala-type roof, inspired by that on Shah Jahan's public viewing balcony at the Agra fort. The use of this curved roof suggests that it was provided after Aurangzeb assumed the throne. After his accession, forms such as the baluster column and bangala roof, once reserved for imperial use, came to be more broadly based. The interior, too, resembles Shah Jahan's palace buildings. On the ground floor, the dado has carved floral sprays, more closely spaced than on imperial prototypes. The net and stellate vaulting of the ceiling is encrusted with mirrors, recalling the decor of pavilions at the Lahore fort's Shah Burj (Plate 107). This area, in front of the older women's quarters, probably served as the raja's quarters.

Although Hindu temples were constructed in various parts of India throughout Shah Jahan's reign, especially in princely Rajasthan, the only region where temple construction has been systematically studied is Bengal. As noted in the previous chapter, terracotta temples there during the Mughal period took on an increasing regional character, borrowing from both the pre-Mughal Islamic architecture of Bengal and also well-established Hindu traditions. During Shah Jahan's period, the regional temple types continued to be constructed. For example, a temple dedicated to Raghunatha at Ghurisa (Birbhum District) is dated 1639. It has a chau chala roof (a vault with four curved sides that meet at a curved central ridge), a type characteristic of Bengali architecture at this time. A second temple-type developed, called a ratna temple, which was surmounted by several spires. The Gokula-Chand temple of 1639 at Gokulnagar and the Shyam Raya temple of 1643 at Bishnupur, both in Bankura District, are of this type. Each is surmounted with a central octagonal pavilion and flanked by a spire at each of the roof's four corners. While temples such as this had virtually no impact on architectural traditions outside of Bengal after this period, they represent an important regional form, indicating the continuing evolution of Hindu architecture under Muslim rulers.

Shah Jahan's active involvement in the design and production of architecture far exceeded that of any other Mughal emperor. Themes initially established in the buildings of his predecessors were finely honed and reached maturity under Shah Jahan. For example, the long-standing notion that imperial Mughal mausolea were symbols of paradise was manifest most precisely in the Taj Mahal. More than any other ruler, Shah Jahan sought to use architecture to project the emperor's formal and semi-divine character. He did so, in part, by adapting motifs found in western art and indigenous Indian architecture, such as the baluster column and baldachin covering, giving them a unique imperial context. The charged meaning of these motifs, however, is only found in Shah Jahan's reign, for they are seen on the earliest non-imperial structures of his successor's reign. He built many more mosques than did his predecessors and used this building type to project his official image as the upholder of Islam. This is a trend which accelerates under Aurangzeb, Shah Jahan's son and successor.

Just as the symbolic content of Mughal architecture peaks under Shah Jahan, so, too, the style favored by this ruler introduces a new classicism in form and medium. Favored is white marble or burnished stucco surfaces that emulate marble. While marble had been used sparingly by Akbar and Jahangir, it dominates Shah Jahan's palace pavilions, mosques, and the most important tomb he constructed, the Taj Mahal. The marble on secular structures, most notably palace pavilions, often is elaborately inlaid with multi-colored precious stones and at times ornately carved. By contrast, the marble surface of religious buildings, especially mosques, remains considerably more austere, suggesting a division between secular and sacred arts not seen previously. Even enormous public structures, such as his Jamic mosque of Shahjahanabad, while faced primarily with red sandstone, were profusely inlaid with white marble. Shah Jahan's architectural style is deeply rooted in the buildings of his predecessors.

The tomb of Mumtaz Mahal marks a return to Humayun's Timurid tomb-type, and indeed the interest in elaborate Timurid vaulting types is heightened in Shah Jahan's reign. Trabeated pavilions, as seen in earlier Mughal reigns, grace Shah Jahan's palaces, hunting estates and gardens.

Now, however, there is an emphasis unprecedented in Mughal architecture on the structure's graceful lines and a harmonious balance among all the parts. Shah Jahan's personal involvement in architecture and city planning appears to have motivated others, especially the high-ranking women of his court, to build. While the emperor provided palace buildings and forts, these women and the nobility assumed responsibility for embellishing the cities. Nowhere is this seen more clearly than in his de novo city, Shahjahanabad, where mosques, gardens, markets, serais and mansions were provided by the aristocracy.

CONCLUSION

As in other reigns, the nobility built in the provinces and areas outside the capital. The number of surviving structures is great, reminding us that the mechanisms of Mughal economy encouraged constant spending and cash flow. Although we know less about the emperor's reaction to these buildings than we do about Jahangir's response to structures built by his nobles in the provinces, we see the strength of the elegant imperial taste promulgated by the emperor: it is widely emulated across India.

7

Aurangzeb and the Islamization of the Mughal Style

Shah Jahan's third surviving son and successor, Aurangzeb, is generally considered the last effective Mughal ruler. Under his successors the Mughal domain diminished. Even in Aurangzeb's reign, persistent warfare in the Deccan and increased factionalism among the nobility had an impact on the empire's stability. Most believe that a lack of vitality in artistic production paralleled this military and political instability. As a result, the architecture of Aurangzeb and the later Mughals has largely been ignored. It should not be. All the same, under Aurangzeb and his successors the framework of earlier architectural patronage was changed. That is, under the earlier Mughals the emperor was the model patron. The nobility generally regarded the type of structures he built and the styles he favored as the ideal to emulate. Under Aurangzeb, and especially under his successors, that changed. There was no dynamic imperial patron, so the nobility and other classes built independently of strong central direction, often employing styles and motifs that still echoed those established in Shah Jahan's reign.

HISTORICAL DEVELOPMENTS DURING AURANGZEB'S REIGN

When Shah Jahan became ill in 1657, most believed that he would not survive. This sparked a war of succession among the imperial princes with Aurangzeb emerging as victor. He first celebrated his coronation in Delhi's Shalimar garden in 1658 and again the same year in the palace of Shahjahanabad, then adding to his name the title

Alamgir (World Seizer). Although Shah Jahan recovered and lived until 1666, he remained a prisoner in the Agra fort for the rest of his life. Aurangzeb's brothers, including the former heir apparent Dara Shukoh, were executed, murdered or, in the case of Shah Shujac, pursued until death.

Until 1681, Aurangzeb maintained his residence in Delhi. Among his most pressing problems were on-going troubles with the rebel Maratha Shivaji which finally ended in victory for the Maratha. Shivaji's death in 1680 did not terminate the Maratha threat to Mughal authority, for his son Shambuji was no less a warrior than his father. It was in pursuit of him that Aurangzeb permanently left Delhi for the Deccan. The second half of Aurangzeb's reign was spent in the Deccan where Shambuji and his Maratha successors continued to plague Mughal forces until Aurangzeb's death in 1707. As a result north India received less imperial attention than previously, changing the nature of architectural patronage there.

By the end of Aurangzeb's fifty-year reign, the Mughal empire covered nearly the entire subcontinent. The only area not under Mughal control was the southernmost tip of India and a small area controlled by Afghans in the northwest. This is comparable to the situation at the end of Akbar's almost equally long reign, when the Mughal empire stretched into the Deccan. However, despite these seeming similarities, the differences were much deeper. Akbar bequeathed to his successors the foundations of a stable empire, unshakable until the early eighteenth century. By the time of Aurangzeb's death, the fabric of the empire had been weakened considerably by continuous warfare in the Deccan, by Sikh uprisings as well as by rebellion of the various houses of Rajasthan. Financially the empire was in dire straits. Aurangzeb also failed to maintain balance in the Mughal administrative system, most notably in the matters of rank (mansabdari) and landholdings. Factionalism among the nobility thus increased. Moreover, Aurangzeb's progressive inability to assimilate local elite chieftains (zamindars) into the Mughal government estranged yet another influential group. The alienation of these groups undermined a critical feature of the Mughal state. That is, Aurangzeb's predecessors had viewed themselves as fathers to their people and made their presence felt through close contact with the highest-ranking nobility, who, in turn, maintained close contact with lesser nobles, petty princes and local landholders. Aurangzeb failed to maintain this system effectively, thus essentially promoting factionalism and, by extension, rival patronage systems.

AURANGZEB'S PATRONAGE

Attitude toward Hindu construction Condemned by some as a religious zealot and praised by others as an upholder of Islam, Aurangzeb and his religious policies are among the most misunderstood of all Mughal history. There is no doubt that Aurangzeb was a devout Sunni Muslim. Highly educated, he spent his leisure reading the Quran and in prayer. Aurangzeb's court also assumed an increasingly orthodox atmosphere. For example, the practice of jharoka, the daily presentation of the emperor to his subjects, was abandoned since it was derived from the Hindu notion of darshan. Court dancing girls and musicians were released, but only ostensibly for religious reasons.

Aurangzeb did not have the resources to maintain them. More controversial than the increasing austerity of the court and its ritual is Aurangzeb's attitude toward Hindu construction, especially temples. Common belief holds that he destroyed massive numbers of Hindu temples and banned the construction of new ones. True, he did not encourage the construction of new temples, continuing a policy already in practice under his father, Shah Jahan. But when Aurangzeb did destroy temples, he did so not out of bigotry but as a political response when his authority was challenged. For example, the Keshava Deva temple in Mathura, built by the Mughal amir Raja Bir Singh and supported by imperial grants, was destroyed to retaliate for seriously disruptive Jat uprisings in the Mathura area in 1669-70.' Mughal losses were heavy. Abd al-Nabi Khan, the commandant of Mathura (faujdar) and the patron of that city's Jamic mosque (Plate 177), was among the Mughals killed. Temples in Cooch Behar were destroyed in 1661 after the local rajas there had defied Mughal authority. Those Hindus who remained loyal were rewarded, indicating that temple destruction in Cooch Behar was politically motivated, not simply an aggressive act against Hindus. The demolition of temples as Udaipur, Jodhpur and other places in Rajasthan in 1679 and 1680, too, was a response to long-term recalcitrance on the part of the ranas there. Similarly the destruction of Raja Man Singh's famous Vishvanath temple in Benares was largely to punish Hindus, especially those related to the temple's patron, who were suspected of supporting the Maratha Shivaji. Many of these temples desecrated by Aurangzeb, including the largest and most notable among them, had been built by Mughal amirs. In each case, Aurangzeb reacted to the violation of a long-established allegiance system binding emperor and nobility by destroying property maintained previously with Mughal support. Thus in a sense Aurangzeb destroyed state-endowed property, not private works.

Some of Aurangzeb's alleged destruction is more legendary than real. He is commonly accused of destroying the caves at Ellora and other sites in modern Maharashtra, but these assertions are made in considerably later sources. They are not mentioned in any contemporary Persian chronicle, where such destruction is generally reported in terms of glorious holy war (jihad). Rather, Aurangzeb's own writings praise the beauty of Ellora. Aurangzeb himself says the caves must be the work of Almighty God,7 indicating that he had an aesthetic sensitivity that many assume he lacked, in fact, a sensitivity not limited to Islamic patronized structures. Moreover, decrees (farman) testify that imperial support was provided for temples throughout Aurangzeb's reign. These orders were issued either to protect the rights of Hindu subjects or to reward service rendered by Hindus. Imperial mosques

Contemporary histories relate that Aurangzeb repaired numerous older mosques. The frequent mention of his repair and construction of mosques suggests that this was the architectural enterprise he most highly valued. He reputedly repaired more mosques than any of his predecessors, not just Mughal mosques but also those built under the Tughluq, Lodi and Deccani sultans as well. In other cases Aurangzeb was attentive to the maintenance of mosques. Once he ordered a lamp for a mosque in an old outpost, and on another occasion he wrote to his prime minister (wazir) to express dismay that the carpets and other furnishings of the palace were in better condition than those of the palace's mosque. After capturing Maratha forts, Aurangzeb often ordered the construction of a mosque. In part they were erected from religious fervor and in part they served as a symbol of Mughal conquest. These mosques were probably constructed quickly of locally available materials. Other mosques he built filled a genuine need. For example, in Bijapur city he built an cIdgah since there was no suitable one there. In the Bijapur palace he added a mosque for his personal use. To gain special merit, the emperor even laid some of the stones himself. Concerned that all remaining materials should not be used for impious purposes, Aurangzeb ordered them buried.

Shortly after his accession, Aurangzeb ordered a small marble chapel, known today as the Moti or Pearl mosque, to be constructed inside the Shahjahanabad fort (Plate 160). Shah Jahan had built no mosque inside this fort, using instead the large Jamic mosque for congregational prayers. Aurangzeb, however, wanted a mosque close to his private quarters. Five years under construction, his exquisite mosque was completed in 1662-63 a t considerable personal expense. It is enclosed by red sandstone walls that vary in thickness to compensate for the mosque's angle, necessary to orient the building toward Mecca, and at the same time to align it with the other palace buildings. Entered on the east, the compound consists of a courtyard with a recessed pool and the mosque building.

Although the mosque and its courtyard are small, about 9 by 15 meters internally, the high walls, over which nothing can be seen, emphasize the sense of compact verticality creating a sense of spatial tension, a characteristic of Aurangzeb's architecture. This is further underscored by the three bulbous domes on constricted necks, the central one rising above the others. These domes were originally gilt-covered copper that resembled gold, drawing attention to the height. They later were replaced with white marble domes, still in place. Closely modeled on the Nagina mosque (Plate 114), the prayer chamber, entered through three cusped arches, is divided into two aisles of three bays each with an ancillary corridor on the north for use by the court ladies. The marble surfaces here and on the courtyard walls (Plate 161) are more ornately rendered than those on Shah Jahan's mosques

(Plates 105, 114, 115 and 124). Here arabesque foliate forms - unique during this period to imperial palace mosques - cusped arches, and even architectural members are elegantly carved. They serve as a contrast to the much more sedate ornamentation of Shah Jahan's religious edifices. The immediate source of this ornate decor is surely Plate 161. Courtyard walls, Moti mosque, Shahjahanabad, Delhi the organic carving on Shah Jahan's later palace architecture, for example, the nearby throne of Shah Jahan's Public Audience Hall (Plate 119). Aurangzeb's Badshahi mosque (Plate 162) also reveals an ornateness and emphasis on spatial tension seen in the Moti mosque, but on a much larger scale. Adjoining the Lahore fort, the Badshahi mosque remains the largest mosque in the subcontinent. An inscription over the east entrance gate indicates that it was built in 1673-74 by Aurangzeb under the supervision of Fidai Khan Koka, the emperor's foster brother. Prior to this time Lahore had no monumental mosque capable of serving the population. Aurangzeb's construction of this mosque follows Shah Jahan's provision of large mosques close to the Agra and Delhi forts.

Situated on a raised platform, the mosque is approached by high steps. The east entrance is a large vaulted gatehouse made of red Sikri sandstone. It opens to an enormous courtyard. Built to hold 60,000 persons, the mosque served an unusual dual function of cIdgah and Jamic mosque. The prayer chamber adheres generally to the plan of Shah Jahan's Delhi mosque (Plate 124) constructed about two decades earlier, although it is considerably larger. While closely modeled on Shah Jahan-period congregational mosques, the Badshahi mosque reveals a greater sense of spatial tension in keeping with the new aesthetic established early in Aurangzeb's reign. This is achieved, in part, by the sheer scale of the complex and by the facade's arched openings that are small in comparison to the building's overall massive size. Further underscoring this spatial tension are the bulbous domes and the minarets at the compound corners that emphasize the sense of verticality.

The ornamentation, like that on Aurangzeb's Moti mosque, is less chaste than on Shah Jahan's religious buildings. Here floral designs, cusped arches and cartouche motifs are outlined with white marble inlaid into the red surface. In lieu of the smooth flowing lines that characterized ornament on Shah Jahan's mosques, a series of short curved lines form the designs, thus creating a sense of ornateness that becomes characteristic of later Mughal design.

The mosque's stucco interior relief, including baluster columns (Plate 163), is polychromed to achieve the effect of inlaid stone seen earlier in Shah Jahan's architecture. Aurangzeb's mosques built in close association with palaces - primarily those dating to the time of his father, Shah Jahan - are considerably more ornate than the mosques of Shah Jahan's reign. Their decor, however, is inspired by Shah Jahan's palace architecture. Ornateness formerly reserved for palaces is now found in mosques which to Aurangzeb were the most significant architectural type. As palaces were less important to him, he curtailed some of the earlier court ritual; for example, in his eleventh regnal year he abolished the practice oijharoka. Significantly after this time, his most elaborate mosque, the Badshahi mosque, was built.

For Aurangzeb, personal devotion and the ritual of prayer were more meaningful than courtly ritual such as the viewing of the emperor at the jharoka that had developed to bolster the semi-divine character of earlier Mughal rulers. Thus, by extension, features formerly associated with royalty were now associated with piety and Islam. Most telling is the use of the baluster column and fulsome floral forms found earlier on the marble throne in the Shahjahanabad palace's Public Audience Hall, but now found in what Aurangzeb must have considered a strictly religious realm.

By contrast to the ornateness of Aurangzeb's palace mosques is the impressive red sandstone cIdgah at Mathura (Plate 164), also certainly sponsored by Aurangzeb. This cIdgah, a mosque for the annual cId celebration, replaced the temple of Keshava Deva, destroyed in 1669-70 by Aurangzeb's command to avenge on-going insubordination by Jats. One chronicler notes that after the temple's destruction a large sum was spent on the construction of a mosque. The patron's name is not mentioned by the Mughal chronicler, but a European visiting Mathura within the decade states that it was built by Aurangzeb himself. The structure's size, 52 by 20 meters, as well as its appearance suggest imperial patronage. Situated high on a hill, the cIdgah is built on the foundations of the destroyed temple. The facade is similar to that of the contemporary Badshahi mosque. For example, all the entrances are cusped, but they have no inlaid marble work. The mosque's double-aisled multi-bayed interior also bears little ornamentation; a large recessed tri-partite central mihrab is its most striking feature.

This mosque bears considerably less ornamentation than do the other two built by Aurangzeb, but they were associated with imperial palaces. The Mathura cIdgah, however, was situated nowhere near a palace. Rather, it was built at Mathura, a city then of secondary importance, on top of a demolished temple, to remind rebel forces that non-Muslims would be tolerated only so long as Mughal authority was obeyed. Tombs Like his predecessors, Aurangzeb visited the dargahs of esteemed saints and contributed sizable sums for their maintenance, especially those of Gesu Daraz in Gulbarga, Mucin al-Din in Ajmer and Khwaja Qutb Sahib Bakhtiyar Kaki in Delhi. But unlike the earlier Mughal rulers, his attitude toward building at these shrines is ambiguous. At one point he comments that the erection of mausolea over graves is not in accordance with orthodox Islamic practice. In fact, he provided no buildings at the Ajmer or Gulbarga shrines. Yet he did order renovation of Bakhtiyar Kaki's tomb in Delhi and had a drawing made of the shrine's layout. Although the dargah dates to the thirteenth century, active Mughal patronage of it commenced under Aurangzeb, when several princes were buried there. The colored tiles with floral sprays inlaid into the west wall of the saint's tomb are probably Aurangzeb's contribution. Toward the end of his life, Aurangzeb noted that visiting graves was not acceptable in orthodox Islam. Nevertheless, the location of his own tomb indicates that he personally never lost esteem for saints. For just before he died, Aurangzeb ordered the construction of his tomb at the dargah of Shaikh Burhan al-Din in Khuldabad, meaning the Abode of Eternity, not far from Aurangabad and the Ellora caves. This area long had been the burial site of esteemed saints as well as some Deccani and Mughal princes. The emperor's open-air grave, in accordance with his final wishes, was marked by a simple stone cenotaph, although in the early twentieth century it was faced with white marble. The top was filled with earth so plants might grow. Its original simplicity followed a form used earlier at Jahan Ara's tomb (Plate 167), one that in the eighteenth century became common.

Throughout his life Aurangzeb was concerned about the maintenance of royal tombs, foreshadowing the interest in his own. He protested bitterly when land containing the grave of one of his deceased daughters was purchased. When a prince, Aurangzeb had written Shah Jahan regarding repairs that he felt were mandatory for the preservation of his mother's tomb, the Taj Mahal (Plate 131). After Shah Jahan's death, Aurangzeb ordered the governor of every province to send 2,000 rupees for the maintenance of this tomb.

Fortification, Palace and Garden Architecture

Despite his primary concern with religious building, Aurangzeb maintained a lifelong interest in secular structures. For example, he built and repaired serais, wells and bridges - structures all necessary for the welfare of the state. In addition, the construction of fortifications was well in keeping with this emperor's interests in territorial expansion. During the first few years of his reign, Aurangzeb constructed outer defensive gates before Shah Jahan's Lahore and Delhi gates of the Shahjahanabad palace. Reputedly the imprisoned Shah Jahan, upon hearing of this, wrote, "You have made the fort a bride and set a veil before her face."19 These monumental gates, composed of red sandstone, obscured Shah Jahan's ceremonial entrances into the fort and their original direct alignment with the city's main bazaar, its canal and Jahan Ara's gardens. They did, however, lend military strength to the fort. Aurangzeb also ordered an outer defensive wall (sher hajji) erected around the Agra fort. It was built in three years under the supervision of Ictibar Khan. Later in his reign, Aurangzeb ordered forts constructed during the campaign against the Afghans, and in 1705 another was built in conjunction with the campaign against the Marathas. In various Deccani cities additional fortification was provided.

In 1683 Ihtamam Khan was charged with building walls around the city of Aurangabad. These masonry walls today have virtually disappeared, but several of the original thirteen gates still exist. The Delhi gate (Plate 165), marked by a wide entrance arch and engaged polygonal turrets surmounted by a domed chattri on each side, follows an older regional form, not one characteristic of contemporary Mughal structures elsewhere in India.

Aurangzeb's concerns extended beyond the military security of a locale. In Delhi he banned any construction that did not have his prior approval and went so far as to dismantle a structure erected by a lady of the court without his permission. Even after his permanent departure from Shahjahanabad, Aurangzeb ordered Aqil Khan, governor (subadar) of Delhi, to maintain its gardens, palaces and serais. The emperor ordered reports on their condition and had drawings of them prepared. The rooms of the palace were cleaned, locked and the carpets stored to prevent damage.

Once Aurangzeb had moved permanently to the Deccan he did not reside in older palaces of the Deccani sultans. He had new ones built, including the palace at Aurangabad. In addition, Aurangzeb repaired the residences of others. For example, in 1685 he ordered renovations to an earlier palace near Ahmadnagar. Aurangzeb, like his predecessors, clearly felt that palatial residences were a necessity for a king. He objected, however, to the misuse of palatial settings, stating that dissipated rulers spent inordinate time in the pleasures of a palace. Like his predecessors, Aurangzeb loved garden settings and rewarded gardeners for good work. He built only a few, mostly when still a prince, including a garden and tank in the vicinity of Bijapur as well as one in Ujjain. Aurangzeb, again like his predecessors, was taken by the beauty of Kashmir and its gardens, although he decreed in the sixth year of his reign that no king should visit there unless on military or administrative business; the pursuit of pleasure, he believed, was inadequate reason for going to Kashmir.

During Aurangzeb's reign, most members of the imperial family were more devoted to the patronage of literature and religion than to the construction of grand edifices and gardens. However, several notable tombs and mosques were constructed by the royal family, including the Bibi-ka Maqbara, or Tomb of the Queen, built in Aurangabad (Plate 166). This monumental white tomb, completed in 1660-61, was built for Rabica Daurani, Aurangzeb's wife, also known as Dilrus Banu, who died in 1657. At Aurangzeb's command, their eldest son, Prince Aczam Shah, built this tomb closely modeled on the Taj Mahal (Plate 131).

Persian inscriptions on the tomb's south entrance gate give the names of the architect, Ata Allah, the supervisor, Aqa Abu al-Qasim Beg, and the engineer, Haspat Rai. Other contemporary documents indicate that the supervisor and others in responsible positions were at the site continuously during this time, Plate 166. Tomb of Rabica Daurani, also known as the Bibi-ka Maqbara, Aurangabad thus resulting in the tomb's completion within four years of the queen's death. The architect, Ata Allah, was the son of Ustad Ahmad, architect of the Taj Mahal and Shahjahanabad fort. This does much to explain the tomb's close resemblance to the Taj. Rabica Daurani's tomb is situated in the middle of a char bagb, typical of most imperial Mughal tombs (Plate 19). Approximately half the size of the Taj Mahal, this tomb is different in notable ways. At Rabica Daurani's tomb there is an emphasis on the building's verticality, not the harmonious balance of proportions as at the Taj. This rapid shift in spatial arrangement occurring shortly after Aurangzeb's accession triggers innovative directions for eighteenth- and nineteenth-century architecture.

While marble is the predominant building material for the Taj, burnished stucco covers the Bibi-ka Maqbara and its adjacent mosques. Only on the tomb's interior is marble used. Unlike the Taj, Rabica Daurani's tomb has no inlaid work. Instead, the tomb's ornate surfaces are carved with panels of intricate floral sprays. Although the mausoleum itself is not painted, rich polychrome decorates the elaborate net vaulting of the entrance gates. The carving, polychrome and the emphasis on the tomb's verticality are characteristic of late seventeenth- and eighteenth-century tombs and elaborate dwellings. By contrast the two mosques inside the tomb's compound bear little elaborate ornament, recalling more the private mosques of Shah Jahan (Plates 105, 106,

114 and 115) than Aurangzeb's contemporary Moti mosque in the Shahjahanabad fort (Plates 160 and 161). Rabica Daurani's tomb is the last imperial Mughal tomb built in the tradition of monumental covered mausolea set in a char bagh. Raushan Ara's structural tomb had been built in Shah Jahan's time with an opening in the roof exposing the cenotaph to the elements. The taste for simple graves uncovered by any superstructure, hence in accordance with orthodox practice, increases throughout the late seventeenth and eighteenth centuries. Aurangzeb's own grave was of this type. So was the one built by Shah Jahan's devoted daughter, Jahan Ara, for many years the most powerful woman in the empire. She is buried in Delhi at Nizam al-Din's dargab, not far from the tomb of the esteemed saint. Enclosed by beautifully carved marble screens, her white marble cenotaph serves as a planter (Plate 167). It is marked by a marble slab carved with a verse demonstrating her humble piety and devotion to the Chishti saints. Forgiven by Aurangzeb after Shah Jahan's death, Jahan Ara regained her position as a significant cultural force. She lived the rest of her life in Delhi writing a biography of Mucin al-Din Chishti and died in 1681.

Simple graves and cenotaphs now mark the burial sites of imperial princesses. Among them was Zeb al-Nisa, who died in 1702, the oldest of Aurangzeb's children and a beneficent patron of poetry and literature, and Zinat al-Nisa, Aurangzeb's second daughter, who was noted for her piety and charity. Each was buried in separate grave sites near or in Shahjahanabad. Their tombs, each destroyed, had simple graves marked by a cenotaph and headstone carved with Quranic verses similar to those at Jahan Ara's grave. In conjunction with her simple tomb, dated 1711-12, Zinat al-Nisa constructed a large mosque in Shahjahanabad (Plate 168). Located due south of the palace and overlooking the Jumna river, it was built on a high plinth. The location and size of this mosque, along with those constructed by earlier ladies of the court (cf. Plate 116), underscore the status of the patron. The mosque's red and white striped domes and high centralpishtaq, among other features, are modeled closely on Shah Jahan's Jamic mosque (Plate 124). Typical of Aurangzeb's architecture, however, are the tightly constricted necks of the domes and cusped entrance arches supported on slender piers, emphasizing the structure's height.

Western India

Ajmer and Vicinity

Aurangzeb paid homage on several occasions at the dargah of Mucin al-Din Chishti and continued his predecessors' practice of generously distributing alms there, but added no structures to the shrine. One, however, was built there during his reign. Shaikh Ala al-Din, who until his death was in charge of the shrine, built his tomb in 1659-60 just outside the shrine on its west. Known as the Sola Khamba (Plate 169), this rectangular marble building derives its name from the sixteen columns that support cusped entrance arches. Its three mihrabs are closely modeled on the central one of Shah Jahan's marble mosque immediately to the tomb's east (Plate 106), again underscoring the impact of this mosque on the subsequent architecture of Ajmer. The Sola Khamba, however, introduces cusping, not seen on Shah Jahan's public architecture in Ajmer. This and the increasing number of columns supporting these cusped arches reveal an elaboration of form common to Aurangzeb-penod works. Another structure bearing the impact of Shah Jahan's Jamic mosque is one provided in 1692-93 close to the dargah by Sayyid Muhammad, an attendant (mutawali) at the saint's tomb. Unlike the Shah Jahan-period mosques on the same street, this small single-aisled mosque (Plate 170) is not on ground level, but located above the shops, following contemporary practice in Delhi, suggesting the scarcity of open land. It bears several inscriptions, including a lengthy Persian one inlaid with black stones into a white marble ground. This elegant inscription, designed by Naji, a well-known poet and calhgrapher of Aurangzeb's time, is similar in appearance, location and design to the one on Shahjahan's mosque at the shrine (Plate 105).

The mosque itself is a simple yet elegant structure whose facade consists of three cusped arches supported on polygonal columns, a form typical of Aurangzeb-period architecture in Ajmer. Ranking in quality with imperial works is an exquisite white marble tomb believed to be that of the wife of Abd Allah Khan (Plate 171). He was the father of the famous Sayyid brothers, who after Aurangzeb's reign were known as the king-makers. Her tomb is modeled closely on those built for imperial princesses, for example, the tomb of Jahan Ara (Plate 167). Like that tomb its cenotaph, surmounted by finely carved screens, is left open to the air.

Today it bears no inscription, but a plaque dated 1702-03, now embedded in the wall of Abd Allah's nearby tomb, refers to the death of a lady and probably once belonged to the white marble tomb. Other inscriptions indicate that a mosque and garden were built in conjunction with the tomb between 1702 and 1704. Later in 1710 Abd Allah's tomb in the same compound was built by his sons. Even structures outside of Ajmer reveal an awareness of current Mughal idiom. Among these is the Jamic mosque in Merta, about 100 km north of Ajmer (Plate 172). It was built by Hajji Muhammad Sultan, the son of a local religious official, in 1665. The mosque, constructed in local red stone, is situated on a high plinth above shops. Very tall minarets, visible from a considerable distance, advertise its presence as do its three bulbous domes. The central one has a tightly constricted neck and is faced with alternating red and white stripes like those on Shah Jahan's Jamic mosque in Shahjahanabad built about a decade earlier (Plate 124). The overall effect is an emphasis on verticality and a clear sense of spatial tension such as we see a few years earlier at the Bibi-ka Maqbara at Aurangabad and the Jamic mosque in Mathura, both products of 1660-61 (Plates 166 and 177).

Abmadabad

Aurangzeb, who was born in Ahmadabad, ordered repairs to both Mughal and pre-Mughal buildings there, revealing his interest in the maintenance of older structures, especially mosques. New buildings were constructed on behalf of the Mughal administration by Muhammad Aczam Shah, a governor of Gujarat. He erected palace buildings on the Sabarmati river, but no trace of them remains. Also at this time Mughal governors, amirs and religious officials erected religious structures to enhance Mughal presence and at the same time to immortalize their own names. Among these are the mosque and tomb of Sardar Khan, a noble who had gained Aurangzeb's favor during the war of succession, when he prevented Dara Shukoh from entering Ahmadabad. Sardar Khan's tomb (Plate 173) and its adjacent mosque bear features typical of contemporary Mughal architecture, for example, bulbous domes with constricted necks (Plate 168).

The mosque's plan, a single-aisled three-bayed form, is common in contemporary Mughal architecture elsewhere but not typical of architecture in Gujarat. The mosque and tomb, however, also display many local features, especially the tomb's screened walls that are modeled on those of the more famous tomb of Shaikh Ahmad Khattu at nearby Sarkhej. The tomb, based largely on local tradition, is domed, unlike the characteristic royal tombs of Aurangzeb's time. Other notable monuments of this time, for example the Hadayat Bakhsh madrasa (1690-1700) and the mosque, madrasa and tomb of Nawab Shujacat Khan (1695), also combine local idiom with standard Mughal vocabulary. Thus in Gujarat throughout the Mughal period most buildings, reign. The tomb's interior arrangement, with a central chamber surrounded by eight smaller ones, is also found throughout the subcontinent at this time. The interior dome (Plate 174), like that of Wazir Khan's nearby mosque, is magnificently polychromed. The tomb is thus a regional version of a general type popular throughout Mughal India.

During the time that Aurangzeb resided in Shahjahanabad, revenue from Kashmir soared, and new serais were needed to support the increased trade. Among these a serai on the road between Lahore and Delhi in Ludhiana District was built in 1669-70 by Lashkar Khan, a general in the military. This serai, known as Serai Lashkar Khan, is a square enclosure entered through massive gates similar to those of Serai Amanat Khan but even larger than the gates of that earlier one. This serai is brick constructed, but devoid of the usual tile ornamentation. Also serving the needs of travelers on this route were deep step-wells (baolis). Shortly after Aurangzeb's accession one was excavated at Mahem in Rohtak District. It was built by Saidu, a mace-bearer in the imperial court. Three stages of steps descend to this extremely deep well. On the second level an arched opening overlooks the circular well beyond and serves as a pavilion to catch cooling breezes. In the foothills north of Delhi, Fidai Khan Koka, the supervisor of the Badshahi mosque in Lahore, built a terraced garden at Pinjaur around a natural spring. Although the exact date of this summer retreat is not known, its pavilions with cusped arches supported on baluster columns, reserved in Shah Jahan's reign solely for buildings intended for the emperor and his immediate family, suggest that the garden was built in Aurangzeb's time. By now such strictures had loosened (Plate 178), probably because Aurangzeb had little desire to associate himself with symbols suggesting a semi-divine status.

Delhi to Mathura

Delhi remained a leading center of culture and learning even after 1681, when Aurangzeb permanently shifted the empire's administration to the Deccan. In Delhi Jahan Ara presided as a patron of sufic learning, and the princess Zeb al-Nisa provided generous patronage for literary figures, theologians, calligraphers and others. Aqil Khan, the governor of Delhi from 1680 to 1696, was a poet and historian, instrumental in maintaining Delhi as a vital cultural center. Delhi's small but wealthy leisure class not only patronized poets and other cultural figures but also built gardens, markets, mosques and magnificent mansions. Among these works was a large caravan serai known as Bakhtawar Nagar, built in 1662 by Bakhtawar Khan outside the city walls.

Although Delhi suffered three major fires in 1662, it was mostly the poor, living in crowded conditions, who were affected, while the spacious mansions of the wealthy, modeled on the imperial residence, survived well. New mansions were built during Aurangzeb's reign, while those erected earlier under Shah Jahan also continued to be used, but not necessarily by the same family. Once a noble died his house became state property and was bestowed upon the next inhabitant by the ruler himself. For example, after the leading noble Ali Mardan Khan died, Aurangzeb awarded his mansion to Jahan Ara.

There was little architectural activity far south of the walled city. True, doors were donated at the tomb of Amir Khusrau in the dargah of Nizam al-Din Auliya during Aurangzeb's reign. But most building was concentrated close to the western part of the walled city, in proximity to its Lahore and Ajmer gates. The mosque and tomb of Nasir Daulat, built in 1658 but no longer surviving, were just outside the city's now-demolished Lahore gate. Inside the city walls, between the Lahore and Ajmer gates, the Anarwali mosque was built by a pious lady. This mosque as well as the mosque of Khalil, just inside the Ajmer gate, still stand although they have been considerably remodeled. The mosque of Khalil, dated 1698-99, is a single-aisled three-domed structure situated on a high elevated plinth with shops beneath. Small mosques such as this, built above shops and towering over the street below, become typical of much mosque architecture from Aurangzeb's period on. Just outside the city walls other buildings were erected. The dargah of Hasan Rasul Nama was established in 1691, some ten years after Aurangzeb had departed from Delhi. A gateway and other additions were made in 1671 at the Tughluq-period Qadam Sharif shrine. This construction, clustered to the city's west and away from the river, was probably on newly developed land, since no earlier Mughal structures were there.

Among these buildings the complex containing the tomb, mosque and madrasa of Ghazi al-Din, immediately beyond the Ajmer gate, is the largest and best preserved. Such a large edifice on this major thoroughfare underscores the notion that this portion of the city had been undeveloped. The school, today housing Zakir Husain College, has been one of Delhi's leading educational institutions since its establishment and is the oldest continuing school in the city. The patron, Mir Shihab al-Din, came to India from Bukhara in 1674. In 1683 he received the title Ghazi al-Din Khan Bahadur for his successful campaigns in the Deccan. Sometime after this date and before his death in 1709 he built his complex in Delhi.

The school is a quadrangular building apparently influenced by traditional Iranian iour-aiwan structures, reflecting the patron's Bukhara origins. The main gate is a massive red sandstone portal, leading to a courtyard on three sides of which are double-storied galleries whose vaulted chambers serve as living quarters. On the east are projecting oriel windows surmounted by curved sloping roofs (Plate 175) inspired by the bangala style superstructures of Shah Jahan's palace architecture (Plate 113). The mosque (Plate 176), on the west, is not an extension of the wall, as is usual in Iranian madrasas, but is freestanding. It resembles Zinat al-Nisa's mosque on the river bank built about the same time (Plate 168). The emphasis on verticality is apparent here as well, and devices similar to those at Zinat al-Nisa's mosque are used to achieve this effect. Its three bulbous domes, originally faced with strips of red and black stone, sit on very high constricted necks.

Ghazi al-Din's simple grave, adjacent to the mosque, is enclosed by marble screened walls but has no superstructure to protect it from the elements. This is similar to the type established for the royal family during this period. The royal court rarely was in Agra, for until 1666 its fort served as Shah Jahan's prison. Thus there was little notable construction here during Aurangzeb's reign. But in nearby Mathura a Jamic mosque (Plate 177) of some significance was constructed in 1660-61 by Abd al-Nabi Khan, the faujdar of the city who later was killed during Jat uprisings. It was in part his death that prompted Aurangzeb to demolish the huge Hindu temple there and to erect in its place the cIdgah discussed earlier (Plate 164). The Jamic mosque, the earliest notable non-imperial mosque of Aurangzeb's reign, is situated on a high plinth in the center of the city. It echoes the verticality and spatial arrangements seen in the contemporary Bibi-ka Maqbara, built by one of Aurangzeb's sons. The mosque's high plinth, tile-covered gateway and towering minarets appear to diminish the small prayer chamber, thus emphasizing the structure's vertical nature in conformity with the imperial style of the time. The courtyard's rectangular pavilions surmounted by bangala roofs (Plate 178) also adhere to forms seen in imperial architecture of the period. During Shah Jahan's reign such pavilions had been associated with imperial presence, but very early in Aurangzeb's reign they lost this meaning and are often found on structures built by non-imperial patrons. The rapid adoption of motifs formerly restricted to imperial use appears to be related to Aurangzeb's relative disinterest in forms that originally had been associated solely with royalty. It thus appears that there was little centralized direction for artists and patrons, allowing them greater freedom in the use of forms previously charged with exclusive meaning.

The bangala roof is also seen early in Aurangzeb's reign on the entrance portal of another sub-imperial mosque. This impressive stone Jamic mosque (Plate 179) was provided in 1664-65 by Muctamad Khan, commander (qalcadar) of the Gwalior fort. Located at the fort's base, the stone-faced mosque recalls the plan and elevation of the slightly earlier Jamic mosque at Mathura (Plate 177), but not its ornamentation. Although mentioned in no contemporary text, the inscription over the prayer chamber indicates that Muctamad Khan destroyed a temple associated with the Hindu sage for whom Gwalior was named and in its place constructed the mosque. Inscriptions of this nature during the Mughal period are not common but a few similar ones can be cited: there is one on the Patthar-ki Masjid in Patna. In both cases, however, the destruction stems from no recorded imperial order.

Benares

Tradition still perpetuated in Benares blames Aurangzeb for destroying many of that city's temples, even though imperial documents indicate that he long had been concerned with maintaining harmony between the Hindu and Muslim communities there. In fact, there is evidence only for his demolition in 1669 of the Vishvanath temple, built almost certainly by Raja Man Singh during Akbar's reign. Aurangzeb's demolition of the temple was motivated by specific events, not bigotry. One was the rebellion of zamindars in Benares, some of whom may have assisted Maratha Shivaji in his escape from Mughal authorities. It widely was believed that his escape initially had been facilitated in Agra a few years earlier by Jai Singh, Raja Man Singh's great-grandson, thus explaining the destruction of this particular temple. Another was reaction to recent reports of obstructive Brahmins interfering with Islamic teaching. The demolition of the Vishvanath temple, then, was intended as a warning to anti- Mughal factions, in this case troublesome zamindars and Hindu religious leaders who wielded great influence in this city. Moreover, the temple had been built by a Mughal amir, some of whose successors recently had abetted the emperor's most persistent enemy.

The ruined temple then was used as the qibla wall of the large mosque constructed in its place, underscoring Aurangzeb's displeasure with Benares' politically and religiously active Hindu elite. Today this mosque (Plate 180), whose facade is modeled partially on the entrance into the Taj Mahal, is known as the Gyanvapi mosque. The name of the patron is not known and its construction is cited in no Mughal text. Tradition holds that another mosque of Aurangzeb's reign was constructed on the site of a destroyed temple, although no evidence supports this. Today known as the Jamic or Aurangzeb's mosque (Plate 181), it dominates the famous Benares riverfront. Located at the top of the very steep steps leading to Panchganga Ghat, the mosque was even more visible and clearly symbolized a powerful Muslim presence in this holiest of all Hindu cities when its very tall minarets still stood. Inscriptions of later date record repairs to the mosque, but none reveals its original construction date or patron. Yet it is characteristic of Aurangzeb-period architecture. The proportionately tall height of this threedomed mosque and its now-missing minarets emphasized the structure's verticality. Unusually refined, the stone-faced mosque is a single-aisled threebayed type usually associated with private, not imperial, patronage. Its brown stone facing is delicately carved with niches and arches. The finely rendered stucco, stone and polychrome work suggest a patron of fine taste and great wealth.

Eastern India

Bihar

The flourishing trade of Bihar and the relatively calm political climate made conditions here ripe for building activity. For example, Dacud Khan Quraishi, Plate 181. Jamic mosque, also known as Aurangzeb's mosque, Benares governor of Bihar from 16 5 9 to 1664, provided structures himself and by example encouraged others to do so as well. He ended the last significant source of on-going opposition to Mughal authority in Bihar by conquering Palamau, inhabited by Chero rajas. Inside the Cheros' seventeenth-century fort, whose elegant gates had been built during Shah Jahan's reign, Dacud Khan constructed a brick mosque in 1660. A single-aisled three-bayed structure surmounted by three low rounded domes, this mosque lacks the sophistication of the fort itself and other contemporary projects, possibly a result of its hasty construction. Nevertheless, it served as a powerful indicator of Mughal presence in this newly conquered territory.

Dacud Khan's serai (Plate 182), in contrast to his Palamau mosque, is finely built. He constructed it with the emperor's permission for the protection of travelers in a robber infested area. This brick serai is in the town still called Daudnagar (Aurangabad District). It remains today the best-preserved example of seventeenth-century secular architecture in Bihar. The serai is entered on the east and west sides by arched portals with chamfered sides, recalling earlier Mughal portals at the Ajmer fort built around 1570. Details, however, such as the stone pillars and cusped arches recalling those on the Sangi Dalan built about a decade earlier in Rajmahal have a more contemporary air. So do the small domed chattris atop the portal roof that probably derive from those on the gateway into the Taj Mahal complex.

A second example of secular architecture was built in Bihar Sharif for Shaikha, a member of the Afghan Ghakkar tribe, many of whom had lived in Bihar since the early sixteenth century. Called the Nauratan (Plate 183), it was built in 1688-89. The main building in the Nauratan compound is a singlestoried flat-roofed square-plan structure. The interior arrangement, however, is familiar throughout Mughal India (Plate 74). That is, a central domed chamber is surrounded by eight ancillary vaulted rooms, a total of nine chambers, the source of the building's name, Nauratan, or nine jewels. Beside this building, others in the compound include a tank with underground chambers, a mosque and domestic quarters, some of which are still extant. The building, today a school, provides a rare view of the predilections of the upper class in the late seventeenth century.

Throughout Aurangzeb's reign, buildings were constructed in Patna, the capital of Bihar. Only one of them, however, is credited, at least by its inscription, to Aurangzeb himself. That is the Rauza mosque dated 1667-68. It is, in fact, the only Mughal building in all Bihar that claims imperial Mughal sponsorship. This simple single-aisled three-bayed mosque was built in conjunction with the graves of two saints. It adheres closely to the form established by the early seventeenth-century mosque of Mirza Macsum. In spite of the brief inscription, the Rauza mosque's unpretentious style and plan suggest that it was built in response to a general order encouraging the construction of mosques, but was not actually paid for by the ruler. Aurangzeb was never in Patna, nor did he construct mosques at sites with which he did not have a strong personal interest. Unlike the simple Rauza mosque, one constructed nearly twenty years later by Khwaja Amber, in the service of the empire's highest-ranking noble, Shaista Khan, features the most elaborate stucco work on any Patna structure of this time. However, the decor of this mosque, dated 1688-89, is considerably more subdued than contemporary ornament elsewhere. Here only the interior of the domes is intricately embellished (Plate 184), recalling similar designs on the Benares Jamic mosque or the Bibi-ka Maqbara in Aurangabad built at the beginning of Aurangzeb's reign. This contrasts with the more characteristically austere architecture of Mughal Bihar, generally unembellished by contrast with contemporary architecture in the Mughal Bengal capitals of Dhaka or Rajmahal.

Bengal

Although most of Bengal had been under Mughal rule since Jahangir's time, Assam, Cooch Behar and Chittagong lay outside the grasp of Mughal authority. Cooch Behar and Assam, territories to the north of Mughal Bengal, were conquered in the early 1660s. At that time temples were destroyed and mosques established, again for political purposes. Assam was eventually lost again, never to be consolidated into the Mughal empire. To the southeast, however, Buzurg Umed Khan, the son of the empire's leading noble, Shaista Khan, conquered Chittagong, on the southeast coast of Bengal. The Mughals long had vied with local rajas and Portuguese adventurers for Chittagong. When Buzurg Umed Khan secured it for the Mughals in 1666, it became a Mughal headquarters. There in 1668 he completed a Jamic mosque modeled on ones at Dhaka, although today it has undergone considerable change. For some twenty years, Rajmahal had been the capital of Bengal under the governorship of Prince Shah Shujac. When Aurangzeb assumed the throne, Shujac was pursued into the jungles of Assam where he died. Aurangzeb's governor then abandoned Rajmahal, by then associated with the nowdisgraced Shujac. As a result, nearby Gaur, too, lost much of its significance, although one notable monument was constructed there, probably early in Aurangzeb's reign. It is the tomb of Fateh Khan (Plate 185), a noble associated with Shah Shujac and his spiritual mentor Shah Nicmat Allah. Fateh Khan's rectangular tomb is surmounted by a deeply sloped bangala roof and appears to be the first extant example in Bengal of a Mughal structure that is entirely covered with this roof type, commonly believed to have originated here.

The capital was moved to Dhaka, which once again became the premier city of Bengal. Construction in Dhaka, long a major trade center, increased. It was at this time that one of Dhaka's most famous monuments, known today as the Lalbagh fort, was built. Its construction is credited to Shaista Khan and Prince Azim al-Shan, Mughal governors of Bengal from 1678 to 1684. Within this compound, designed as a four-part garden, they built the tomb of Bibi Pari, an audience hall (Plate 186) and attached hammam, a tank, enclosure walls and gates. Since the mosque within the walls is dated 1649, however, the present compound was probably built on the foundations of an earlier site. There is considerable empty space within the walls, and no residential quarters are apparent.

The structures in this compound as well as their axial layout adhere to the imperial Mughal idiom. The appearance of the audience hall closely follows that of the Sangi Dalan in Rajmahal (Plate 155) as well as the viewing pavilion in the Agra fort. Bibi Pari's tomb is modeled on that of Shah Nicmat Allah in Gaur, which in turn is inspired by the tomb of Ictimad al-Daula in Agra (Plate 71). However, the placement of Bibi Pari's tomb adjacent to the audience hall is quite out of place. Although it reputedly contains the remains of Shaista Khan's favorite daughter, Bibi Pari, that does not explain the unorthodox location of the tomb.

Despite the fact that the compound is almost universally called the Lalbagh fort, it more closely resembles an elaborate walled garden, for example, the Amm Khass Bagh in Sirhind, though the Lalbagh is not terraced. No structure in the compound is inappropriate to a garden. As was the case with most imperial gardens, it appears originally to have been intended for ceremonial and administrative purposes as well as for pleasure. In the life of a prince, these functions were not entirely discrete. Dhaka, like the other Mughal urban centers, has several surviving mosques belonging to Aurangzeb's reign. Among them is the Satgumbad mosque (Plate 187), uninscribed but traditionally credited to Shaista Khan. Others include the mosque of Hajji Khwaja Shahbaz built in 1678-79, the mosque of Kar Talab Khan (the future Murshid Quli Khan) constructed between 1700 and 1704, and the mosque of Khan Muhammad Mirza dated 1704-05 (Plate 188). All these are single-aisled, multi-bayed mosques surmounted by domes. Both their interior and exterior surfaces are significantly more articulated than Bengali buildings of Shah Jahan's time, in fact more elaborate than mosques of eastern India in general, which are conservatively embellished (Plates 94 and 151). Their surface is usually a plaster veneer over a brick core, not the more impressive stone facing used for many imperial structures.

Increased articulation of surfaces is seen, for example, on the projecting corner turrets of the Satgumbad mosque. On Kar Talab Khan's mosque, the rectangular chambers surmounted with deeply sloped and curved bangala roofs flank the north and south ends. These recall the tomb of Fateh Khan in Gaur, built at the beginning of Aurangzeb's reign (Plate 185). Earlier mosques in Bengal have only two engaged columns on the east facade, while there are four on the Hajji Khwaja Shahbaz mosque, six on the Khan Muhammad Mirza mosque dated less than forty years later, and even more on the larger Kar Talab Khan mosque. Other innovations of the period include cusped entrance arches on the facade and mihrabs with cusped arches supported on engaged colonettes with bulbous bases. More elaborate is the interior of the Hajji Khwaja Shahbaz mosque (Plate 189). Its mihrabs have ornate cusped arches supported by slender colonettes and cusped transverse arches that contrast to the plain ones of Shah Jahan's time. Burdwan was another city in Bengal long associated with the Mughals. Here Nur Jahan's first husband was killed and buried. Later the capture of Burdwan gave the rebel prince Shah Jahan all Bengal. In 1698, Khwaja Anwar-i Shahid, a noble in the service of Prince Azim al-Shan, then governor of Bengal, was ambushed and killed in Burdwan. It is popularly believed that after this incident the prince built the Burdwan Jamic mosque, dated 1699-1700, as a gesture of thanksgiving, since apparently he was the target, not the Khwaja. However, Azim al-Shan's name is not mentioned in the inscription, and the heavy unrefined features of this mosque do not suggest princely patronage. Although the mosque in Burdwan is not an outstanding structure, the tomb complex of Khwaja Anwar-i Shahid is the most refined monument in all Mughal Bengal. This complex includes a splendid gateway, tank, mosque, madrasa and the tomb itself (Plate 190), all within a walled enclosure. Even though tradition states that the tomb complex was built in 1712 by the future emperor Farrukh Siyar, also in Burdwan at the time of the ambush, it may have been the product of Azim al-Shan's princely patronage. The three-bayed mosque's highly articulated interior is replete with cusped niches. Such ornateness is unprecedented on any seventeenth- or early eighteenth-century Bengali mosque and is probably inspired by imperial architecture such as Aurangzeb's Badshahi mosque in Lahore (Plate 163). The interior of this Burdwan mosque probably served as a basis for later eighteenth-century architecture in Murshidabad. The tomb, however, is the most creative structure in the complex. Its format, unique in India, consists of a square single-domed central chamber with rectangular-plan wings on the east and west sides crowned by bangala roofs. The tomb's plastered facade is covered with cusped medallions and niches as well as finely incised geometric patterns that recall the exterior of Sultan Nisar Begum's tomb in Allahabad.

Despite Aurangzeb's reputed anti-Hindu stance and ban on temple building, in fact terracotta temples were constructed in Bengal in unprecedented numbers. There are nearly forty dated terracotta temples and many others as well. A variety of types was produced. The facades of most of these temples are profusely embellished with images of deities and genre scenes indicating the strength of the Hindu visual tradition. The founding of Calcutta by Job Charnock in 1690 and its subsequent fortification, although of little significance during Aurangzeb's reign, were ultimately to affect the future of the Mughal empire and its successor states. For the next 150 years in Bengal, three rich building traditions - Mughal-type mosques, Hindu temples and British secular structures - made this eastern area the most diverse in all north India.

Aurangabad

Although Aurangzeb spent the last twenty years of his reign in the Deccan, and Aurangabad served as the primary royal residence after the move south in 1681, little survives from this time. Unlike the north, where nobles generally followed imperial lead in providing architecture, few apparently did so in the Deccan. The Mughal situation there was not sufficiently stable to make architectural construction a prudent investment. Among the few structures provided by nobles at this time are two mosques constructed in Aurangabad shortly after 1661, when Rabica Daurani's tomb was built (Plate 166). In 1661-62 the Chowk mosque was provided by Shaista Khan, noted for his architectural patronage throughout the empire. A doubleaisled structure of five bays each, the simple mosque is surmounted by a single dome. It is modeled on the nearby Jamic mosque dated 1615-16, built before Mughal presence here, and so shows few Mughal characteristics. Shaista Khan probably used a locally trained architect and took little part in its construction. Much more in the Mughal mode is the Lai mosque (Plate 191) provided in 1665-66 by a government official, Zain al-Abidin. The plan of the Lai mosque is almost identical to that of the Chowk mosque built in the local idiom.

However, the cusped arches of the facade supported on bulbous balusterinspired columns are within the Mughal tradition. The use of these features was probably inspired by a mosque in the compound of Rabica Daurani's tomb. Other structures in Aurangabad that appear to date to Aurangzeb's time include the Panchakki, a garden and reservoir complex built around a saint's shrine, and a small white mosque, now part of a girls' school, with cusping and columns similar to those on a mosque at Rabica Daurani's tomb.

CONCLUSION

Aurangzeb was much less involved in architectural production than his predecessors were, but he did sponsor important monuments, especially religious ones. Most notable are mosques that date prior to the court's shift to the Deccan. Some of these, such as the cIdgah at Mathura, were built by the ruler himself, others by his nobles to proclaim Mughal authority in the face of opposition. On Aurangzeb's palace mosque we see an elaboration of floral and other patterns derived from those on Shah Jahan's palace pavilions. But these forms are no longer intended to suggest the semi-divine character of ruler, a notion that little concerned Aurangzeb. Early in Aurangzeb's reign the harmonious balance of Shah Jahan-period architecture is rejected in favor of an increased sense of spatial tension with an emphasis on height. Stucco and other less expensive materials emulating the marble and inlaid stone of earlier periods cover built surfaces. Immediately after Aurangzeb's accession, the use of forms and motifs such as the baluster column and the bangala canopy, earlier reserved for the ruler alone, are found on non-imperially sponsored monuments. This suggests both that there was relatively little imperial intervention in architectural patronage and that the vocabulary of imperial and divine symbolism established by Shah Jahan was devalued by Aurangzeb. At the same time architectural activity by the nobility proliferated as never before, suggesting that they were eager to fill the role previously dominated by the emperor.

8

Architecture and the Struggle for Authority Under the Later Mughals and their Successor States

HISTORICAL DEVELOPMENTS

Aurangzeb died in 1707, but the Mughal empire endured, at least officially, for another 150 years. It lasted until the British exiled and imprisoned the last Mughal ruler after the uprising in 1858. Shah Alam Bahadur Shah succeeded Aurangzeb in 1707. Continuous political turmoil prevented him, however, from entering the long-standing Mughal capital, Delhi, after his coronation. Delhi again became the imperial residence in 1712, but the empire continued to suffer seriously from financial problems, political intrigue, inadequately prepared rulers, and invasions.

Moreover, Delhi experienced difficulties that reflected on the entire state. In 1739 the city was sacked by the Iranian ruler Nadir Shah and again in the 1750s by Afghans who entered India four times. In fact, as Delhi became increasingly vulnerable, it also became virtually all that was left of the Mughal empire. By the beginning of the nineteenth century, two Delhis emerged - the older Mughal city where the king still resided in Shah Jahan's fort, and British Delhi which increasingly encroached upon and transformed the older city. As the empire weakened, the nawabs of Murshidabad, Awadh and Hyderabad established their own successor states, while Sikh, Jat, Maratha and other Hindu rulers asserted their independence, carving out numerous little kingdoms from what once had been a single empire. The architecture sponsored by the rulers and inhabitants of these new domains is heavily dependent on the Mughal style established under Shah Jahan and Aurangzeb, yet in each case new formal interpretations and meaning are given to older forms. The results are often highly creative expressions, reflecting these houses' political allegiance and religious affiliation.

Delhi: the Capital

The city before 1739

For the first half of the eighteenth century Delhi remained the unrivaled center of Muslim culture in north India, although eventually many poets and artists seeking more secure and lucrative patronage went to such stable courts as Awadh and Murshidabad. While no Mughal ruler so much as entered the city between 1679 and 1712, Delhi's allure remained so great that an order was issued prohibiting those in the army from going there without permission. Literature, music, mystic thought and humanistic learning continued to flourish, although painting and architecture had suffered from a lack of imperial patronage well before Aurangzeb left Delhi. Between Aurangzeb's death and Muhammad Shah's reign (1719-48), little of consequence was constructed in the walled city of Shahjahanabad. In any event, no later Mughal ruler was a prolific provider of buildings. Rather, princes, queens, nobles and, increasingly, otherwise unknown citizens provided structures along with the ruler. Thus the study of architecture here will not be divided into imperial and sub-imperial categories as earlier in this book.

From the time he succeeded Aurangzeb, Shah Alam Bahadur Shah never entered Delhi. He did, however, commission the construction of a mosque and his own simple screened yet roofless tomb in the dargab of Bakhtiyar Kaki, just behind the famous thirteenth-century Qutb Minar. The continued importance of this dargab is attested by buildings provided there by some of Bahadur Shah's successors and the fact that the last Mughal resided in a mansion attached to the dargab. Qutb Sahib Bakhtiyar Kaki, a follower of the

Chishti order, had been a fourteenth-century saint. His dargab was a venerated shrine even before his death, though never as popular as the dargab of Shaikh Nizam al-Din, also in Delhi. Before Aurangzeb's reign there is virtually no evidence of Mughal patronage at Dargah Bakhtiyar Kaki, although Babur did visit the shrine. By praying there upon his entry into Delhi in 1526, Babur may have confirmed its sanctity for the Mughals. Commencing with Shah Alam Bahadur Shah, Dargah Bakhtiyar Kaki enjoyed unprecedented Mughal patronage. The reason for this remains unclear. In general, however, Mughal patronage at shrines in the vicinity of Delhi expanded, because Mughal authority outside Delhi was increasingly challenged.

Both the shrine of Bakhtiyar Kaki and also the emperor benefited from the close association that developed. On one hand the Mughal kings legitimized their rule by this intimate contact with the spiritual heirs of Shaikh Qutb Sahib Bakhtiyar Kaki; in turn, the shrine itself reaped economic and social benefits from imperial patronage. Once the Mughal rulers invested there, so, too, did high-ranking Mughal nobility and, by the eighteenth and nineteenth centuries, the nawabs of independent or vassal states. shrine of Bakhtiyar Kaki, is known as the Moti mosque. Probably built several years before Bahadur Shah's death in 1712, the marble mosque is situated in a walled enclosure to the west of the saint's grave. Unlike the double-aisled Moti mosque in the Shahjahanabad fort, this is a single-aisled structure. It is surmounted by three bulbous domes on constricted necks. On each corner of the east central bay is a slender engaged baluster-like column, a feature by now used in religious architecture.

Bahadur Shah's successor, Farrukh Siyar (r. 1713-19), further embellished the dargah by building a screened marble enclosure around Bakhtiyar Kaki's grave and two marble entrance gates leading to the grave site. He also rebuilt in white marble the dargah's original stucco mosque situated to the east of the saint's tomb. The marble gates (Plate 193) are inscribed with inlaid black marble characters, thus drawing upon forms and materials first introduced by Shah Jahan at the Ajmer Chishti shrine (Plate 105). The one closest to the tomb, dated 1717-18, is characterized by rounded cusped arches in whose spandrels are large floral medallions and arabesque creepers. Beyond Farrukh Siyar's gates the devotee goes through a series of passages from the first entrance to the grave. This architectural complexity helps emphasize the saint's importance. Since dargahs have inherent authority, the Mughals, as a result of their patronage, draw upon that authority.

Farrukh Siyar's additions radically changed the shrine's appearance. Visually the Chishti dargah of Bakhtiyar Kaki now more closely resembled the premier Chishti shrine of Mucin al-Din in Ajmer, where during Shah Jahan's reign many of the major structures had been built by the royal family. But the shrine in Ajmer received no new support from the late Mughals due to unfavorable political conditions. Instead Bakhtiyar Kaki's shrine was revitalized by the later Mughals in white marble and building types that evoked a glorious Mughal past. Festivities at the shrine also underscored Mughal affiliation with the Chishti order.

For example, Raushan al-Daula Zafar Khan, by far the most influential amir in the court of Muhammad Shah, more powerful even than the prime minister (wazir), spent vast sums, much of them embezzled, on the cUrs ceremony at Khwaja Qutb Sahib Bakhtiyar Kaki's dargah. By providing elaborate lighting devices along the road that led from the palace in Shahjahanabad to the dargah some 15 km south, he created a spectacular visual link between the Mughals and this shrine. These celebrations, popular with Muslims and Hindus alike, appealed to a wide section of the population. Muhammad Shah assumed the throne in late 1719, reigning twenty-nine years, until his death in 1748. He was the third monarch to rule after Farrukh Siyar; his two predecessors did not survive even a full year. Muhammad Shah is credited with constructing a wall around Dargah Chiraq-i Delhi in 1729 and the construction of a wooden mosque inside the Shahjahanabad palace. He also built his own tomb (Plate 194) inside the shrine of Nizam al-Din in Delhi. This white marble screened tomb is modeled closely on the nearby tomb of Jahan Ara Begum (Plate 167), although this tomb-type long had become standard. Muhammad Shah's enclosure reveals more profuse floral ornamentation and highly carved surfaces, for example along the screen's base.

It is only commencing with Muhammad Shah's reign that considerable building activity is witnessed again within the walled city of Shahjahanabad. Significant construction occurred both before and after the invasion of Delhi by the Iranian Nadir Shah in 1739, suggesting that his attack had less devastating long-term effects than is commonly believed. Among the structures erected before Nadir Shah's invasions is the Sunahri or Golden mosque built in 1721-22 by Raushan al-Daula, who provided lavish celebrations at the cUrs ceremony of Bakhtiyar Kaki. This three-bayed single-aisled mosque is situated next to the Mughal police station (still in use today) in Chandni Chowk, then across from Jahan Ara's great serai. The mosque was provided at the beginning of Raushan al-Daula's rise to power. The location alone, close to the main entrance of the Shahjahanabad palace, indicates his close ties to the emperor. An inscription over the structure's east facade indicates that the mosque was erected to honor Shah Bhik, his spiritual mentor, who had died two years earlier.

Reached by a flight of narrow steps, the structure is elevated above the ground. Its slender minarets that rise above the roof line and the gilt metalplated bulbous domes resting on constricted drums added a delicate air to Shahjahanabad's skyline. The emphasis at this time was on delicacy and refinement, not just on the sense of awesome height that had been a major factor in late seventeenth-century taste (Plates 177 and 179).

The mosque's facade (Plate 195) and interior are embellished with molded stucco arabesques and floral motifs. Panels of elaborate floral sprays similar to those on the Badshahi mosque form a dado along the base of the facade. The bases of the fluted engaged pilasters flanking the central bay are elaborately covered with floral tendrils. Thus floral sprays that were earlier reserved for Aurangzeb's palace mosques are now used outside the palace, yet by the highest-ranking nobility.

The use of hitherto imperial motifs reflects the increasing power assumed by the nobility - at times overshadowing that of the ruler himself. Although Raushan al-Daula provided more buildings than any other noble during Muhammad Shah's reign, his was not the finest in Delhi. That superb building is the Fakhr al-Masajid, or Pride of the Mosques (Plate 196), provided by a noblewoman. The mosque was built in 1728-29 by Kaniz-i Fatima entitled Fakhr-i Jahan (Pride of the World), to commemorate her deceased husband, Shujacat Khan, a high-ranking noble under Aurangzeb.

Situated on a high plinth, not far from Delhi's Kashmir gate, it is one of the few stone mosques built in Delhi during the eighteenth and nineteenth centuries. This red sandstone mosque, faced with white marble, is clearly modeled on the major mosques of the city erected during the reigns of Shah Jahan and Aurangzeb (Plates 124 and 168). Most of those mosques, too, had been provided by the court ladies. Fakhr-i Jahan, by erecting this mosque, continues an earlier tradition. While the emphasis on the mosque's height due to its tall minarets is typical of the period, the delicate inlay and carved niches of its interior recall the uncluttered aesthetic of Shah Jahan's earlier religious architecture.

Other notable mosques of Muhammad Shah's reign built inside the city before Nadir Shah's invasion show the continued vitality of the evolving Mughal style, one that persisted even in the absence of strong central leadership. These include the mosque and school of Nawab Sharaf al-Daula dated 1722-23 and the Muhtasib's mosque (Plate 197) provided in 1723-24 by Abu Sacid, the hereditary inquisitor (muhtasib) of Delhi. Both of these are singleaisled three-bayed mosques entered through openings with cusped arches and surmounted by bulbous ribbed domes. These domes recall those on the Moti mosque at Bakhtiyar Kaki's dargah (Plate 192) and are similar to many during this period. Nawab Sharaf al-Daulat's mosque is situated on a high plinth with chambers beneath, today shops, that may have served as the school. The mosque of Abu Sacid rather unusually for this time is not atop a high plinth. Unlike Sharaf al-Daula's solid appearing edifice, it bears delicate stucco ornament similar to that on Raushan al-Daula's mosque built only two years earlier. Not all mosques inside the city were adequately large to serve an entire locality; rather, they were built for personal use. One such example is the mosque of

Tahawwur Khan (Plate 198), dated 1727-28, built by a major landholder of Delhi. The area of the city in which this simple single-aisled flatroofed mosque is located is named for Tahawwur Khan and was the site of his mansion. On its facade three cusped entrances are supported by bulbous pilaster columns. Thus a variety of mosques was erected before 1739; possibly the lack of a strong imperial pattern accounts for this diversity in form and ornament. Delhi. That is because mostly sacred buildings remain, although serais, gardens and markets continued to be built. The surviving ones are outside the city wall. For example, an extensive bazaar known today as the Tripolia with a massive triple-arched entrance gate at either end was built in 1728-29 north of the walled city along the major highway leading to Lahore. This compound was built by Nazir Mahaldar Khan, superintendent of the women's quarter in the palace of Muhammad Shah.

At Muhammad Shah's request, the raja of Jaipur, Sawai Jai Singh Kachhwaha (1699-1743), provided Delhi with an extraordinary observatory known as the Jantar Mantar (Plate 199). This able statesman and astrologer constructed the observatory about 1725 in an area to the south of the walled city known as Jaisinghpura, probably the locale of his own estate there. Subsequently he built similar observatories with comparable sophisticated structural instruments in Jaipur, Benares, Mathura and Ujjain. Constructed of brick and plaster, the juxtaposed circular and angular shapes of these enormous instruments produce an effect unlike that of any other architecture of the period. Their forms as well as their scientific sophistication remain appealing to twentieth-century sensibilities. Muhammad Shah's desire for such an observatory speaks highly of his interest in promoting scientific knowledge, not simply the literary arts for which he is well known.

In 1739, the Iranian ruler Nadir Shah invaded Delhi. This was the city's first invasion in almost two centuries. From Raushan al-Daula's Sunahri mosque, Nadir Shah ordered the city plundered - a sack that lasted less than twelve hours. Many were killed, regardless of religion. The markets and buildings in the vicinity of Chandni Chowk as well as the fort suffered great damage. The psychological jolt given to the complacent citizens of Delhi was never fully forgotten.

Poets many years later continued to lament this event as if it had happened yesterday. The Iranian ruler remained in the city for about two months, taking on his departure the money from the royal treasury, jewels - including Shah Jahan's Peacock Throne and the Koh-i Nur diamond - and many other valuables. However, the loss of this wealth, essentially noncirculating, ultimately had little impact on the city's economy since trade continued to prosper.

Indeed, Delhi recovered quickly, and new buildings replaced those destroyed. The very patron who had provided the mosque from which Nadir Shah issued his order for the destruction gave the city a second mosque. Raushan al-Daula Zafar Khan provided it in 1744-45. By now the former influential amir had fallen from favor and was no longer active in politics. His second mosque, like his first one (Plate 195), is known today as the Sunahri or Golden mosque, and, like it, was also built in honor of the religious figure Shah Bhik, who had died some years earlier. Situated south of the fort along the main road that led to the Delhi gate, now an area known as Daryaganj, it is a singleaisled three-bayed mosque (Plate 200). Originally it was surmounted with gilt, copper-faced domes. However, the metal was subsequently removed and placed on the mosque Raushan al-Daula had constructed earlier in Chandni Chowk. Today even the domes are missing. This mosque is more robust in appearance than the one he provided some twenty years earlier. It also bears considerably less stucco ornament. Whether this change in aesthetic was conscious is unclear, but the solid yet austere appearance suggests an infusion of new stability into the city. In 1748 Muhammad Shah was succeeded by his son, Ahmad Shah. The new ruler's mother, Udham Bai, also known as Qudsiya Begum, wielded considerable influence over Ahmad Shah, as she had done in the early stages of Muhammad Shah's reign when she was that ruler's favorite consort. Now, in fact, this shrewd queen and her confidant, Javid Khan, the prime minister, held the true reins of power. Qudsiya Begum was an enthusiastic provider of architecture, best known for her palace and garden complex, Qudsiya Bagh. It was probably commenced when Ahmad Shah assumed the throne in 1748. Located just north of Delhi's walled city, this garden housed a substantial residence that overlooked the river Jumna. The mansion has since been destroyed, but late eighteenth-century engravings of its riverside facade indicate its splendor and size. A large two-storied edifice, the mansion had polygonal turrets at each end. The facade was marked with projecting oriel windows surmounted with sloped bangala-type roofs, indicating that this roof type continued to be used on secular architecture. Today only an entrance gate and mosque remain, both made of stucco-covered brick.

The massive gate, probably that of the entire compound, is surmounted by unusually large kungura. Detailed ornamentation of the gate's stucco work contributes to an overall elaborate appearance. Beyond is the mosque (Plate 201), whose plan is similar to that of others in the later Mughal period. It is richly adorned with molded and polychromed stucco, marked by elaborate faceted patterns and exaggerated floral designs found at the base and apex of arches. Engaged pilasters are flattened and highly articulated with chevron-like designs. Such ornamentation is usually termed decadent, as if to reflect Qudsiya Begum's own character, generally considered low and unrefined. She was, however, a highly cultured woman. In any event, this ornamentation is simply a more exuberant expression of that developed under the earlier Mughals.

During her son's short reign, Qudsiya Begum provided a second mosque (Plate 202), with Javid Khan, in 1750-51. Like the two mosques provided by Raushan al-Daula, this one, too, is known as the Sunahri mosque after its once metal-plated domes. Located along the main road just south of the palace, the compound is entered by a red carved stone gate. The red stone mosque is small and delicate, though flanked on either side by extremely tall minarets. These and the bulbous domes emphasize the mosque's height, giving the small building a grandiose air. It is decorated with more subdued ornament than that of Qudsiya Begum's private mosque on her mansion grounds. In the year the queen mother provided the Sunahri mosque she also built several structures at a Shia shrine known as Shahi Mardan in Delhi, about 9 km south of the walled city. These included an assembly hall, a mosque and tank as well as a walled enclosure.

Little is known about the shrine before Qudsiya Begum's patronage there, but it is probable that the queen mother erected these structures to augment a Qadam Sharif, a building housing a footprint revered as that of Ah, who according to the Shia sect was the rightful successor of Muhammad. The current Qadam Sharif was built in 1759-60, probably renewing an older one. Although most of Qudsiya Begum's buildings here have been rebuilt, her mosque (Plate 203) remains a well-preserved example of eighteenth-century religious architecture.

It closely resembles the overall plan and elevation of her private Qudsiya Bagh mosque. Lacking is the profuse stucco ornament, suggesting that more austere decor was considered appropriate for public buildings such as the Sunahri mosque, built concurrently. Qudsiya Begum's patronage here may have been an attempt to give this Shia shrine similar status to that enjoyed by Sunni shrines of Bakhtiyar Kaki and Nizam al-Din.

By the mid-eighteenth century Delhi was virtually all that remained of the once great Mughal empire. Nevertheless, that small empire and its emperor remained the model for Muslim culture and administration throughout north India. In Bengal and elsewhere, former provinces were transformed into autonomous states. In the case of Awadh, however, the ties with Delhi were broken gradually. For example, Safdar Jang, the Mughal governor of Awadh, never regarded himself as independent, but part of the larger empire. After his death in 1754 his body was transported a considerable distance to the imperial capital, Delhi, which Safdar Jang always considered his home. There his son, Nawab Shujac al-Daula, built an enormous mausoleum (Plate 204).

Not only was Safdar Jang's tomb built in the Mughal capital, it was, moreover, closely modeled on Humayun's tomb, the first imperial Mughal mausoleum (Plates 18 and 19). This square plan tomb is in the center of a walled char bagh complex. Although the tomb's layout, plan and its exterior, faced with pink and white stone, recall Humayun's tomb, Safdar Jang's tomb bears many features characteristic of mid-eighteenth-century architecture. These include complex stucco ornament on the interior, cusped rounded entrance arches, central pishtaqs surmounted by a series of bulbous domes and a central dome that rests on a tightly constricted drum. The structure presents a balance between increased surface articulation and mass. Commonly referred to as the last vestige of an older Mughal architectural style, this tomb exerted considerable influence on the mausolea of the subsequent nawabs of Awadh and their queens, who were buried in either Faizabad or Lucknow (Plate 216). This older imperial-type tomb appealed to the ruler of Awadh, the tomb's patron, who had adopted with minimal change many of the customs and regulations of the Mughal court.

Although the Mughal empire became increasingly impotent politically, Delhi continued to flourish even into the late eighteenth century. Much of Delhi's construction at this time was financed by persons employed by the East India Company or by businessmen. Into the nineteenth century, the growth of wealthy Jain, Jat and other non-Muslim communities increased. In what was once the heartland of the Mughal empire, these non-Muslims constructed their own buildings that reflected Delhi's new elite. For example, almost directly in front of the Shahjahanabad fort several Jain and Hindu temples were built, and elsewhere in the walled city Hindu temples were erected in prolific numbers. The Mughal emperors and their subjects continued to build, although not as extensively as before. Some mosques were added inside the walled city, among them one provided in 1779 by Qasim Khan, a high-ranking noble in the reign of Shah Alam II. But increasingly construction occurred south of the walled city, in part because the esteemed Chishti dargahs were there. In 1755-56 the emperor Alamgir II himself wrote an inscription now inside the tomb of Nizam al-Din indicating that he had made repairs and additions to the shrine. South of the city, moreover, there was vacant land suitable for the construction of garden complexes and tombs. Here, about 1730, Shah Alam II buried his mother and daughter in a walled enclosure that contains three red stone tombs (Plate 205). Each of the single-story buildings is surmounted with a bulbous ribbed dome standing on a constricted neck. Internally they are arranged with eight smaller chambers surrounding a large central one, a plan common in Mughal tombs and dwellings (Plate 74). Known as Lai Bangala or the Red Pavilion on account of their color, they are today within the compound of the

Delhi Golf Club. They are rare examples at this time of domed mausolea for imperial family members.

In 1803, the British gained control of Delhi, and Mughal authority existed in name alone. The Mughal emperors, however, assumed their regal responsibilities as best they could, for they remained symbols of a way of life and refined culture whose significance even the British recognized. They continued to construct religious and palace edifices when possible. In 1811 new stone masonry bridges replacing older wooden drawbridges were placed before the Lahore and Delhi gates of the Shahjahanabad palace. Erected under the auspices of the Mughal ruler Akbar II, their construction was supervised by an Englishman, Robert Macpherson. These immovable bridges served British interests, for their presence meant that the fort could not be completely isolated by Mughal inhabitants. An increasing number of religious buildings was provided by citizens identified only by name. For example, in 1837-38 Saddho, a woman who describes herself as a humble milkmaid, erected religious structures within the old city that no longer remain. Still standing, however, is a red sandstone mosque (Plate 206) built in 1822-23 by Mubarak Begum, known as Lai Kunwar, the consort of an Englishman residing in Delhi. This small singleaisled three-bayed mosque is probably the best surviving example of early nineteenth-century Mughal architecture in Delhi today. Its facade is marked by rounded cusped arches, above which is a tri-lobed arch whose central bay recalls the baldachin covering on Shah Jahan's throne in his nearby Public Audience Hall (Plate 119). The interior transverse arches are tri-lobed, the shape of decorative arches on the mosque's exterior. Tri-lobed arches also appear on the mihrab. The mosque's interior is finely but chastely carved with shallow recessed arches and cusped niches. This small but well-balanced structure suggests a waning taste for highly ornate surfaces in Delhi, while in contemporary Lucknow and Murshidabad, Mughal successor states, the desire for ornate surfaces was at a peak.

The last significant Mughal building erected within the old walled city is the mosque of Hamid Ali Khan (Plate 207), the prime minister of Bahadur Shah II (1837-58), the last Mughal emperor. Hamid Ali built it in 1841-42 not far from the Kashmir gate. Its inscription was written by Ghalib, the most famous poet of the time. This large mosque, situated on a raised platform, reveals a sense of spatial tension. Here the emphasis is on the horizontal, while spatial tension in the later seventeenth century had a vertical emphasis. Yet the sense of visual imbalance is similar. The facade bears three large cusped entrance arches. The central bay, marked with a large arch whose central lobe forms a curved cornice, recalls Shah Jahan's throne in the nearby fort. Its flanking side-wings are surmounted with a parapet of miniature domes based on earlier Mughal entrance gates, in particular the entrance into the Taj Mahal. The mosque's interior (Plate 208) features cusped arches supported on baluster-type columns derived from those first used in Shah Jahan's architecture.

This evocation of forms from the past was intentional, for Hamid Ali chose not to include any of the increasingly apparent westernized features on his mosque; instead he looked back to motifs manifest most clearly during the height of Mughal power. In this same manner, Bahadur Shah only a decade later commissioned the poet Ghalib, the very poet who wrote the verse embellishing Hamid Ali's mosque, to write a history of the entire Mughal house commencing with Timur. The vision of the last Mughal and those associated with him was to the past, not to any future.

Ghalib himself laments the passing of the past, a major theme in his verse and letters, evoking Shah Jahan's reign as a golden age. Yet, while Hamid Ali's mosque shows features based on those of earlier Mughal buildings, they are here combined in a unique manner. This innovative structure suggests that even at the very end of the Mughal period architectural forms and decor maintained a deep debt to the aesthetic of Shah Jahan and Aurangzeb; yet at the same time these forms continued to evolve in a highly experimental and creative manner. The last Mughal emperor, Bahadur Shah II, a sufi himself, constructed his own red sandstone mansion adjacent to the dargah of Bakhtiyar Kaki. It was known as Zafar Mahal after the king's poetic name. It is no accident that the residence was constructed close to the dargah. Just as tombs were built in the compounds of these shrines so that the interred might receive the divine power (baraka) of the saint, so the last Mughal, with little authority of his own, hoped to derive some from the inherent authority of the dargah.

Western India

Rajasthan

For generations the Mughals had patronized the dargah of Mucin al-Din Chishti in Ajmer, but due to political difficulties did so no longer by the beginning of the eighteenth century. Not much later the Mughals lost Ajmer to Hindu authorities, who held it until 1818, when the British took control. All the same, the importance of Ajmer's Chishti shrines attracted support from Hindus and Muslims alike. Moreover, Mughal authority, while in reality impotent in Ajmer, remained symbolically important. For example, in fulfillment of a vow made during an illness, Ali Jah, the nawab of Karnataka, constructed a white marble pavilion (Plate 209) at the dargah of Mucin al-Din in 1793. The flat-roofed rectangular pavilion is largely modeled on Shah Jahan's Jamic mosque in the dargah (Plate 105), including even details such as the inscription inlaid in black marble lettering.

The inscription evokes the Mughal emperor's name, even though he had no political authority in Ajmer, reflecting his continuing role as a figure-head of Indian Persianate culture. Mucin al-Din inspired patronage even outside the dargah. A large cIdgah (Plate 210) was constructed some distance from the shrine to honor the saint according to the inscription embedded in its qibla wall. Only on the city outskirts was there adequate open space for this large structure. It was provided in 1773-74 by Nawab Mirza Chaman Beg, the governor of Malwa under the Sindhia rajas, then the masters of Ajmer. An impressive interpretation of a bangala-msp'ireA roof forms the upper portion of this vast wall mosque's upper central bay. Beneath this curved form is a pavilion depicted in stucco relief that resembles Shah Jahan's balcony from which he presented himself to the public (Plate 113). Subsequent variations on this pavilion type were used frequently in the palace architecture of the Rajasthani princes, but in all cases this paviliontype maintained a royal or religious connotation. Its use here serves as a reference to Mucin al-Din, who in the cIdgah's inscription is called "king of the dominion."

Tombs built earlier in Ajmer continued to be embellished. Abd Allah Khan, father of the king-maker Sayyid brothers who were so very prominent during the first half of the eighteenth century, had built a garden, mosque and tomb for his wife in Ajmer at the end of Aurangzeb's reign. Abd Allah Khan's own tomb (Plate 211) was added to this garden complex in 1710 by his son, Sayyid Husain Ali Khan.

Five years later, in 1715, he added a large arched entrance to the compound. The tomb is loosely modeled in plan and elevation on the Aurangzeb-period Sola Khamba, or tomb of Shaikh Ala al-Din, just outside the dargah of Mucin al-Din Chishti (Plate 169). A dome and four corner chattris, however, surmount the roof of Abd Allah Khan's tomb, while the roof of the earlier tomb is flat. On Abd Allah's tomb, the cusping of the arches is tighter, less exaggerated, and the supporting pillars are less ornate. While architecture under the later Mughals is generally considered a more exaggerated version of earlier Mughal material, here is one of several instances where the opposite pertains. Construction in the city continued as well, the most notable example being the mosque of Mir Sacadat Ali, today across from the railway station. This two-storied mosque, dated 1852-53, when Ajmer was part of the Britishgoverned Rajputana Agency, is built in an eighteenth-century Mughal idiom with cusped arches and delicate stucco work. Its inscription, like that on its more experimental counterpart in Delhi, is also composed by the famous poet Ghalib. While most cities grew randomly within and outside their confines, Jaipur, founded in 1727, was completely planned. Sawai Jai Singh (1688-1743), a remarkable statesman and head of the Kachhwaha house, built it on the plain below Amber, this house's older capital.

The layout of his new capital was praised widely in contemporary sources. Based on ancient Hindu texts, the resulting walled city, with broad regular streets dividing it into quadrants in a grid-like pattern, is far more organized than the Mughal city of Shahjahanabad. Sawai Jai Singh's interest in astronomy as indicated by his observatories also had an imprint on the city's plan.

The focal point of the city is the palace. It is designed along the lines of a traditional Rajasthan mansion, but different from the residential part of Mughal palaces. Chambers for residential, administrative and courtly functions are all contained within these multi-storied walls. Even more graceful than Mughal palaces, this one has a light appearance. This is achieved through the use of numerous cusped arches on slender columns, screens containing very delicate carving, and many pillared pavilions with curved roofs surmounting the roofline. These features emphasize the sense of height and also create a graceful skyline.

Much of the city and its uniformly designed buildings were constructed under Sawai Jai Singh, but his successors continued to build there as well. In 1799 Maharaja Sawai Pratap Singh built the Hawa Mahal (Plate 212). This residential building, constructed to take advantage of the cooling breezes, was dedicated to the Hindu deity Krishna and his consort, Radha. Its six stories of clustered, articulated and projecting oriel windows, all surmounted by curved roofs, resemble a honeycomb. The building's top floor reflects each of the smaller roofs. This in essence utilizes traditional Indian building concepts of reduplication of forms, yet maintains the characteristic late eighteenth-century height, grace and lightness.

North India

Lahore to Agra

The Mughals were able to hold Lahore and most of the Punjab until the mideighteenth century, when political instability made their rule there tenuous. By 1768, Sikh chiefs had replaced the Mughals until the British, in turn, superseded them in 1849. Few notable monuments were erected in the Punjab during the later Mughal period, possibly reflecting the unstable conditions as well as the lack of imperial intervention there. The tomb of Sharaf al-Nisa Begum, known as the Sarvwala Maqbara, or Cypress tomb, after its dominant ornamentation, is Lahore's best-preserved monument from the post-Aurangzeb period. Sharaf al-Nisa was the sister of Nawab Zakariya Khan, a governor of Lahore under Muhammad Shah. This tomb purportedly was used during her life as a meditation chamber. A unique structure, the building is a tapering tower surmounted with a pyramidal vault. Cypress trees and floral motifs rendered in glazed tile mosaic embellish the upper portion. Glazed tile is not new in Lahore, but the stiff, rigid quality of the design is a marked departure from the free-flowing arabesques of earlier periods.

Under the Sikhs building accelerated considerably. Many new buildings, often faced with marble stripped from older Mughal structures, were erected by the new government and leading Sikh citizens. The styles of these Sikh buildings in Lahore correspond with those found elsewhere in contemporary north India. That is, cusped arches, fluted domes, slender carved columns and curved cornice roofs dominate. For example, the Baradari (Plate 213) in the garden facing Lahore's Badshahi mosque is a delicate marble edifice whose columns and cusped arches belong to the Mughal tradition. This is a squareplan pavilion constructed in 1818 by Ranjit Singh. The most important Sikh monument is not in Lahore but in Amritsar. This is the Golden temple, commenced in the late eighteenth century and completed largely during the nineteenth century. Situated in the middle of an enormous tank connected to land via a long causeway, the shrine is known as the Harimandir. This two-storied structure is entirely gilt-covered, glistening in the sun and giving the impression of extraordinary opulence. The temple's square plan and two-storied elevation surmounted by a small domed pavilion and chattris appear to derive from Mughal tomb-types as well as some palaces, for example, the one at Datia (Plate 99). However, the result is characteristic of Sikh shrines alone. Other features, however, such as the fluted domes, curved cornices and multiple small domes that surmount the shrine's parapet are pan-Indian devices of this period that transcend sectarian lines.

The Mughals lost control of Agra and its surrounding area to the Jats early in the eighteenth century. Here the older established Muslim families suffered more than those of Delhi as they were replaced by Jat and Maratha Hindu elites. However, many Muslim artisans still found patronage since the products they originally produced were now demanded by the new Hindu elite, insuring a continuity of style. Little Muslim construction was witnessed in this area during the eighteenth and nineteenth centuries, but temples, palaces and gardens constructed under Hindu patrons now embellished the Agra region. This area flourished under these new rulers while they constructed their headquarters at Dig, Bharatpur and other localities. The area's association with the birthplace and childhood of Krishna further stimulated its vigorous revitalization. For example, members of the Jaipur royal family are credited with providing a number of temples in Brindavan, while the subsequent Jat rulers of the area also maintained these structures and added their own as well. Nearby at Govardhan multi-storied cenotaphs embellished with cusped arches, bangala-rooied pavilions and ribbed domes were built to memorialize the rajas of Bharatpur.

But by far the most impressive work is the palace at Dig in Bharatpur District (Plate 214). It was constructed as the new Jat headquarters under Badan Singh (1722-56) and his family, most notably Suraj Mai (1756-63) and his successors. Although built in several stages and under different patrons, the palace and its garden setting adhere to a symmetrical formality derived from Mughal gardens. A central square char bagh is surmounted on all four sides by pavilions, recalling the organization of Mughal gardens. Massive tanks on the north and south ends of the palace complex, however, recall Hindu temples more than any Mughal palace. The palace pavilions are characterized by an air of solidity and grace. Badan Singh's portion of the palace, known as the Purana Mahal, consists of a series of rectangular pavilions surmounted by deeply sloped curved roofs topped with spiked finials, creating a highly articulated yet elegant skyline. Another portion of the Dig palace is the Keshav Bhavan, overlooking one of the large tanks. It is a single-storied open building with baluster-like columns supporting cusped arches on each facade. Short and somewhat squat, these fluted columns rise from bases out of which emerge large lotus petals. Not simply a mirror of structures executed at the nearcontemporary city of Jaipur, the buildings of Dig appear more substantial, with less emphasis on height. Their reflections mirrored in the nearby tanks, however, lend them an illusionistic quality. Mechanical devices to emulate rain and thunder were incorporated into Dig's architecture. The purpose was to evoke the yearning of lovers, a Hindu theme stimulated by painting and poetry. Structures at nearby Mathura, built in the nineteenth century during the period of British supremacy there, are of a style similar to contemporary material in Delhi and Rajasthan. Among these is a cenotaph built as a memorial to a deceased Hindu, Parikhji, who died in 1837. In plan it is similar to the octagonal tomb-type of the Lodi and Sur kings. The ornamentation, however, is typical of nineteenth-century architecture here and in Delhi. Cenotaphs such as this were originally associated only with Muslim custom. Then, around the sixteenth century, they were erected by some of the Hindu princely families of Rajasthan to commemorate their ancestors. This cenotaph at Mathura has been adapted to non-royal Hindu use, blurring the distinction in architecture reserved for one religion or another as well as that reserved for the monarch on the one hand and his subjects on the other.

Faizabad and Lucknow: architecture under the nawabs of Awadh

The Mughal governors of Awadh became increasingly independent so that soon after the time of Safdar Jang (d. 1754) ties with central authority remained in name only. The governors administered Awadh from Lucknow, the Mughal headquarters, which soon became the premier city of Awadh. However, Faizabad, some 120 km to the northeast, was the initial residence of Safdar Jang and his immediate successors, the nawabs as they were called, in recognition of their original role as deputies to the Mughal emperor. During the reign of Safdar Jang's successor, Shujac al-Daula (1754-75), Faizabad became such a significant city that contemporary chronicles, probably exaggerated ones, claim that it equaled Shahjahanabad in beauty and magnificence. Most of the city has long since disappeared, but a mosque and the tombs constructed for Shujac al-Daula and his wife remain notable reminders of Faizabad's early splendor.

During the initial period of the nawabs' power, buildings were modeled closely on Mughal prototypes, for Delhi, still the center of courtly Muslim culture, remained the ideal to emulate. This is evident in buildings of the central market place {chowk), commenced about

1765 by Shujac al-Daula. He provided this chowk with an elaborate triple-arched entrance. In the market, Hasan Reza Khan, later to be one of the chief ministers of Awadh, built a mosque, known today as the Chowk mosque (Plate 215). The three bulbous domes and two minarets of this single-aisled three-bayed mosque, situated on a high plinth, dominate the skyline. This emphasis on the building's height recalls Mughal buildings of Aurangzeb's reign (Plate 179). Other aspects, however, relate to more contemporary architecture of Delhi, for example the stucco work above the cusped arches and the ornate treatment of the mosque's parapet (Plates 201 and 204).

Tombs in Faizabad also were inspired by Mughal models; particularly the tomb for Shujac al-Daula, built about 1775, and one for his wife, Bahu Begum (Plate 216), constructed about forty years later, after her death in 1816, show Mughal features. Both of these tombs, like the tomb of Safdar Jang (Plate 204), Shujac al-Daula's predecessor, have bulbous domes and are set in char haghs. The ornament on these tombs, like that on the Chowk mosque, is deeply rooted in earlier Mughal traditions. At the same time, these tombs reveal original characteristics such as multiple entrances on the facade and elaborate parapets on the roof, significant features in the developing independent Awadhi style. Asaf al-Daula, Shujac al-Daula's son and successor, moved his residence to Lucknow, in part to distance himself from the powerful Bahu Begum. From the time of Asaf al-Daula onwards, that is from 1775 to the abolition of the house of Awadh by the British in 1856, Lucknow remained the seat of the nawabs. Although construction was considerable under the nawabs of Awadh, architecture in Lucknow can be placed generally in two broad categories. Those structures built by the nawabs commencing about the later eighteenth century for their own residences or as public works often reflect considerable European influence, while religious structures are usually based on the architecture of earlier Indo-Islamic houses.

Apart from bridges, whose parts were actually ordered from Europe and then assembled in Lucknow, it is the palace architecture that bears the most noticeable European characteristics. Such features as Paladian-style columns, triangular pediments, and Adam-style fanlights were all widely used in Lucknow's residential architecture. Even structures such as a zenana, whose purpose precluded numerous tall windows on the facade as favored by contemporary Europeans, reflect an awareness of European styles. Instead of windows, the architects provided niches with statues or fresco paintings of men 0 Such ornamentation, however, was only a superficial adaptation of European tradition, for the buildings' interiors continued to follow traditional plans essential to indigenous modes of living.

The European features suggest the nawabs' superficial display of regard for the British, yet at the same time an uneasiness with both British dominance and British artistic styles. A series of palaces was constructed in Lucknow, from Asaf al-Daula's defensively viable Macchi Bhavan, built about 1774, to the Kaiser Bagh, built about 1848 by the last king of Awadh, Wajid Ali Shah. Today only isolated structures that once were part of the extravagant palatial Kaiser Bagh complex remain (Plate 217).

Highly influenced by European art, the fine ornate stucco work in the shape of fish (the nawabs' royal emblem), and the floral motifs standing out along exaggerated cusped arches, are characteristic of the Kaiser Bagh buildings. While the well-fortified Macchi Bhavan was a symbol of the nawabs' power, the pleasure-garden nature of the last palace, the Kaiser Bagh, reflected the impotent nature of the politically moribund nawabs 1 Thus the increasingly extravagant nature of each subsequent palace, culminating in the Kaiser Bagh, must be seen as reflecting a developing need to project an image of strength. The Europeanized mansions in each palace complex perhaps reflected an image of political power, one often more inflated than real. The nawabs and their architects seem to have felt greater ease in constructing religious structures, even though they were often part of the palace grounds.

In 1784 Nawab Asaf al-Daula commenced an enormous Imambara, a hall used during the Shia celebrations of Muharram and for storing movable shrines (tacziya) used in these ceremonies. This complex adjoined the Macchi Bhavan palace. It was erected to provide work and income for citizens who were suffering from a serious famine. The nawab himself participated in the construction process as an act of religious merit, thereby encouraging even the high-born to labor 2 The compound consisted of the huge Imambara, a large free-standing mosque, a step-well and elaborate entrance gates. Even in these gates the complex's vast scale is emphasized. Nowhere is this better expressed than in the Rumi Darwaza (Plate 218), the gate serving as the west entrance to the Imambara. This enormous gate's high rounded pishtaq is enveloped by a series of projecting green glazed ceramic finials from which water once spouted. Typical of the Awadh nawabs' architecture, the gate was highly creative, characterized by a sense of dynamic articulation never expressed in the more orderly structures of the Mughals.

The Imambara was at the time of its construction a technological achievement, for it had the largest vaulted hall that ever spanned an uninterrupted space. Yet other aspects of Asaf al-Daula's Imambara belong to a vocabulary of standard ornament found on mosques and madrasas throughout north India. For example, it is adorned with magnificently rendered high stucco relief, numerous arches edged with deep cusping and crowned by a parapet of bulbous domes. While these features, seen on many of Lucknow's religious buildings, are arranged in a manner unique to Awadhi architecture, they are all established forms used earlier on Mughal and other Islamic buildings.

Thus in the architecture of Lucknow, just as in the other well-established Muslim house of north India, Murshidabad, long-standing Islamic forms served as the basis of religious structures, while European sources stood behind administrative and residential structures. European forms were meticulously avoided for religious architecture. Rather, the models for religious buildings were structures that had been erected by earlier Indo-Islamic houses. These models were, however, associated not with a dynasty but with the very essence of Islam.

Benares

Mughal rulers held Benares until the mid-eighteenth century, when the city and the region around it fell to Hindu zamindars who had been awarded the title raja by the Mughal emperor. The new ruler's authority, however, was less than absolute, for the territory held by the Benares raja was under the larger umbrella of the East India Company.

Construction in Benares by Muslims diminished during this period. Although mosques continued to be built, the most noteworthy Islamic structure is the tomb of Lacl Khan (Plate 219), dated 1768-69. It overlooks the Ganges at the site where today the Mughal Serai bridge spans the river.

The form of this square-plan tomb surmounted by a dome and four chattris is highly conservative, adhering closely to Mughalperiod monuments. Glazed-tile decoration on the tomb's surface produces a striking polychrome effect. While glazed-tile embellishment is not generally associated with Mughal and post-Mughal architecture in eastern India, it is also used in a mosque almost precisely contemporary in date, the one built by Mir Ashraf, dated 1773, m Patna. There, however, the tiles are on the floor. In Benares, the most sacred of all Hindu cities, temples were erected in prolific numbers during the late Mughal period and the years of rule by zamindars.

Most important of these was the Vishvanath temple, whose predecessor had been razed by Aurangzeb. A small structure, with delicate reduplicated spires that emphasize the temple's height, it was once again revitalized as the major site of pilgrimage in the holy city. In addition to temples, the ghats, often leading from massive edifices facing the waterfront, were built by Hindu rajas, some residing at a considerable distance, as a means of establishing their own standing in this sacred city.

Eastern India

Bihar

The finest late Mughal mausolea in Bihar are modeled on the tombs of Iftikhar Khan in Chunar and Shah Daulat in Maner, each built during Jahangir's reign (Plates 89-92). Among these are tombs built for Shamsher Khan (Plate 220) and Ibrahim Husain Khan, both following the plan and elevation of the tombs from Jahangir's time but embellished with motifs characteristic of eighteenthcentury ornament. That is, each tomb has a domed central chamber surrounded by an open veranda. Ibrahim Husain Khan's tomb in Bhagalpur bears no date, but its interior and exterior walls, ornately articulated with stucco ornament, reflect the increased surface elaboration seen in much eighteenth-century architecture across north India. Also showing the new motifs is Shamsher Khan's tomb. Among these new features is the dome's high drum with screens that are surmounted by bangala roofs. Shamsher Khan served for some time as governor of Patna (then known as Azimabad) during the reign of Shah Alam Bahadur Shah. He, like his uncle, Dacud Khan, founded a town in his own name, Shamshernagar, not far from Daudnagar. There he built his own tomb, a serai and well before his death in 1712. Only the tomb remains.

In contrast to the fine late Mughal mausolea of Bihar is the austere Jamic mosque of Silao in Nalanda District. This single-aisled three-bayed mosque, constructed in 1741-42 by a father and son, Sayyid Muhammad and Sayyid Ghulam Najaf, is enclosed by high walls, not common in eastern India at this time.

On each of the exterior walls are inscriptions, again unusual. Like the exterior, the mosque's interior is sparsely ornamented. Cusped mihrabs and a more complex form of pendentives than seen before in Bihar are the sole decorative devices. The contrast with such contemporary monuments as Ibrahim Husain Khan's tomb in Bhagalpur indicates that in eighteenth-century Bihar no single ornamental style prevailed, probably because there was no single strong patron or model.

Patna remained Bihar's leading commercial center. The city was even enlarged under Prince Azim al-Shan, governor of Bihar in the early eighteenth century. He renamed the city Azimabad, proclaiming his desire to create a second Delhi. His efforts failed, as did his bid for the throne, but Patna still continued to benefit from the patronage of political figures and wealthy merchants.

Among the structures they provided, the most elegant is the mosque of Mir Ashraf (Plate 221), constructed by a Patna businessman in 1773-74. Its articulated facade with petal-like kungura, cartouches and arched niches is characteristic of those seen throughout India in the eighteenth century. The interior, too, is ornate, for cartouches and arch motifs embellish the walls and dome. The floor of the prayer chamber is composed of multicolored tiles of the sort used on pre-Mughal Bengali structures.

This unique flooring is in keeping with the mosque's articulated surfaces, related to that of contemporary architecture in Murshidabad, for example, Munni Begum's Chowk mosque built in 1767 (Plate 224). Whether ornate or austere, religious architecture in Bihar, as in Awadh and Murshidabad, reveals virtually no European influence. There is no better example than the Bawli Hall mosque (Plate 222) on the estate of a nineteenthcentury residence. The mosque's central facade has a tri-lobed entrance arch and a parapet of domed kungura, recalling features of the 1841-42 mosque of Hamid Ali Khan, Delhi's last significant Mughal mosque (Plate 207). No European forms are used on the Bawli Hall mosque; rather, its design reflects contemporary work at the Mughal capital more than anything seen in the closer centers of Awadh and Murshidabad. By contrast, the residence reveals considerable European influence following patterns set forth in Lucknow and Murshidabad. Bawli Hall, the nineteenth-century residence of Nawab Luft Ali Khan, was once an extensive mansion little different from contemporary British buildings in India. Now abandoned, it shows the extent that British architecture served as the model for houses of important figures in later Mughal successor states.

Bengal: architecture under the nawabs of Murshidabad

The architectural landscape of Bengal after Aurangzeb's death was dominated by three active groups, each responsible for different forms and types of buildings. Wealthy Hindu bankers, landholders and merchants built splendid terracotta temples in unprecedented numbers. An entire new city, Calcutta, developed under the British in a European idiom.

Concurrently the Mughals and their successors, the nawabs of Murshidabad, embellished their own capital, only 200 km north of Calcutta. Under previous Mughal rulers the capital of Bengal had fluctuated between Rajmahal and Dhaka. In 1703 Murshid Quli Khan, a high-ranking amir, shifted the administrative center from Dhaka to Murshidabad. By 1717 he had given himself unprecedented powers, paving the eventual break with the Mughal court. Murshid Quli Khan never ceased to regard himself as a Mughal agent, even though he manifested signs of independence. For example, he annually remitted revenue to the imperial court in Delhi, but named the new Mughal capital after himself, in contrast with the earlier Mughal capitals of Bengal, Rajmahal and Dhaka, that initially had been named Akbarnagar and Jahangirnagar for the ruling Mughal monarchs.

Murshid Quli Khan's first architectural project in this new city was a Jamic mosque (Plate 223) constructed in 1724-25. This impressive structure, originally surmounted by five domes, is today known as the Katra mosque. Its single-aisled plan is typical of the Mughal idiom in Bengal. However, several features recall the ornamentation of pre-Mughal Bengali architecture, for example, the facade's numerous niches. The mosque thus stands in contrast to the more refined buildings developed in Bengal during the time of Shah Jahan and Aurangzeb (Plates 154, 187 and 188).

This break with the Mughal ornamental style parallels the patron's assertion of independence. Surrounding the mosque are domed cloistered chambers used as a madrasa. The construction of this madrasa-cum-mosque, one of the very largest mosques in all Bengal, endows the city that hitherto held little religious significance with a dominant sacred importance - possibly an attempt to rival the traditional centers of piety in Bengal, Gaur and Pandua.

Less than fifty years later another Jamic mosque (Plate 224) was constructed by Munni Begum, the de facto ruler and highly influential wife of the recently deceased Nawab Mir Jacfar. Known as the Chowk mosque, this elegant structure was built in 1767-68 in the tradition of Mughal, not pre-Mughal, mosques. The graduated size of the five rounded domes and two end-vaults flanked by slender minarets yield an overall appearance of restrained majesty. The interior and exterior are embellished with thickly applied plaster ornament. While more elaborate than that on the earlier Burdwan tomb, stucco ornamentation on structures erected under the Murshidabad nawabs remains considerably more subdued than that on buildings built by the nawabs of Awadh. The Chowk mosque, constructed at the height of Munni Begum's influence, was the most important religious structure in the city. Located on the ground of Murshid Quli Khan's former audience hall, this mosque may have been envisioned as the focal point for a politically rejuvenated Murshidabad under Munni Begum's leadership. In fact, however, the real power of Munni Begum and the succeeding nawabs had been eclipsed by the British.

From this time on, many mosques modeled on Munni Begum's were built in the city, although the embellishing motifs are less ornate. These mosques were almost always inscribed with the name of a patron, otherwise unknown, but never the name of the ruling nawab or British overlord.

This suggests that mosques were no longer built as a means of gaining the favor of the ruler or of a powerful figure. While mosques were the building type most commonly constructed in Murshidabad, two important religious complexes, each associated with the Shia sect, were built under private patronage in the late eighteenth and early nineteenth centuries. One is the Husainiya, located on the east bank of the Bhagirathi, in close proximity to the palace.

This structure was intended to house portable models (tacziya) of a building associated with the martyrdom of the Prophet's grandson, which were carried in procession at the time of Muharram. The Murshidabad Husainiya was commenced in 1804-05 and enlarged in 1854-55. A highly placed court eunuch, Amber Ali Khan, was responsible for the initial construction, while another, Darab Ali Khan, was responsible for the later enlargement.

Although they built the Husainiya as private citizens, they were nevertheless intimately linked with the court. The construction and renovation of a Husainiya facilitated the celebration of a religious rite observed in Shia Islam, the sect followed by the Murshidabad nawabs. The celebration of such rites appears to have become an increasingly important aspect of official ceremony under the Murshidabad nawabs. Since all important secular and political ritual was controlled by the East India Company, it is not surprising that the nawabs might seek to foster religious ceremony. In Awadh, too, the nawabs promoted religious ceremony, having largely lost their authority over secular ritual. Patronage by court eunuchs also was provided at Murshidabad's Qadam Sharif complex. The principal structure there is a shrine housing an impression said to be that of the Prophet Muhammad's foot. It was built in 1788-89 by Itwar Ali Khan, chief eunuch of Nawab Mir Jacfar. This impression, said to be from Arabia, was removed from a shrine in Gaur; before that it had been housed in nearby Pandua. These cities each had served as the capital of the independent sultans of Bengal before Mughal times. In Gaur, the shrine housing this impression had been the focus of the city's sacral significance.

Erected during the Husain Shahi dynasty, its importance continued into the Mughal period. Thus the transfer of the footprint to Murshidabad was intended to bolster the religious status of the city, whose administrative and economic role had been badly undermined six years earlier when government offices were shifted to Calcutta. Just as Murshid Quli Khan, the first nawab of Murshidabad, had attempted to transfer to Murshidabad the sacral significance that had been associated with Gaur, so, too, in the late eighteenth century, when the city's importance was greatly diminished, a similar attempt was made. The shrine's significance increased even more after 1858 and into the early twentieth century, when it was revitalized in an attempt to infuse new life into this waning city, now almost entirely eclipsed by British power centered in Calcutta.

By the early nineteenth century, Murshidabad was the nawab's residence, nothing more. His powers continually reduced, he had to rely on the East India Company for his paltry annual stipend. The nawabs' utter dependence on the British is reflected in the residence of the nawab (Plate 225) constructed between 1829 and 1837. Designed by a European, Duncan McLeod, it follows the model of Government House in Calcutta, which in turn was modeled on Kedleston Hall in Derbyshire. Yet, ten years after the completion of the palace, the nawab built to its north an enormous Imambara signaling his autonomy in matters religious. The Imambara's sheer size - some 80 meters longer than the palace itself - underscores the notion that the patronage of religion and religious rite were among the few means for the nawabs to show authority independent of the British.

According to an inscription, the patron, Nawab Feredun Jah, appointed Sadiq Ali Khan as supervisor for the massive structure. He designed this Imambara, the largest in eastern India, with European features, in keeping with the palace opposite. Thus the appearance of the Imambara, an official structure part of the palace, stands in marked contrast to the city's privately patronized religious structures, all of which lack European motifs and forms. That Europeanized features largely were reserved for official architecture is suggested by another mosque (Plate 226) commenced by the same architect who designed the great palace Imambara. This mosque completes an understanding of architecture in Murshidabad. Known as the Chotte Chowk-ki Masjid, it stands in an area earlier associated with Murshid Quli Khan's palace.

An inscription over the central entrance ascribes its initial design and construction to Sadiq Ali. Since he died in 1850, much of it must have been completed by then. Contrary to what might be expected from the designer of the Imambara, this mosque is devoid of Europeanized features at a time when the near-contemporary mosques of Calcutta reveal considerable European influence. In fact, in plan and elevation it resembles Mughal-period structures in Bengal dating to Shah Jahan's time (Plate 154). That is, its simple cusped arches and plain facades have more in common with earlier Mughal structures than with the ornate facades of early nineteenth-century buildings in Murshidabad. This is characteristic of late non-imperial mosques of Murshidabad, those patronized by persons other than the nawab. They adhere to forms developed in Bengal much earlier in the Mughal period. This suggests that here, as in Awadh, the architectural styles developed under the Mughals came, in Mughal splinter states, to be associated with the true architecture of piety, of Islam, and of the old social order, a style that by now had shed association with one or another ruling house. It was a style that stood in contrast to that built by the rulers, increasingly dominated by Britain as much in their architecture as in their authority.

Bibliography

Asher, Catherine: *Architecture of Mughal India*, Cambridge, New York, 1992.

Barrucand, Marianne, and A. Bednorz: *Moorish Architecture in Andalusia*, Cologne, London, 1992.

Blair, Sheila S., and Jonathan Bloom: *The Art and Architecture of Islam, 1250-1800,* Pelican History of Art. New Haven, 1994.

Creswell, K. A. C.: *A Short Account of Early Muslim Architecture*, Aldershot, Adlohoc, 1989.

Crowe, S.: "*The Gardens of Mughal India*", Oxford, London, 1972.

Garlake, Peter S.: *The Early Islamic Architecture of the East African Coast*, British Institute of History and Archaeology in East Africa, Nairobi, 1966.

Goodwin, Godfrey: *A History of Ottoman Architecture,* Oxford, New York, 1992.

Hambly, G.: "*Cities of Mughal India*", New York: G. P. Putnam's Sons, 1968.

Koch, Ebba: *Mughal Architecture: An Outline of Its History and Development (1526-1858),* Munich, London, 1991.

Michell, George, and Mark Zebrowski: *Architecture and Art of the Deccan Sultanates,* Cambridge, London, 1999.

Moynihan, Elizabeth B.: *Paradise as a Garden In Persia and Mughal India.* New York, George Braziller, 1979.

Okada, Amina: *Indian Miniatures of the Mughal Court*, New York, Harry N. Abrahms, Inc. Publishers, 1992.

Papadopoulo, A.: "*Islam and Muslim Art*", New York, Harry N. Abrams, 1979.

Prussin, L. Hatumere: *Islamic Design in West Africa,* Berkeley, 1986.

Tillotson, G. H. R.: *Mughal India*, New York, Penguin Books, 1990

Index

□□□